Praise for AMERICA'S DAUGHTER

Meeting Maria Nhambu (when she was Maria Bergh) and having an African as my high school teacher influenced me and inspired me in so many ways. She awakened and encouraged my interest in Africa that led to five different trips to Africa. She helped spark my search for my own heritage and identity. She planted seeds for my art and community awareness and activism. To read about that time in our lives and learn in depth about her life is a revelation to me. Just as she opened new pathways for me, **America's Daughter**, book two in her incredible life story will do the same for others as she relates a true American story!

—Seitu Jones, visual artist and sculptor, B.S., MLS
Loeb Fellow Harvard Graduate School of Design

From Tanzania to America, Nhambu's story of determination continues to emphasize the power of education. Nhambu has never forgotten her roots and has had a life-long passion and commitment to the education of Tanzanian children. As a board member for OBA she was able to give valuable insight into the challenges facing families and communities in Africa as they seek a brighter educational future for their children.

—Diane Jacoby, Executive Director
Operation Bootstrap Africa

What a story! Maria Nhambu makes her soul available to her readers to see and enter into issues of race, identity, love, motherhood, career and creativity. She gives us insights into how she survived a rough childhood of abandonment and mistreatment. Her story exemplifies the power of faith in God, in others, and in oneself. Her memoir series will inspire many!

—Rev. Toney Jackson, Pastor of Bethlehem Baptist Church, Newark, NJ
Spiritual counselor; Workshop and Seminar Leader

Maybe because of my age, my ethnicity, and my own life experiences, everything in Maria Nhambu's second book is RELEVANT, especially today in our multi-cultural, multi-ethnic, multi-religious, multi-gender America. She deals with topics that speak to each one of us living here—immigration, prejudice, mixed-race marriage, education, adoption, motherhood and the importance of listening to your inner self. In her language classroom, she was way ahead of her time integrating culture with language as the only way to teach language effectively! That is why her students wanted to learn from her, bonded with her, and loved her.

—*Dr. Margaret M. Wong, Foreign Language Teacher,*
Director of International Education

I've known Maria Nhambu since 1976 when she came to teach at Central High School where I was principal. With my encouragement, she created and taught an African Studies program. I now understand how much of Africa she brought to her students. Her story is intimately tied to Africa's story, America's story and history. An invaluable book for anyone passionate about Africa and the human condition.

—*Joyce Taborn Jackson, Ph.D., Licensed Psychologist*

Maria Nhambu instinctively knew that she belonged to God although her life told her she belonged to no one. How many other children never believe in themselves and give in to the outside voices of the world that falsely tell them they are bad, unwanted, not valuable, and not loved?

—*Marian Wright Edelman, President and Founder*
Children's Defense fund

Nhambu's plight is not hers alone; her fight against odds is not hers alone; her right to be free is not hers alone. As America's Daughter, Nhambu's journey to America becomes for her as well as for millions of others, "the home of the brave." Her quest continues to illumine not only to herself, but for herself. Answers, bold and clear, are within reach for all who purposely, definitively declare: I am who I am wherever I am, daughter, son of the universe. Entitled by birth and by birthright, Africa's child growing in stature and wisdom by virtue of origin, I am because we are.

—*Grace Hill Rogers, Retired English Secondary teacher and principal;*
Recipient of Teacher of the Year by Minnesota Alliance of Black Educators

Maria Nhambu's unique writing style...puts the reader face to face with the truth about racism, prejudice, and cultural differences. It asks the question: Is it different today?

—*Marie-Thérèse Reed, Docteur d'Etat ès Sciences (Ph.D.)*
University of Rennes, France, Officer National Order of Merit

Maria Nhambu's memoir with European colonialism and American racial segregation and its impact make **America's Daughter** a must read. The author brings to readers her own middle passage story as a biracial child brought up in an African orphanage coming to the United States. This second book of her trilogy provides readers with many perceptions and insights. Her struggle with identity in America raises profound questions we would do well to ponder today.

—*Benjamin Mchie, Educational Consultant, Writer, Historian,*
Founder and Executive Director of African American Registry

Foreign students are so eager to get on with their education and learn about America, but many, I'm sure, will resonate with Maria Nhambu's description of her adventures and experiences in her new country. The story she tells in **America's Daughter** lets us see ourselves in a new light and creates bridges to understanding diverse experiences.

—*Coventry Cowens, Assistant Director, Multicultural and*
International Programs, Saint Catherine University

The truths that Maria Nhambu shares with her readers in America's Daughter are revealing, but for different reasons to both African-Americans and the white community. We have so much to learn from each other and about each other. Nhambu teaches from a unique and powerful perspective and the lessons are of great value to us all.

—*Vera Farrington Founder, The Spady Cultural Heritage Museum.*

Reading **America's Daughter** will change my life forever. Nhambu's journey is incredible and filled with adversity that most could not endure. Yet she has been blessed to see and love from the inside out always redefining who she is meant to become.

America's Daughter is a reawakening of the issue of race and ethnicity in this country. Nhambu lives through the familiar and unfamiliar prejudices in every aspect of her life, and with grace and dignity teaches us how to be better than what we have been taught to dislike about others. This book spoke to my soul. It let me know that deep inside of us is strength and courage to overcome anything. I am grateful for her life's journey. It has meaning beyond what I could ever have imagined.

—*Sue Anderson, Director, (Retired),*
Office of Equal Employment Opportunity (EEO)
Centers for Disease Control and Prevention (CDC) Atlanta, Georgia

An incredible and inspiring story. Maria shares her continued struggles in the second book of her trilogy. **America's Daughter** tells how she deals with issues of racism and prejudice that still exist in America today. It is full of heartbreak, humor, and determination. Her writing is from the heart. Maria's faith and trust in God continues to give her the strength to endure and not give up. A must read!

—*VJ Jackson, Marketing Manager, Best Print and Design,*
Atlanta, Georgia

America's Daughter pulses with the energy and determination of a woman, displaced and alienated as a child, who with astounding energy and determination forges a life from the fires of deep fear growing up as a half-caste African in an abusive environment. The text burns with a vengeance, not for the adults who raise her, but for a seemingly impossible path into adulthood. She is gifted not only by the energy of survival but her unyielding and intelligent seeking for a life in which she proves her mettle, moves through seemingly unyielding barriers, ultimately to a marriage, a career and motherhood, all against the backdrop of an internal relationship with her alternate soul-spirit who unfailingly discerns the truth and brings it to her in loving clarity.

This second part of a trilogy reveals her talents, creativity as an artist and business woman, committed motherhood to her son and daughter, staunch fighter for her marriage, and her people of origin. The text bristles with images and color, all against the backdrop of international settings vividly described, from Norway, the home of her husband, to Tanzania, to her home base of Minnesota.

—*Denise McCollum Scott*

Maria Nhambu's second book, **America's Daughter**, delivers the same masterful writing and honest emotional journey as **Africa's Child**. Mary/Maria journeys to America with more heart-wrenching challenges, adaptations, education, culture questions, searching for love and acceptance. Her strong, determined soul carries her through each situation with hope. Her humor adds much flavor to the book. How in the world could she succeed without it? I could not put **America's Daughter** down. From the first sentence to the last I was captured, satisfied, entertained, encouraged and left wanting more. A thoughtful journey written from raw honesty, sure to delight and fill your heart.

—*Anna Fitzsimmons*

From growing up in an orphanage in Africa, to studying in America, marrying and starting a career, Maria Nhambu's story is amazing. She sheds light on what it is like to be deprived of knowing any family, especially a mother, or even knowing one's tribe in Africa, as well as how difficult it is to be a newcomer in the U.S. We should all be more aware of how deeply these things can affect someone. Encounters with culture shock and racial bias are deftly described.

—*Janet Brownell*

I find **America's Daughter** DELIGHTFUL—so very funny, and also very poignant—sometimes both at the same time.

—*Natasha Vaubel*

America's Daughter has a special appeal to our generation. It is a thoughtful book, or perhaps more properly, thought-provoking, on several levels. Very large topics, from the intensely internal (and therefore universal) to historical and societal issues are presented in a manner that leaves us to soul search for our own truths and open up paths to understanding other cultures.

—*Walter Graff, LL.B.*

America's Daughter is an extraordinary book. Nhambu continues her amazing life journey after arriving in America along with her beloved "Fat Mary" as she did in Book One of her trilogy. This book will inspire all human beings. Nhambu had to endure and maneuver her way around racial prejudice, cultural complexities and stereotypes that were brand new to her. She tried to fit in not only as an American but a Black American as well.

Her story is heartwarming—sometimes funny and sometimes painful. Her inner strength and wisdom shine through her writing as she faces many hardships and obstacles. **America's Daughter** is educational, fascinating, and unforgettable. A true testimony to what we can accomplish when we love and believe in ourselves.

—*Carletta Smith, MSW, Retired Minneapolis Public Schools*

Maria Nhambu's humor, innocence and determination not to be racially excluded from her surroundings are all part of her maturity. In **America's Daughter**, she becomes the very cultured, savvy traveler and the center of many friendships around the world. I love Fat Mary, Maria's second conscience. Her relationship with Fat Mary had me wishing that I too could talk to her.

—*Dale Breise, Retired Bank Executive,*
Chairman, Delray Beach Chamber of Commerce

Dancing Soul Trilogy ☆ Book Two

America's Daughter

A Memoir

Maria Nhambu

Delray Beach, Florida

Published by

Dancing Twiga Press
Delray Beach, Florida
www.MariaNhambu.com

ISBN 978-0-9972561-3-0 soft cover
ISBN 978-0-9972561-4-7 mobi
ISBN 978-0-9972561-4-7 ePub

Cover and text design by Bookwrights
Cover chalk drawing by street artist, Acapulco, Mexico, 1976
Back cover author photo of Nhambu by Daphney Antoine
Printed in the United States of America

To Catherine Murray Mamer, my adoptive mother.
You are the embodiment of the Power of One.

Dancing Soul Trilogy

Africa's Child
America's Daughter
Drum Beats, Heart Beats (to come)

Map of Africa Showing Tanzania

Map of Tanzania Showing
Locations Mentioned in Text

Contents

Foreword

It was a snowy February day in Minneapolis, Minnesota, when the letter arrived from Morogoro, Tanganyika, East Africa. Margaret Rose, my roommate at college, was teaching for the Maryknoll Sisters there, and I was an English and speech teacher at Regina High School in Minneapolis. Each week we exchanged the letters of our students who had become pen pals.

"We need another English teacher here," she wrote. "Why don't you come?"

I replied that same evening with my first cablegram, taking care to use the minimum number of words to save money: "Regarding pedagogical position, affirmative!" That decision changed my life.

I grew up in Onamia, Minnesota, the only child of older parents. My mother died when I was thirteen, leaving me alone with an alcoholic father. I was always looking for family. The tightknit community of my tiny town provided that for me. I loved my time at the College of St. Catherine in St. Paul, where I found sisters in my dorm mates and people I thought of as family. Speech and Theater were my majors.

I arrived at Marian College, the Maryknoll High School for girls where I was hired to teach for $75 per month. My job description included teaching Oral English to every student in Forms 1 through 4, tutoring five students who qualified to take the Cambridge Exam in Oral English, codirecting The *Mikado* which was already in rehearsal, producing a one-act play, and moderating the Drama Club and the Bridge Club.

Mary Rose Ryan was one of the students I tutored. Without that close association, I would not have gotten to know her so well as I asked her questions while working to improve her spoken English. As I learned her story and came to know this remarkable young woman, I felt a need, a calling if you will, to help her achieve her full potential. I learned she was not among the handful of students the Sisters planned to send out of the country for further education. With the optimism and naïveté of youth and an empathy that demanded action, I began planning to adopt and bring her home with me. We would become the family we both wanted.

Less than two months after arriving in Africa, I wrote my father, asking what he thought of my plans and suggesting that the $3,000 I had inherited from my Aunt Rose could be used for expenses. I made it clear to him I would never feel right leaving her behind.

Finding a way to get Mary Rose to the United States took nearly nine months. Once I learned she was eligible for an American passport, I worked endlessly to secure it. In exchange for that information and assistance, I made promises that were extraordinarily difficult to keep, and I am proud to say I kept my word.

America's Daughter has been a very difficult read for me, even though I know and have lived a great deal of the story. I am stunned at my naïveté about all I should have provided to this young African woman who knew nothing about living in the United States. How could I have been so unaware of all she was going through? How could I have dashed ahead of her on the escalator on her first day in America? How could I have had no clue to what she was experiencing and have thought things were going along well?

Years later I found out that Mary Rose would rather stumble along, enduring racial and cultural prejudice, than let me think for one moment I wasn't the best thing that ever happened to her or that anything was my fault. Rather than talking about her problems with me, she discussed them with her own "Fat Mary," whom we have already met in *Africa's Child,* her earlier book.

Little in my background prepared me to be a mother to a beautiful, mixed-race nineteen-year-old from Africa.

Growing up with parents who were forty-four when I was born was very lonely. Onamia, however, was a wonderful place to be raised. Our town had a vibrant school system and was full of amazing people who loved and took care of one another and of me.

We lived nine miles from the Mille Lacs Indian reservation, and I was fascinated with the Ojibway culture. We had one Black family, consisting of Mrs. Winch and her daughter, Princellyn, and they lived on my block. Mrs. Winch cleaned house for a lot of families in town. She stood out because she had a wig; Princellyn was crippled and wore an elevated shoe. A friend pointed out to me recently that "No one ever told us that Mrs. Winch was Black."

I also grew up a devout Roman Catholic, and after my mother died, the Crosier fathers in many ways reared me as my father was frequently away for treatment for alcoholism. I knew nothing about sexuality other than what I learned in health and home economics classes. My mother died soon after telling me never to let a boy touch me!

I was indeed ill prepared to protect and guide Mary Rose, to help her cope with life in America in the 1960s. Mary Rose and I arrived in St. Paul, and I began to learn what I didn't know about racism, setting boundaries with a beautiful young woman sought out by young men, all the while struggling with a job teaching junior high English in a suburban school miles from where we lived and learning how to live as a family of two. There is no doubt I would do it all again.

Our family of two grew to three when I married John Mamer the year Mary Rose graduated from St. Catherine's. John immediately accepted her as his daughter, and he became her father. We gave birth to our daughter Eleanor after nine years of marriage. I love the family I created. Even though Mary Rose is some thirty years older than her sister, Eleanor, they are as close as sisters can be.

My expanding family now consists of my two daughters, son-in-law, four grandchildren, and three great grandchildren. Cheers to Family and the power and the knowledge that we all can choose to create families of our own when we find ourselves alone.

Catherine Murray Mamer
Former Director, Peace House Community

A Note from the Author

I have always been amazed at how I functioned my first few years in America. I can honestly say I was lost, confused, and bewildered most of the time. I lived in my own world that was neither Africa nor America. I felt alone and isolated despite having Catherine Murray as my mother and a semblance of family. Almost everyone I met assumed I knew all about American life and culture and explained little to me. Consequently, I interpreted life from my limited understanding of my environment and ended up embarrassing myself and others numerous times.

I worked hard at fitting in and becoming an American, but then I discovered that being an American was not enough. I had to be a Black American because that's how Americans, especially whites, saw me. The process of becoming Black was hardest of all. I knew nothing about the history or culture of Blacks in America, but because of our pigment affinity, I was seen in most settings as a representative of that racial group. It was a huge undertaking and I often missed the boat completely and got lost along the path to becoming America's daughter. But today, some fifty years later, I can finally say I feel just at home as an African American as I am as an African.

Of course, my relationship to white culture hasn't changed since I was born. In Africa, I was a mixed-race African and in America I am Black. White society, for the most part, doesn't understand that Black American culture is as different from my own African culture as African culture is from the predominant white culture in the United States.

As challenging and complicated as my cultural assimilation was, it put me in a situation I have frequently encountered—bridging the gap of knowledge between my old world and my new one for classmates and others. It was a mixed blessing, often requiring soul-searching to find common ground, but once found, opened doors of communication and mutual understanding and encouraged respect of both cultures.

At first I wondered why Cathy let me fend for myself as I plowed through the many layers of new and foreign-to-me cultural issues. There were very good reasons, but perhaps the most important was that she was twenty-three years old when she adopted me and brought me to her country. She had hardly left adolescence herself when she decided to "raise" a nineteen-year-old from a culture that couldn't have been more different from her own.

It was Cathy who taught me the true meaning of the word "risk." Whenever I see that word written or hear it spoken, I see her face. I see her faith. I see her love and her youth when she took on this challenge. She perceived a need and didn't wait for everything to fall into place before doing something about it. She did not wait until someone wrote the manual on *How to be a Mother to a 19-Year-Old African Orphan When You're Only 23*. She rose to the occasion and gave it everything she had.

Cathy often says that the greatest achievement of her life—adopting and bringing me to America—was accomplished when she was twenty-three. That is not true. The decision she made long ago was simply the initiation of an ongoing, lifelong achievement. She has continued to be that devoted, most loving, and selfless person every day and every year through my life and the lives of my children and grandchildren. She created a family for me and for herself where there was none before. That's an incredible achievement!

Because of Cathy, I finally understand the African saying we repeated as children: "Whoever thinks that one person doesn't make a difference, hasn't slept under a mosquito net with one mosquito."

I hope this story proves the Power of One and inspires us to follow her example however and wherever we choose to make a difference in the lives of others and in the world.

Prologue

The story I tell in the following pages might appear to be that of any immigrant coming to America and learning a new culture. It's not. As a college-aged foreign student, I had more than the usual struggles because I came from a less-than-usual background.

I was left at an orphanage for mixed-race children when I was only a few days old. The orphanage in Tanzania, East Africa, was run by German missionary nuns. Moved by the plight of biracial children, who at that time often suffered ill treatment and outright rejection by both African and white societies, the nuns established the Don Bosco Children's Home and Boarding School at Kifungilo for children like me.

My story began in a country (then called Tanganyika) yearning to be independent of British colonialism and to forge its own identity. I tell about growing up there, about my longings and struggles and my own search for identity in *Africa's Child,* the first book of my memoir series, Dancing Soul Trilogy.

Our physical needs were provided for by the nuns and benefactors, yet I had to face my personal realities: I had no identity, no tribe, no family, and no mother. Most children at least had a mother to visit them. Bullying and cruelty on the part of other children, and especially at the hands of the older girls in charge of us, were daily experiences. The discipline administered by the nuns was frequently harsh and occasionally brutal.

To survive, I created my own Fat Mary ("Fat Mary" was my detested orphanage nickname). She was my inner voice, and spoke from the heart rather than from the mind. She loved me unconditionally and saved my experiences for me until I could process, understand, and come to terms with them. I trusted and relied on her guidance.

Discovering dance and its power to heal my soul played a key role in my survival. From the restrained German waltz to the many tribal dances of my country, I learned and loved them all and depended on dance to make me feel alive and fill me with joy.

My love of learning and longing for further education kept me focused, motivated, and hopeful. It also brought me into contact with many inspiring and supportive teachers. One of those teachers, only four years older than I was, took me back with her to America and arranged for a college scholarship. I now had a mother. My greatest childhood longing was fulfilled. With her by my side, I believed it was possible to choose to belong to and create a family.

On the plane leaving Africa, I had a vision of Mama Africa, a powerful and proud African woman carrying the abundant fruits of Africa in a basket. She accompanied me as I gazed down on the continent I was leaving. She would be with me in my new country, Mama Africa assured me, and I would forever be a child of Africa.

Let me tell you the story of how a somewhat bewildered, often overwhelmed and confused nineteen-year-old Mary Rose Ryan (a name I chose for myself) from East Africa dealt with the challenges of a new life in America and what she made of the generosity of others, the opportunities she encountered, the gifts she was born with, and the legacy of her known and unknown past.

1

Where's the Statue?

When we arrived in New York, I wondered if Cathy had played a joke on me. Had we come to America after all? There was no Statue of Liberty anywhere in sight at the airport. I looked everywhere. I guess I expected that as soon as my feet touched American soil, someone representing her and holding the torch of freedom would welcome me. No one had told me to look for her out in the harbor from the plane.

I followed Cathy as we rushed through the crowd, listening to her admonitions to stick with her and hang onto my bags, when what I really wanted to do was to kneel and kiss the ground right there, savoring that I was indeed in the Promised Land.

A steel-toothed escalator loomed in front of me. I could hear the nun who taught English at my American-run Maryknoll high school in Africa telling us that an escalator was a "moving staircase," but I had imagined a wooden staircase, like the one in the orphanage at Kifungilo, blended somehow with the wildly swinging ladders we made from thick forest vines.

This staircase was moving all right. Steps appeared from nowhere as I stood on the metal platform. I tried to walk up the stairs, but I missed a step and fell. As the step's metal teeth bit into the skin on my thigh, the precious items Cathy had bought in Ireland tumbled down behind me. Instead of helping me up, people kept pushing me back down as they walked over and around me. I couldn't see and could barely breathe. I finally grabbed onto the trousers of some man who had no choice but to drag me up to the top before shaking me off like a piece of rubbish stuck to his shoe.

"Where are you?" I heard Cathy's voice. "What happened?"

"I fell and couldn't get up. I'm sorry I dropped your packages."

"Are you okay?" she asked, then joked, "Thank God I shipped my precious Belleek china home from Ireland!"

I went to the restroom to clean up. By then I had figured out that "restroom" meant toilet. Once I got the paper towels out of the dispenser, I marveled at such a wonderful invention. Imagine using these sturdy towels only once and not having to wash and reuse them! And I could use all I wanted because no one was watching. I took a sheet, dabbed it on a bleeding cut, and since they were free, put a couple more around my thigh and fastened them with a safety pin. Sister Silvestris, the nun in charge of us at the orphanage, had taught us to always travel with a safety pin and a rosary.

We walked among the skyscrapers of Manhattan in mid-July. The sudden gush of cold air conditioning that engulfed me every time I entered a building reminded me of the orphanage's cold cement floors and the chilly winds that gave Kifungilo its name. Everything I touched was cold—from the walls to the counters to the tables and chairs. Where were the trees, bushes, and flowers, I wondered, and why did Americans put plastic plants and flowers in pots or stick imitation trees in holes cut in the polished marble floors?

If the American nuns who taught me had compared skyscrapers to our tall, many chambered anthills, I'd have imagined them better. People in the buildings were just like the ants busy coming and going, working and minding their own business in the cold corridors of their maze of sky-high concrete towers. Most people didn't notice me. They didn't nod, smile, wave, or say "Good morning," and they looked confused when I greeted them.

My American history classes with the Maryknoll nuns had failed to prepare me for Grand Central Station. Where were the *wazungu*, the white people? The vast hall was filled with bustling people of every shade of black, brown, and yellow, not just the shades of pink and white I'd expected. They were speaking more foreign languages than I'd ever heard, even considering Tanganyika's many tribal languages. Most of the Black people I saw were light-skinned, like half-castes, and many had even lighter skin than mine. I recognized Arabs, Latinos, and people from India and China. But to my puzzlement, I saw no Native Americans. Where were they? Wasn't this their country, and if so, shouldn't they be the majority of people living here? Did the American *wazungu* take their land from them like the British *wazungu* took ours? Were they fighting for independence like many African countries? Why hadn't our American teachers taught us about them?

The next thing I remember about my arrival in America is visiting the home of Janice and Jim Baker in New Haven, Connecticut. Janice, Cathy's childhood friend, was pregnant with her first child, and Jim was in the seminary, studying to become a Methodist minister.

Janice welcomed me with hugs and kisses. She knew so much about me, I felt I didn't have to speak. Did Cathy write to her about every conversation we'd had? In this first American household I developed my paranoia that everyone already knew my parents had abandoned me and Cathy had adopted me. I was sure people speculated about whether she had acted out of love or pity, although I never felt she pitied me. While Cathy always made me feel wanted and even needed, many Americans I met resurrected in me the insecurities of my childhood I had thought would disappear because of her love for me.

I decided the Bakers must be very rich indeed because they had many shiny appliances on their kitchen counter that I had never seen. As I sat at the breakfast table marveling at the babbling sound coming from the electric coffee pot, two slices of toast suddenly popped out of a silver toaster, startling me. I jumped up from my chair declaring, "I didn't do it! It happened all by itself!"

That evening in bed I reflected on my journey so far with Cathy. She had been very excited about the three-week tour through Egypt, the Holy Land, and Europe she planned for us on our way to America. I was in a daze and didn't remember much of it. I knew we'd landed in Zanzibar and then in Nairobi, where we spent the night with Thecla, a classmate from Marian College, who was already married. Once we boarded the plane in Nairobi, my reverie about Mama Africa that began as I soared from the land of my birth continued. I came back to reality when we landed at midnight in Khartoum, where Cathy fainted in the 110-degree heat. She recovered in time to take off for Cairo, and I easily picked up where I had left off with Mama Africa, her abundant gifts and powerful presence representing the strength and beauty of the continent I was leaving.

When we arrived at the Cairo airport, an older American businessman fell in love with Cathy and accompanied us for much of our three-day visit in Egypt. He took us to the pyramids. I was impressed with the sound and light spectacle during which thunder and lightning dared to interrupt pharaohs and ancient Egyptian sages reciting history. I wondered why, even though Egypt was in Africa, there were no African-language versions of the performance.

Cathy's American businessman showed up in Tel Aviv, where he wined and dined us and arranged for tours to all the Christian holy places. The most memorable impression I have of the Holy Land, unfortunately, is of the merchants who, having flung their olive-wood rosaries around the garden of Gethsemane and other places they said bore the footprints of Jesus, assured us that purchasing these rosaries guaranteed a top spot in heaven.

The gentleman followed us to Rome and paid for our tour of the city in a cozy carriage pulled by two ornately outfitted white horses. We visited too many museums with too many gold and silver objects and too many buildings with too many paintings of people I had never heard of on the walls and ceilings! I remember being separated from Cathy in the huge crowds at St. Peter's Square during the installation of Pope Paul VI and the long embrace that erased our mutual panic when we found each other after two hours.

Cathy finally told our businessman benefactor that we were grateful for all his help, but now we had to travel alone. I wondered why she didn't let this rich man, who obviously adored her and would do anything for her, continue with us to America and pay for everything. She'd told me several times that we could never afford to "live it up" the way we did without his "footing" the bill. I had no idea what she meant on either count.

We almost missed our train to Holland. Cathy pushed me up the steps of the narrow train doorway and threw our suitcases in behind me. Then I had to drag her with her fifty-pound purse into the train. In Nijmegen, we visited three Kifungilo girls who were in nursing school, and went on to shop for winter clothes in London. We then flew to Dublin, Ireland, which was Father Michael's country. I had hoped that by the time I left Africa I would have forgotten him and our relationship, but being in his country brought back memories of the stories he used to tell me about Southern Ireland and how I had naively imagined I would someday visit him in Cork.

For me, the trip across the Atlantic Ocean was the dividing line between Africa and America. The heaviness of leaving the African continent dissipated in Europe, and by the time we flew over water, I felt free and light as a feather. Once again, I was sure I was personally piloting the huge plane across an ocean I'd only seen on maps. Now it was speeding me away from my country and delivering me to the Promised Land. I reached for Cathy's hand and said, "Thank you." As she often did, she smiled, squeezed my hand, and gazed at me with her large, expressive blue-green eyes.

I was about to start the chapter of my life that Fat Mary and Sister Martin Corde had envisioned for me because we believed in miracles. I relived the last page of my life in Africa that held my farewell gift from Mama Africa. She made sure it was her long-suffering soul, generosity, love, and unparalleled dignity I would remember when I was far away from her. Many times I have felt no one would miss me or even care whether I was here, there, or anywhere, but I knew a mother would miss her departing children no matter how many she had. I knew Mama Africa would miss me, but because she'd live in my heart forever, I wouldn't miss her too much. Was this a taste of the bond between mother and child?

I heard a loud knock on my heart. It was Fat Mary, my soul friend. Here we were in America, just as I had promised her. It was unusual for her to knock with such urgency.

You have hardly acknowledged me since we left Africa. You need me now more than ever. Mama Africa and your new American mother cannot replace me. Don't forget I am your childhood, and your childhood follows you wherever you go. I am here to give back to you the lessons of our most meaningful conversations at the orphanage. I have to warn you, though, that in America you will not only face challenges from your past, but you will experience the blessings and complexities of becoming America's daughter. Together we will forge on into adulthood—stronger, wiser, and happier.

With tears of joy, I recalled her role in my childhood. She had been my consoler and counselor since the day I understood I was alone in the world and had no one who loved me or wanted me. I had decided back then that I would love me, fat me, just as I was. The abandonment, beatings, and insults I endured as little Fat Mary wouldn't matter. I created a soul companion, another Fat Mary, who loved me and whom I loved in return. I took care of her, and she carried the emotional and psychological pain that came at me every day. She took all that I couldn't understand and kept it to give back to me when I was ready. Her role was also to safeguard the meaningful and happy moments of my childhood and bring them to me when I needed to remember life's goodness. She was my constant companion who would never abandon me. My responsibility to her was to shower her with unconditional love.

I was happy when our stay in Connecticut ended and we finally boarded the plane that took us "home" to Cathy's father, Mr. Eugene Murray. He was at the Minneapolis-St. Paul International Airport to meet us. He was only a little taller than Cathy, and his nose was bumpy and blue as if bruised. I wondered what kind of a father he would be to me when I saw in his face the same sincerity and acceptance I'd seen in Cathy's. He too hugged me as if he'd known me his whole life. He kept repeating, "Welcome to America, my princess, welcome to America." His loving and warm welcome made up for the missing welcome from the Statue of Liberty in New York. I felt I had indeed arrived in the land of my dreams, and I had just met the third member of my new family. Fat Mary applauded my growing family and acknowledged that I was home.

As Cathy and her father talked in the front seat of the car, I watched the features of my new land pass before me—the buildings that gave way to houses, to spacious fields and farmhouses. We were going to Onamia, Minnesota, but first we stopped in Princeton, a tiny town en route.

2

The Dairy Queen

"Oh, you dear, dear soul, you're back. You're back from Africa!" After the car came to a stop in the driveway of a small brick house, a petite older woman with neatly coiffured, neck-length, wavy blond hair greeted us in a deep, husky voice as she clutched Cathy's outstretched arms.

"Sophie, Sophie!" Cathy jumped out of the car and hugged the woman for a long time.

So this was Sophie. Cathy had told me I'd love her because she loved her, and that ever since Cathy's mother died, she wished her dad would marry Sophie.

"Catherine Anne, just look at you! You had to go all the way to Africa to look this good! You've lost weight. Didn't they feed you there? And there's Mary Rose!"

I loved Sophie right away. This tiny woman shook her head when she spoke and managed to get her very short arms completely around me, saying, "I know all about you. Don't pretend you're not as excited to meet me as I am to meet you!"

She got in the car without waiting for my response, and the two of them talked all the way to Onamia, often becoming hysterical with laughter and tears as they discussed their tiny town and its inhabitants. I knew I'd like old Mabel and her sister Mildred—I thought her name was "Mildew" and I called her that for several years. It would be nice to meet Mabel's daughter, Margaret, who eased my fears that everyone in Onamia was over seventy. Mr. Murray spoke only occasionally to remind the chattering Sophie of some fact she'd forgotten to mention as she dramatized the happenings in Onamia during the past year.

7

Every so often Mr. Murray, who had paid for our flight to America along with our travels in Europe, asked me about the trip. All I could tell him was that it was very long, and I was sorry, but I had already forgotten the names of most of the places he'd made possible for us to visit during our three weeks in Europe. Then Cathy recited where we had been and what we had seen and done. During the trip, I had concentrated more on people and figuring out if the *wazungu* of Europe were different from the *wazungu* in Africa, while Cathy focused on sightseeing. Once I left Africa, my main concern was getting to America.

I tuned out the chatter and tried to imagine Mr. Murray's house. Would it be like the big houses I'd seen in magazines at our school library or like some of the ones we'd been driving past? How many floors would it have? Would I have a whole room to myself? Would I be eating the same food they ate, as I did at Janice and Jim Baker's house? Were Americans in America as nice as the Americans I knew in Africa? When would I meet the Black Americans who came to America from Africa? Would I be able to identify their tribe as easily as I could in Africa? What if they asked me about my tribe? Would they believe I didn't belong to one?

"There it is! The Dairy Queen! My favorite Dairy Queen," Cathy shouted, jumping up and down in her seat. I looked around and didn't see any queen, only a small shop with big windows. I wondered whether "dairy" was an American word I'd never heard or the name of some queen Cathy knew. I figured the place had something to do with ice cream because of the pictures plastered on it and because Cathy was so happy. Mr. Murray stopped the car right in front of the small building, and Cathy entered her usual ecstasy in the presence of this beloved treat.

"Wait until you taste it. This is no ordinary ice cream!" she said to me, convinced I'd experience the same sensual delight in that violently cold food. Didn't she remember our baffled reaction when she introduced her Oral English students to ice cream at her house in Africa? Nonetheless she ordered a large strawberry ice cream dish for me. I ate only the syrupy strawberry topping, being careful not to touch the ice cream beneath it. As I listened to the appreciative noises she made with each spoonful, I wondered whether her ice cream was warmer than mine. I walked toward the trash can, but before I could lift the lid, Cathy grabbed the ice cream from my hand.

"No! No, no, no! You can't do that! That's a sacrilege! Imagine throwing out ice cream from the Dairy Queen!" She had forgotten that I would never eat or drink anything that cold even if the Dairy Queen herself made it.

"It's cold," I reminded her.

"It's eighty-five degrees outside. Don't tell me that a Dairy Queen isn't just what the doctor ordered!"

What was she talking about? What doctor? Sophie and Mr. Murray were enjoying Cathy's reunion with her beloved ice cream. Although the words "Dairy Queen" appeared in big white letters on a sign in the shape of huge, bright red lips on the roof of the little building, inside I saw only two American girls about my age. Neither one looked like a queen. Would Cathy's Dairy Queen make an appearance to chastise me for intending to throw her cold gift in the trash? Based on the last time I witnessed Cathy with a bowl of ice cream, I didn't even try to rationalize her excitement about it.

Over the years, Cathy continued to stop and worship at Dairy Queens wherever we went, and I continued to see myself at nineteen, confused and disappointed that the Dairy Queen was only a place to buy a certain brand of ice cream and there was no reigning queen.

In 1963, Onamia, cradled in the bosom of Lake Mille Lacs in central Minnesota, was a town that, if you weren't paying attention or if you blinked three times as you drove down Main Street, you'd completely miss. Its population can only be described as old, older, and ancient, and its favorite activities summed up as eating, ate, or will eat.

I was so happy to meet Sophie's two daughters, Bonnie and Nin, who were about my age. They quickly proved my assessment wrong when they introduced me to some of their friends, who talked about a whole lot more than food.

Mr. Murray's store, nestled under the gigantic orange and blue REXALL DRUGS sign on its flat roof, dominated the row of nondescript, attached commercial buildings that included a bakery, a clothing store, and a hardware store. I worked for Mr. Murray at his drugstore, and that first summer I'm sure I dissuaded several customers from ever ordering ice cream again by the disgusted look on my face as I stared at them eating the unbearably cold treat.

Although I thought I spoke English well, it was hard to participate in the older customers' conversations because they talked about food, church, and the nursing home. When I was addressed, it was usually in question form: Had I ever had a hamburger or a hot dog? Had I been to the movies? Wasn't America big? What kind of food did I like? Was I eager to start college?

Throughout my first year in America, this type of interrogation from curious, clueless, yet often sincere people intimidated me. As a result, I almost forgot how to initiate or carry on a normal conversation. The little self-confidence that I'd acquired through Cathy's assurances dissipated, and I became introverted and fearful that I wouldn't be able to answer yet another question from another stranger I'd never see again. The only questions I enjoyed answering were Mr. Murray's: Was I warm? Cold? Did I need money? Would I like something from his Rexall Drugstore? Was I afraid to be so far from Africa? Was I lonely? Did I understand him? Would I sit with him and watch Verne Gagne wrestling on his black and white television set?

I answered questions with monosyllables or very short sentences. By the time school started in September, I knew how to answer all the questions I would be asked. Without fail, every time I met someone new I seized the opportunity to practice my answers and gauge from their reaction if I should memorize that response. I had to be careful, though, and listen well because sometimes I'd answer questions in the order I'd memorized the answers, and I made no sense.

Before we moved to St. Paul for the school year, Mr. Murray asked me to give a talk to his Rotary Club.

"A talk? Me? You mean a speech? In English?"

"I think it would be wonderful. They know about you and are proud that the people of Onamia were the first to welcome you to America."

"You don't have to talk for a long time," Cathy added. "Just tell how we met, a little about our trip, and what you like about America and Americans so far."

"You mean I have to stand in front of people I don't know and say something to them?"

"Well, you can say anything. They'll be happy to hear from you."

I must have talked about something and they probably clapped, but I remember nothing. Cathy always reminds me that the first talk I gave in America was to the Onamia Rotary Club.

3

Winter Boots

Cathy had a list of places to go, people to see, and things to do for every day of my first summer in America, spent in Onamia.

"J. C. Penney is having a sale on lingerie and sleep-wear. We'd better get you a flannel nightgown." I had never felt as hot in my life as I did in the summer of 1963 in Minnesota. I imagined that winter would be a welcome relief.

Cathy's friends in Onamia had collected boxes of used clothing, shoes, purses, and God knows what else for me. I found only two dresses, three skirts, and a few blouses out of the predominantly size 14-18, very old-fashioned styles, that even came close to fitting. Jewelry that I'd considered beautiful in Africa now seemed gaudy as it glittered among the donated items. Going through those boxes took me back to Kifungilo at Christmastime and the way we children searched for clothes in the boxes from Germany.

Sophie helped me sort through the clothes and took the opportunity to tell me yet another of her stories about Catherine Ann as a child. Holding up an emerald-green rhinestone bracelet, she began her story. "I don't believe old Susan parted with this. Catherine Ann, you remember it, don't you?'

"Should I?" Cathy answered, rolling her eyes behind her thick glasses. I knew she was wondering what mischief Sophie was up to now.

I put the tattered petit-point purse I was looking at on my lap to listen to her. I loved her stories and the way she'd stand up and address her audience and act out the main characters be they nine or ninety years old. She'd often forget the order of events, then shake her head and start over again. She made me laugh until I cried, though I usually wasn't sure what was so funny.

"You mean you've forgotten this bracelet? Don't you remember how your mother almost died of shame when you went to old Susan, curtsied, looked up at her with your big eyes, tugged at her skirt, and asked, 'When you're dead and you don't want your bracelet any more, can I have it?'"

Cathy laughed as if she were hearing this for the first time.

"Let me tell you, Mary, Catherine Ann has a huge trunk, and she has begged for everything in it in similar fashion! Her father's attic is full of church hats with net veils, plastic-fruited straw hats, velvet purses, high-heeled shoes, moth-eaten black funeral dresses, evening dresses that look like sequined tents, corsets, and costume jewelry!"

Sophie continued. "I know for a fact that her requests were honored. Many bequeathed these items to her with their dying breaths. Old Susan is definitely an exception. Mary, would you be so kind as to let Cathy have this much lusted-after emerald bracelet?"

Cathy was laughing hard, and I awaited the inevitable ear-piercing siren sounds she made when she blew her nose, cleared her throat, and wiped the tears from her eyes. She didn't have any more Kleenex, so she used her ever-present but impractical nylon handkerchief. She had several of these, and if you wanted to rank high on her list of friends, you'd give her one.

"They're impossible to find," she'd say every time she received one enclosed in a letter. She'd incessantly feel it with her thumb and fingers, but when she got nervous, she'd rub it furiously with both hands, reminding me of Arabs and their worry beads. She literally went into a full-fledged panic attack if it disappeared, even for a moment. Once when we were driving to Onamia, she forgot her hanky. She drove the whole ninety miles with one hand on the steering wheel and the other fingering the end of the nylon scarf tied around my head.

I imagined the mother role Sophie played when Cathy was growing up. While we were still in Africa, a few months after Cathy told me that she would adopt me and take me to America, she told me that her own mother had died when she was thirteen. I recall wondering how she could be a mother to me when she hadn't had her own mother as a role model. Yet I also felt that even though she was only four years older than I, she would be the mother I needed because she had already walked in my shoes. Her parents were forty-four when she was born, and she grew up surrounded by their old and ancient friends, whose funerals she attended and who supplied her with a steady stream of items that explained her particular sense of style. I envied her a little. She was so comfortable among the old that she probably would never fear old age herself.

One day toward the end of the summer, Cathy announced, "Today, it's off to Kinney Shoes to buy your boots."

At the store, she handed me some ugly brown things: "Try these. You'll love them, and they'll be warm and comfy. Your feet will never be cold."

"I don't want boots. Can I have a watch instead?"

"A watch won't keep you warm in winter. Look how wonderful they are." She slid her hand inside the boot that was furry inside and out, put it up to her cheek, and rested her head on it as if it were a pillow.

I had never seen such awful things. I ignored her blissful expression. "I don't want to try them on. I'll never use them."

"Oh, yes, you will! But how can I expect you to have any idea how cold it gets in winter and what you have to wear to stay warm?"

"It was very cold in Kifungilo, and we were barefoot most of the time, so I don't think I'll need these."

She recruited the help of the salesman, who was only too eager to impress upon me the necessity of boots in Minnesota. I gave in as I usually did with Cathy.

"Promise me you won't make me wear these heavy, ugly things outside the house."

"These things are winter boots, and they're only worn outside. Mark my word, Mary, you will have to wear them."

She bought the third pair I tried, and I grudgingly carried them to the car under my arm. I had flashbacks to Kifungilo and how the nuns sometimes dressed us—and how Sister Silvestris beat us when we misbehaved. I convinced myself that since Cathy had never punished me, I would disobey her and give the ugly boots away to the first person who admired them.

4

College of St. Catherine

Mr. Murray gave me a hundred dollars when I left Onamia to attend the College of St. Catherine in St. Paul. That was more money than I had ever possessed in my entire life! I was sure I would be one of the richest girls in school.

We made several trips from Onamia to search for an apartment near St. Catherine's. There were many vacancies near campus. We looked at and liked several, but it took many weeks to find an apartment. Much later, after I had graduated, Cathy told me that my being Black had been the issue. One landlord told her, "You have a pretty Black girl there, and probably many Black guys will be coming here for her, and we don't want that."

We attended the freshman orientation program, and I met Sister Mary Edward, the president of the college. The habit of the Sisters of St. Joseph of Carondelet, who ran the school, was even uglier and more cumbersome than that of the Precious Blood Sisters. Why did nuns have to wear starched, round white bibs and square white headpieces across their foreheads, topped by sheer black veils? I worried that their headgear put pressure on their heads and necks and interfered with proper brain function.

I also met Sister Rosalie, who, Cathy told me, was instrumental in getting me a scholarship to the college. I wanted to thank her and express my deep gratitude and appreciation. With both hands on my heart, I said, "Thanks a hell of a lot, Sister!" Cathy and her friends used that phrase frequently, and I had made a point to remember it so I could use it too.

Sister's smiling face instantly became puzzled. "That's not what you mean, is it?"

"Yes, it is! I am very grateful for what you did for me."

"Then just say thank you."

"Thank you, Sister," I said, wondering why I couldn't use "hell of a lot." I decided it must be because she was a nun and was scared of hell.

For all of freshmen year, I wasn't sure exactly what was happening around me. Another African student who had been a year ahead of me at Marian College, our high school run by Maryknoll Sisters in Africa, was also at St. Catherine's on a scholarship. Although I had known her only casually in Africa, I made an effort to stick with her in hopes that she would facilitate my adjustment to American college life. Unfortunately, she had kept intact all of her African prejudices against half-castes, and it seemed she was ashamed to be associated with me. We performed some tribal dances we'd learned in school at the Annual International Students Festival, and that was the extent of my association with her.

My teachers wanted me to speak in more than short sentences and were not satisfied with the memorized answers I gave in response to their questions. They wanted my opinion on so many topics, especially as someone from Africa. How could I explain to them that the educational system I'd come from did not value my opinion? My only encounter with this kind of give-and-take approach was with the Maryknoll Sisters, and as wonderful and patient as they were, they could not erase my primary and middle school education by German nuns who rewarded me for having no opinion at all. The clever student was the one who repeated what was taught verbatim, while these teachers encouraged me to speak for as long as I wanted ed and did not embarrass me when I couldn't speak or when I was outright wrong.

Didn't I speak English? I hardly understood my classmates even though I tried hard to remember all the slang a fun-loving and easy-going nun at my African high school had taught us. I had received a distinction in English—a First Class Pass in the Cambridge Exams—but all day, every day, incomprehensible conversations raced around me. I felt isolated and confused. With effort, I understood my teachers but avoided conversation with them, resorting to monosyllables and sign language.

The classrooms were often uncomfortably small such as the room in Derham Hall where we studied Sacred Scripture with Sister Mary Virginia. There I felt that Jesus and his Apostles were sitting right next to me, wondering why, with all my Catholic upbringing, I had no idea how to interpret the Bible and retell its stories in my own words. Or the rooms were large like those in the huge, tomb-like science building, Mendel Hall, whose pungent biology labs held sickening odors. In Mendel Hall, I sensed the same odor that seeped into my pores in the hot African air when, as a child, I stood holding my breath at the edge of a fresh grave during a funeral in the Wasambaa villages. Every time I entered that hall, I became preoccupied with death. The inevitable dissection of dead specimens for study did not help.

Everyone else in my classes was a *mzungu* (white). My white *wazungu* classmates were mostly friendly and kind and helpful, but sometimes they confused me by the questions they asked. When did I first start wearing clothes? Did I ever live in a tree? Why wasn't my face black and scarred, my nose flat and wide, my lips thick? Did I live in a real house in Africa? Why was my hair soft and brown instead of coarse and black?

I gave different answers, depending on the day and the person. Sometimes I asked my own questions. "Why is your skin pink? How come your hair is almost white when you're so young? Where are your lips?" To my surprise, they often acted insulted when I asked what I assumed were questions as innocent as theirs.

After a few months in America, I stopped bracing myself for the stereotypical inquisitions, but I was still confused. Weren't Americans among the most educated people on earth? Didn't they know that Africans lived in houses? Why must they insist on calling them "huts"? Didn't they know that only a few tribes practiced skin scarification, and hadn't they ever seen a light-skinned African?

How could they ask me, "Where is Tanganyika?" when I knew the name and population of every state in America? I could name governors and capitals, and was familiar with each state's topography, main industries, and chief exports. Couldn't their geography and current affairs teachers at least tell them that Tanganyika was a country on the east coast of Africa? That Dr. Louis Leakey called it "The Cradle of Mankind" after his 1957 discovery of the skull of Zinzanthropus in Olduvai Gorge? Wasn't that important? Did they even know that Africa is three times the size of the United States? With so many required courses, why wasn't world geography one of them?

I hated my English classes in America as much as I had loved them in Africa. Literature classes were the worst. I could count the number of books I'd read in Africa on both hands. My classmates seemed to have read all the books ever written—except for those by Africans and non-*wazungu* authors. I was as ignorant of Western literature as they were ignorant of geography. I had never owned a book, and until I reached high school, the only books I'd seen were old German volumes neatly set in a wooden bookcase in the convent receiving room when I was being shown for possible adoption. I had admired them at a distance, and my little hands yearned to touch them, but I didn't dare. The first non-textbook I read was *Kateri Tekakwitha: Mohawk Maiden*, which I borrowed from our high school library at age seventeen.

In order to retain my annual scholarship, renewable if I maintained a B+ average, I studied around the clock and was hardly aware of life outside my books. However, I still failed most classes, tests, and exams.

Because I never had a tribal language of my own, I decided to take French, even though an additional language was not required of foreign students. We had all we could do to learn English, or I should say, American. I did poorly in French my first year—I got a D minus. I assumed Sister Marie Philip, my teacher and the head of the department, didn't have the heart to fail me! The first almost-failing grade of my life shocked me into deciding to major in French. I had never failed any subject, and now that it was imperative I do well to keep my scholarship, I had no choice but to study my brains out. It never occurred to me that maybe I had no aptitude for language. In my opinion, there was nothing I couldn't learn with hard work.

Sister Marie Philip was speechless when I told her I wanted to major in French. As I sat in her classes, I hoped she would understand and support my decision. She supported me eventually, but the look of frustration and worry on her face convinced me I had to earn her trust. I improved very slowly after spending interminable hours in the language lab, memorizing and imitating the native French speakers. Like a parrot, I repeated what I'd learned every day to Sister Marie Philip, who didn't seem to care whether I understood a word of what I said, which I didn't. She encouraged me by saying, "Keep it up, keep it up. Your French accent is absolutely delightful."

I continued to do badly in tests. Since I wanted French as my major, Sister Marie Philip became my advisor. One day she called me into her office. I was petrified. I thought she was going to tell me to drop French if I wanted a respectable grade point average. Instead she asked me about a test I'd just failed. She rephrased the questions as though we were having a conversation about the *passé composé* tense. I answered her questions correctly and even went into more depth with my answers to assure her I understood all we'd studied in class.

"Très bien, Marie Rose, très bien, très bien, my sweet *Marie Rose."* A joyful and contented expression had slowly replaced the worried, exasperated look on her face as our session progressed. An hour later we were both smiling and she was outright laughing.

"Madame Reed," she called over the wall to a native French professor, *"Viens, viens! Viens, voir ce que j'ai decouvert!"* ("Come see what I've just discovered!") Marie Therese rushed into Sister Marie Philip's office. Even though I'd only seen her in the hallways and hadn't had her for class, she gave me a big hug before she sat down.

"I must say *bonjour* first. I emm Meeeessis Rrrrreeed, and I'll tell you one sing, you're verrrry prrrrety."

As Sister Marie Philip continued asking me questions about French, she and Mrs. Reed exchanged looks and nods.

"Brrravo!" Mrs. Reed shouted when we were done. "Next semester you will be in my Frrrrench conversation class, and I know you will be my staarrh student."

For the rest of the year, Sister Marie Philip tested me in her office instead of in class with the other students, and I got mostly A's with an occasional B. But no matter how much I studied, I still had trouble with tests in English literature, history, biology, and government. The true/false sections were the worst. How could a fifty-page chapter in a book be reduced to ten true-or-false questions? I usually analyzed and then rationalized all aspects of a question and came to the conclusion that the answer could be true or false depending on the circumstances. I had a better chance of passing a test if I ignored the questions and arbitrarily answered half of them as true and half as false. I changed my ratios each time and did significantly better.

Much later, Mrs. Reed told me that, as my advisor, Sister Marie Philip had taken the time to analyze my poor academic performance and requested that my instructors give me "subjective rather than objective" tests. She convinced them that, unlike the average American student who was petrified by long essay questions, I'd welcome them. She explained that I didn't know how to respond to multiple-choice, fill-in-the-blank, circle-the-correct-answer, or true-and-false questions. If they gave me a chance, I would prove I was as good a student as my high school transcript indicated. If not for Sister Marie Philip, my scholarship would surely have been revoked due to poor academic performance. I am eternally grateful to her.

I eventually learned how to take objective tests, and to my delight I found I didn't have to study so hard or think so critically to get an A. I rediscovered my lifelong hunger for and joy in learning, and in my heart, I thanked the college every day for my scholarship.

Of the required courses, I was most disappointed in history. In Africa I had studied history all through primary, middle, and high school. I found my college classes to be Eurocentric and expected history would be the same, but I wasn't prepared for the shock my textbook gave me. After paying thirty-nine dollars for a heavy, thick book called *World History*, I turned to the table of contents with excitement to search for the section on Africa. Once, twice, three times I leafed through the volume and passed Africa without realizing it. No, this couldn't be right. There must be another section, or maybe the huge African continent had its own book with its own course number. Imagine, only six out of over one thousand pages devoted to Africa! Six pages! And why was Egypt discussed in its own section as though it didn't belong to Africa? Had the book's authors, the teachers who used it, and the students who studied it ever looked at a map of the world? I began to understand why most Americans asked me such ignorant questions about Africa. Maybe it was not their fault. They hadn't studied Africa the way I'd studied America, Europe, Asia, and Australia.

5

Inventing Stories

The ignorance about Africa evidenced by some of my classmates rekindled a lot of the pain of my childhood. Questions by inquisitive but mostly sincere classmates cut through the truth about the life I mistakenly thought I'd left behind. Simple questions such as "What did your father do for a living? How many brothers and sisters do you have? What kind of house did you live in? Will your family come to visit you?" caused me pain.

I told you that we will often revisit the issues of your childhood in America, but I also said we are equipped to deal with them, Fat Mary interrupted my ruminations. She was more assertive, and her vocabulary, which reflected Americanisms as mine did, was improving though she looked the same.

It was difficult to answer classmates' questions truthfully for two reasons. First, it was hard to admit to strangers that I had no family and that I was brought up in an orphanage. I had no tribe or language, no village, no mother or father, no brothers or sisters. Second, nine out of ten students either did not believe me when I told them the truth and continued asking me questions as if they hadn't heard what I said, or they believed me, but then stopped talking to me because they felt sorry for me. During my first year in college, I feared having to answer those awful questions, often several times a day. It was hard for me to concentrate on my studies when I was trying to forge an identity to satisfy my classmates' curiosity.

The second half of sophomore year in college I met Jackie in Sacred Scripture class taught by Sister Mary Virginia. I couldn't stop looking at Jackie because she was the most beautiful girl I'd seen in

America. Her skin wasn't as pink as that of the other students, her deep-set, dark-brown eyes shone with an intelligent understanding of me that at first intimidated me, and her hair was cut close to the scalp like that of an African. No matter where she sat, she'd wave at me when she walked in and give me a genuine and joyful smile that made me feel we were kindred spirits. We'd sometimes stay after class and talk. To my surprise, she never asked me the usual questions. She asked me about school and how and when I learned English. Did I live on campus? Would I like to come home with her for lunch? Where did I find such a pretty sweater? Were my feet cold? Had I studied Sacred Scripture before? Though it was one of my least loved subjects, I looked forward to ten o'clock Tuesdays and Thursdays because of Jackie. One day I confided in her that I had picked her to be my friend because she liked me even without knowing the truth about me.

"And what's the truth, Mary Rose?" she asked.

"That my parents didn't want me, so I was raised by German nuns in an orphanage. You know, I also don't belong to any tribe, and many Africans treated me badly because I was a half-caste. I don't like to talk about my past, but every day it seems I'm forced to face the unpleasant facts of my life because I am asked so many personal questions by people I hardly know."

"They're curious, that's all. You don't have to explain everything to them. Just say that you don't know your parents and try to change the subject."

"But I feel bad when I refuse to answer."

"Most of the time they're just trying to make conversation with you, and it doesn't matter very much what you say. Listen, try this. Next time you're asked about your family, invent a story and see if it really makes a difference to them."

"Like what?"

"Tell them what they expect to hear—you lived in a tree and walked around half naked or tell them that your father was a chief, and you lived in a tribal compound with fifteen brothers and sisters and all your servants!" Jackie couldn't hide her delight as she elaborated on African stereotypes.

In the back of my mind, I resolved to try Jackie's idea, but I had one worry. "What would Cathy think?"

"She doesn't have to know, and who'd tell her anyway?" She changed the subject. "Why don't you ever speak or raise your hand in class?"

"In most classes I don't because of my English, but in this class I have no idea why we're supposed to take the Bible apart. Whenever someone answers a question and Sister says, 'Good, good,' I wonder how many versions of the Bible there could be because that's not what I would have said. I thought there was only the Word of God in the Bible."

"Your understanding of the Bible matters because you're from a different culture. I think Sister Mary Virginia would like you to participate more in our discussions. Just try, okay?"

I agreed but remained as quiet as a church mouse for the rest of the class. I took profuse notes, memorized everything, and spit it back word for word with little or no comprehension in the tests and papers I had to write to pass the required course.

I did act on Jackie's previous suggestion, but I stayed closer to the truth—or to the rumors and innuendos I'd heard growing up in the orphanage where kids mocked me for wanting to find my mother. They insisted my parents were dead. And why did I declare myself an "Amelican girl"? My newly made-up family story went like this: My parents were both killed in a car crash. My mother had been a teacher, and my father a farmer. My two brothers and one sister were in school in our small village in eastern Tanzania. We were rich because we could afford school fees and owned the only brick house in the village. My story changed depending on the question and my mood.

Jackie was right. Students were satisfied with my answers and felt they knew me so much better now that my family was no longer a mystery. I had peace of mind and was better able to concentrate on my studies until one Sunday, out of the clear blue as we were driving to church, Cathy spoke without looking at me. "I heard you've been telling people things about your family that you know aren't true."

"Who told you?"

"It doesn't matter who told me. Well, it was a nun and she was very upset about it."

"Was it Sister Rosalie?" I thought she'd be the one since she'd worked hard to get me the scholarship to St. Catherine's.

"No, but is it true you're making up stories and telling lies?"

"Yes."

She said nothing more, but I felt like everyone, and now even Cathy, hated me. Should I try to explain to her the need I felt to have come from a family like the other students? Had she ever been interrogated repeatedly about a past she'd struggled first to forget and then to accept? And if I didn't know the truth about my past and only had vague rumors to go on, was I really lying? How could she reproach me like this? I thought for sure she'd understand.

"Don't lie, Mary. You can get into a lot of trouble."

Trouble? Did she say trouble? Doesn't she know that my whole life has been one big trouble? What kind of trouble could compare to it? I was at once angry with her for taking the nun's side and resentful that she hadn't noticed how much happier I'd been since inventing my stories. I decided not to talk to her about things that bothered me and only talk to Fat Mary. I'd take my life story into my own hands and do with it as I pleased because in the end it really didn't matter to the Americans, who were just making conversation anyway.

Deep down I didn't want to upset Cathy, so I asked Fat Mary if there was another way for me to handle the questions, and she counseled me. *It's hard for others who don't know your soul to understand. Sometimes in life we do what we have to do to preserve ourselves. You're an expert at that! And don't you remember? It was the Americans in your high school who taught you about "white lies."*

6

Sandals in the Snow

How can I forget my endless curiosity about the wonders of American living my first year in Minnesota? Cathy had told me not to let anyone into the apartment when she wasn't home, but one day I saw a man coming up the steps carrying something big and heavy. I thought it was a delivery for her, so I opened the door even before he knocked. He stretched out his hand and said, "My name is Tom Anderson, and I'm with the Hoover Vacuum Company. I want to demonstrate for you this top-of-the-line vacuum cleaner."

Cathy had a small, lightweight vacuum cleaner. I sensed an opportunity to learn how it worked. "Yes, please. I'd like to see how it works."

He sprinkled the living room carpet with sawdust, then proceeded to vacuum it. Not a speck of the sawdust remained. "See how powerful this vacuum is?"

"How does it work?"

"Didn't you see how well it worked?"

"Yes, but how does the vacuum pick up the sawdust?"

He turned the vacuum upside down and showed me the rows of tiny brushes underneath.

"But how does it work?"

"Excuse me?

"What makes the brushes rotate and clean the carpet?"

He looked at me a little skeptically and said, "It's powered by electricity, of course."

"How?"

"You plug the cord into the wall outlet, then turn on this switch and push the vacuum over the carpet," he said slowly and distinctly.

"How does electricity get behind the wall?"

"What?"

"I've seen toasters make toast, coffee pots make coffee, and electric frying pans fry food. But how does plugging a cord into the wall make everything happen?"

He was exasperated. "Miss, you don't have to understand electricity in order to use your appliances."

"I'd really like to understand it."

"Sorry, it's not my job to explain electricity. I just sell vacuum cleaners." With that, he abruptly unplugged the cord from the wall, packed up his vacuum cleaner, handed me some Hoover literature, and left.

Whether I was completely bewildered by my new life or totally fascinated, I was always observing it. As I had done all through my childhood when I didn't understand situations or people, I often stored my experiences away to reflect on them later. Cathy was my mother now and getting to know her gave me much to observe, ponder—and relish once I caught on to her mannerisms and rituals. This was especially true since we were sharing an apartment and doing nearly everything together.

"Grandma Bergquist makes the best tapioca pudding in the world," Cathy announced as she carefully unwrapped a glass jar enclosed in newspapers sent home with us after dinner in Minneapolis with her best friend's grandmother. Handing me the pudding, she admonished me to hold it with both hands as I carried it from the kitchen counter to the refrigerator, four feet away. I rose to the occasion and successfully set the jar in its designated spot farthest from the door, just underneath the light, near the mayonnaise, but not touching it. The next time we returned from an evening with Grandma Bergquist, Cathy decided to transport her beloved pudding herself. She dropped the jar somewhere along the treacherous path from countertop to refrigerator, then proceeded to cry real tears as she painstakingly separated the broken glass from the white mush on the dirty floor and put the now "just pitiful" pudding in a Tupperware bowl.

She also entrusted me with the transportation of the care packages from Onamia, and sometimes she even let me unpack them. "I swear I don't know how I survived in Africa without Sophie's pickles!" She had a comment for everything she unpacked. I hated pickles and wondered how anybody could eat what resembled biology lab specimens preserved in formaldehyde.

"Let's have some of Mabel's strawberry jam." She reached for the breadbox but changed her mind when she realized that Mildew's (Mildred's) angel-food cake was next to be unpacked. She measured a thin slice of cake, then said, "What the heck," and cut almost a quarter of the golden cake, set it on the counter, and spread a thin layer of jam on it.

"What the heck," she said again, and smothered the cake with more strawberry jam until it oozed onto the counter. "Mary, quick! Get me a plate!" Before I could get it to her, she said, "What the heck" again and ate the cake right off the counter. When she finished, she asked, "Do you want some? You know you can always help yourself."

I wondered about the meaning and use of "What the heck." Should I say it before or after I cut my piece of cake?

In the meantime, I was losing weight. I lost twenty-five pounds my first year in America. Although I loved American food, I must have left my appetite in Africa. In school, the Sisters always asked if I was well, but the students told me I looked great. "How did you do it?" they'd ask. In Africa a thin person, especially a woman, was not considered attractive or desirable, so I had no idea why being thin seemed so important to them. Cathy insisted I see a doctor for a complete physical, and when I did, the doctor found nothing. I could have told him what was ailing me: I was suffering from a profound disease called culture shock and a severe case of homesickness.

My brain was exhausted trying to figure out a lifestyle and living standards that everyone took for granted and few bothered to explain. The cold Minnesota wind blew, bit, and chewed on my bones until they ached. Our apartment was only two blocks from school, but my feet froze every morning by the time I arrived and stayed frozen all day. I saw the other students wearing the cumbersome clothing and boots that Cathy thought I also wore to school every day. These students could still move and think and pretend the cold didn't bother them. I decided to wear the bulky coat, hat, and mittens, but not over my frozen body was I going to wear those boots!

The first few times it snowed, I walked to school in my sandals but decided to call a taxi when my classmates told me not to walk in the snow without boots. The taxi driver flatly refused to take me the two blocks to school. He just shook his head and sped off mumbling and swearing. I finally learned to walk in the ugly boots that Cathy insisted on buying for me, but I removed neither my hat nor my mittens as I sat in the classroom. I removed my right mitten only to take notes. After prompting, urging, advising, and outright telling me to take off my hat and mittens indoors, teachers and students gave up. I was sure that if I removed my hat, my head would turn into a solid block of ice. If they knew how mercilessly the cold gnawed at my bones, they'd leave their hats on too, no matter who laughed at them and said they were "cute."

I longed for the free movement of nonrestrictive clothing and the simplicity of getting dressed for school in Africa. I longed to hear Swahili and to sing the songs we used to sing. Most of all I longed to dance. Didn't anyone in America dance unless it was at an organized occasion? In the months since I'd come to the United States, I hadn't danced at all. How could I live without dancing? We had a dance at school, but it was a disappointment. Everyone danced with a male partner, and those who didn't have a partner hung onto the chairs, neatly arranged along the walls of Marian Lounge. Why couldn't I dance with my girlfriends—one, two, or three at a time, like we did in Africa?

Most of the dances reminded me of the ones we had seen in the American movies during my high school days. We had to be told that the couples on the screen were dancing because we couldn't figure out why they were glued to each other with eyes closed, taking tiny steps back and forth and not covering any ground. Even the German waltz that I learned from the nuns in Kifungilo seemed exciting compared to this slow dancing. When African students from Macalester, Hamline, or St. Thomas came to St. Catherine's and we danced our way, I felt my soul come alive again.

Cathy worked hard to provide for all my needs—physical, emotional, and cultural. She taught English, speech, and journalism at Oltman Junior and Senior High School in Cottage Grove, often leaving our apartment to drive to work when it was still dark. She came home tired and spent but always cooked our meals because that was one skill I was not excited to learn. She also found time to take me shopping at department stores like Dayton's, Donaldson's, and J. C. Penney. I loved shopping in the huge buildings with multi-levels connected by elevators and escalators, with the overly friendly salespeople who greeted every customer like a long-lost friend. I was consistently overwhelmed by the sheer size of the stores and the amount of merchandise available to buy.

Just before my first Easter in America, Cathy took me to Penney's to buy a spring coat. We found a beige, loosely woven, three-quarter length coat with three huge buttons in front and spacious pockets. I loved it! When we got home, I quickly hid it in my closet because I was afraid Cathy would remove the label and price tag attached under one arm with a small safety pin. She had a habit of removing the tags immediately, so I seldom got to savor the fact that the clothes she bought me were new. On Easter Sunday, I ceremoniously put on the coat, making sure the tag was visible. I tucked my hands in my pockets to cover the tag so Cathy wouldn't see it, and off we went to church. During Mass, a woman in the pew behind me tried to be discreet as she pulled on the tag. "You still have the price tag on your coat," she whispered.

With a contented smile, I turned to her and replied, "I know."

7

Piña Coladas

I dated African and American guys, but I didn't enjoy it much. Why should I go to a bar for vicious drinks whose names I couldn't pronounce when I could stay home and study? Yet there were certain dates from my college years I'll always remember—such as the guy Cathy liked the most because his name was Gad. One day after Gad had called asking me to the movies, Cathy asked, "Who is that calling so late?"

"Gad," I replied.

"What'd you say?"

"Gad. We're going to the movies on Wednesday."

"Just a minute. Did you say his name was God?"

"Yes, he's from Kenya. I met him at our school dance." I usually told Cathy only the minimum about my dates because she wanted to know more about them than I did.

"But is his name really God?"

"Yes. Gad."

"Jesus Christ! You can't date God. Nobody dates God!"

Here we go again. Will I ever understand Cathy? Only after hearing Cathy and her friends laugh uproariously when she told them I was dating God did I realize my Swahili pronunciation of Gad was the same as God in heaven. Even I thought it was funny when she watched for the expression on people's faces as she introduced us as "Mary and her boyfriend God!"

I got drunk for the first time in my life with Richard.

"I want to take you to the Waikiki room at the Nicollet Hotel downtown Minneapolis. Have you ever had a piña colada served in a fresh pineapple?"

"What's a piña colada?"

"Do I have a treat for you! You'll love it. Pick you up at eight."

I spent the rest of the week wondering what a piña colada was and what was the correct way to eat the fresh pineapple. Should I peel it first or just slice off the top? I was tempted to ask Cathy but changed my mind in case she thought it was something bad and would tell me not to have it. Then I'd have to disobey her and lie if she asked me about it and that would make me feel miserable.

The drink was "magnificent" as Cathy would say. It was in a real pineapple all right, but the flesh was scooped out. In its place was a sweet, intoxicating mixture of coconut and pineapple juice that reminded me of fresh coconut, which I hadn't had since coming to America. I almost inhaled it after I removed the long straw that interfered with the taste when I tried to act ladylike and sip it. The decorative paper umbrella and other plastic paraphernalia camouflaged the pineapple spikes, so I removed them too and enjoyed my piña colada.

"You like it, don't you?" Richard ordered another one for me.

"Without a doubt, this is the best drink I've had in my entire life!" I heard myself imitating the superlatives Cathy applied to the contents of her care package from Onamia. I wondered why she never made it for me or even told me about it. I'd tasted bourbon, gin, scotch, vodka, and wine with my other dates, but all those drinks were bitter and unappealing. I felt ugly as I drank them because my face mirrored their unpleasant tastes.

I drank my second and third piña coladas just as quickly and told Richard I was full and ready to go home. I counted on his being like most other men I'd dated—he'd insist that I have another one—but he moved the empty pineapple from my place and said, "We came for dinner, and we're not going anywhere until we've eaten, if it's okay with you."

"Can I have more piña coladas with dinner then?"

"You like them that much, eh? Of course, you can have as many as you wish, but eventually you won't taste them because you'll be drunk."

"I've never been drunk, and it's impossible to get drunk on pineapple and coconut juice."

"And some rum and probably other liquors as well."

"No way. I'd be able to taste them because I don't like liquor." I thought Richard didn't want to order more because they were expensive, so I asked for hot tea with my meal.

After four piña coladas, I really wasn't hungry, and I was uncomfortable because I had to go to the bathroom. I discreetly cased the room, found the restroom sign over to my right but couldn't figure out why it was moving as if being blown by wind. I excused myself and headed for the sign, but when I got there it had moved, and there was a wall in its place. I found the sign again, but this time it was sitting on an empty table to my left. I went toward it, but because my feet couldn't keep up with my head, I walked past it and back again several times. Now why doesn't that sign stay still? Thank God somebody walked beneath it. I quickly followed her.

We entered the restroom together, and with a loud bang of a door, she disappeared. Three handles danced on a door to my right. I reached for them several times before I caught one, which delivered me to the toilet seat. It felt great to sit down. When I got out I found myself looking at a row of multiple sinks on the wall. I tried to remember what I was supposed to do with them and their shiny silver faucets. In the mirror in front of me, someone was imitating everything I did and making faces, so I made faces back.

On my way to our table, my knees buckled every few steps, but that was because the room was moving and swaying. I thought it was funny that I kept missing my chair and wondered why Richard wasn't laughing. He tried to help me a few times, but I told him I was old enough to sit down by myself and he should get me another piña colada. I asked him if he had seen the dancing restroom sign and told him the doors all had three handles.

As we talked, Richard's face became distorted, and all I saw was his mouth full of threatening canines as he accused me of being drunk.

"So you think I'm drunk? Ask me to stand on the table and dance. And then ask me to speak French. See, you know I'm not drunk. I know when people are drunk. I've seen many drunk Wasambaa in Kifungilo. They talk soooooo loud and they fall down . . . and they chase weemen and get them very badly pregnant. Then they vomit all over and fall asleep, and the priest forgives them at confession on Friday, and they start again on Saturday. So, you see I am not drunk."

At some point, I saw someone who looked like Cathy wiping the tub. The bathroom resembled ours, except that the toilet seat was on the ceiling and little children were singing "Ring around the roses" and running around the bathroom but never falling down.

When I woke up, my head hurt so much that I imagined the devil picking at it with his huge, rusted pitchfork. I wondered what was happening to me and why I felt so sick.

Cathy had gone to church, so I crawled on all fours to the phone to call Richard. I asked him if he also had a terrible headache, felt dizzy and weightless. Could it be something we ate? I suggested we go to a different restaurant next time. Richard sounded like a stranger. He told me I had a hangover, and he wanted to make it perfectly clear that unless he called me first, I was never, ever to call him because "in America, women do not call men for dates." Then he said, "I will call you later in the week," and hung up. After a minute or two of gazing at the phone with an open mouth, I remembered to close it and crawled back to bed.

"What's the matter with me?" I asked Fat Mary. She pulled my sweaty, matted hair from my face. *You got drunk just like some of the Wasambaa of your childhood. You made a mistake, that's all! With each mistake comes an opportunity to learn. The first lesson is that everybody makes mistakes. The mistakes you made won't change your character or your beautiful soul. That's the second lesson. The third is you must resolve never to make the same mistake twice.*

That episode precipitated agonizing, tearful lectures from Cathy about drinking and men and how lives had been ruined by alcohol. She cried when she told me that one of the biggest crosses she'd had to bear was that her father, Mr. Murray—my favorite man in America—was an alcoholic. I'd heard her use that word when she talked about her cousin Mary Jane. I couldn't understand why she'd think her father did the same crazy things Mary Jane did—like never cleaning her house, not knowing where anything was, hiding liquor in Coke bottles, passing out at ten in the morning and need-ing someone go to her house to see if she was still alive.

I revered Mr. Murray. I spent my first two summers in America working for him at his drugstore, and I never once saw him drink al-cohol. He'd hug me and tell me I was his beautiful princess and give me twenty dollars and tell me not to tell "Pal," his name for Cathy. "Save it," he'd say. And when I tried to give it back saying that I didn't need it, he'd say, "Here's twenty more. Save it for a rainy day." For a long time I wondered why I had to save money to give to a rainy day, then Jackie explained the idiom. He was right. I had several "rainy days" when his gifts came in handy.

For my first Christmas in America, Mr. Murray asked me what gift I wanted. I said I wanted a watch. He sent me a thick jewelry catalog from which he purchased merchandise for his store with a marker in the ladies' wristwatch section. He said to pick any watch I wanted. Cathy had trained me to look at the price of something I wanted before reading its description. I found a dainty gold Hamil-ton watch with a black leather strap for sixty-eight dollars. Knowing that Cathy would disapprove of it since there were others less ex-pensive that were "just as good, if not better," I didn't show it to her. I went straight to Mr. Murray, who bought me the watch for Christmas.

I wore the watch for special occasions and still have it today, fif-ty years later, even though it doesn't work and can't be fixed. Cathy's lectures on "saving things for good" never made the slightest im-pression on me except for that watch.

I also saved the beat-up old suitcase Mr. Murray had sent mon-ey to Cathy to buy for me. The zipper was rusty and broken; the vinyl-covered cardboard showed an accumulation of scratches and scars acquired on its long trip from Tanzania to America in 1963. Unfortunately, it fell apart when I tried to stick one more piece of duct tape on it to hold it together for my move from Minnesota to Florida in 1998. That dilapidated suitcase had held all my earthly possessions when I was nineteen. Over the years, it reminded me that with the contents of my suitcase, Cathy, and Fat Mary, I had everything I needed to live and fulfill my dreams in America.

Cathy must have been mistaken about her father, though once Sophie had called and asked me to "Tell Catherine Ann that he's at it again. We've taken him to Hazelden."

Was I an alcoholic after that night, I wondered? I was miserable for a whole week and couldn't understand why anyone would become an alcoholic by choice. Since Cathy was so sensitive about the subject, I discussed my fears with Jackie, who assured me I was not.

8

Dating Game

 "There's no way I'm going to let you go out with that crazy old man again," Cathy warned me after I made the mistake of telling her I'd double-dated with a friend, and my date was fifty years old and had been in prison. Cathy hung up the phone on him when he called, even though I said Howard had treated me nicely and hadn't tried to kiss or touch me. I almost mentioned that he reminded me of Father Antonio and even Father Michael, but I realized she'd ground me for life if she knew I'd kissed a priest!

"I don't care if he brings you Belleek cups, gold chains, and ruby rings. He probably stole them anyway! It will be a cold day in hell before he gets past our door again."

I liked Howard. I decided not to tell her that he served time for molesting a thirteen-year-old girl. After he explained the whole story to me, I thought I understood what molesting meant. I believed him when he promised not to molest me, whatever that was. Eventually I understood his crime. Then it dawned on me that probably what Father Antonio and Father Michael did to me also belonged in the "molesting" category. I knew that what they did with me was forbidden by the Catholic Church—but was it illegal only in America? Did it make a difference that I was a neglected young girl starving for love and attention and didn't see it for what it was? Was that why Howard's age didn't matter to me? I told him Cathy was upset about him. He said he understood and stopped calling me.

After my arrival in America, I corresponded with Father Michael only once a year, to send him a Christmas card. He always responded in the usual noncommittal way I remembered so well. When I was a junior in college, he wrote to say he was visiting a friend in Illinois and would love to come to Minnesota to see me. Previously I would have taken such a visit as proof that he cared enough to travel across the ocean to see me. Fortunately, I had taken Fat Mary's advice to leave him in Africa because my suitcase would be too heavy otherwise. The days leading to my departure had been agonizing because I had come to realize Father Michael was using me for sexual gratification, and his feelings for me didn't come close to what I felt for him.

As he walked off the plane, I felt a twinge of joy, but it was quickly replaced by the pang of his betrayal. Cathy was happy to see him, and the three of us went to Onamia to spend a few days at a cabin near Lake Mille Lacs.

He tried to kiss me when we were alone, but the game we had played so long ago was over. Now I had only feelings of gratitude for everything he had done to further my education and to help Cathy get me a passport. He wasn't upset or angry when I pulled away. He simply said, "You've become more beautiful than I remember, and I will always long to hold you in my arms." His words went in one ear and out the other.

I was surprised at how emotionally detached from Father Michael I had become, but then Fat Mary wanted to talk. *Father Michael came into your life for many reasons. Those reasons no longer exist. Keep your good memories. Keep the lessons. Believe in the innocence of your early love and trust. Forgive him for hurting you and forgive yourself for believing in him.*

"Thank you for making the effort to visit me. It was good to see you," I said to him at the airport. On the way home, I wondered how I would have felt if Father Antonio had visited me. After our final goodbye in Africa, Father Antonio appeared only in my dreams. I never saw or heard from him again.

I dated Amin, a student from Sudan, off and on for two years. I just couldn't let him go, even though we often disagreed and quarreled about every topic, especially religion. He would recite passages from the Koran with fire and drama, then challenge me to recite anything from the Bible so he could prove that the Bible and the Koran were similar. I could quote a few psalms and had learned to tell stories from the Bible in my own words. He'd then recite supposedly the same story from the Koran. The only problem was that he recited them in Arabic. How was I to know he wasn't repeating some government ordinance or the words from the love songs he sang to me?

He'd sing and dance, swaying his hips, lifting his high buttocks as he undulated his torso and raised his chest, while his hands caressed an imaginary feminine figure, following her contours from head to toe. His thick, very black lips were cracked and loaded with Vaseline. After a song, he'd wipe his lips and smack them several times to moisten them in anticipation of what I usually did when he danced that way. When I was intoxicated by the grace and splendor of his body in motion, I'd join him with my own variations even though Sudanese dancing was different from my own. He laughed at me, and I jumped on him, kissing and hugging him until he couldn't move or sing anymore. "Mary, Mary," he'd say, "let us marry."

I loved Amin. He wrote me long love letters that I hardly understood because his English was unrecognizable. He was on a scholarship studying engineering at the Dunwoody Industrial Institute in Minneapolis. One of our favorite pastimes was spending the evening in his apartment, transcribing that week's letter to me. His body language as he read his letter left no room for misunderstanding. I would correct his grammar, vocabulary, and punctuation mistakes with my red pen, rendering the letter illegible. Then he'd say, "See, my blood is bleeding from my heart to the words, and it can be stopping only when we married together."

Then we'd kiss and he'd carry me to his bed and tell me he wouldn't make love to me, not only because I wouldn't let him but also because he wanted it to be "holy in the blessings from Allah" on our wedding night. He'd ask for "a visit" to my "forbidden fruits," and we lay there in total bliss, often forgetting to go out for dinner or to a dance at one of his friend's apartments arranged every Friday night by the Sudanese students at Dunwoody.

Amin was proud of me. We'd start dancing, and then he'd stop, take a few steps back, fold his arms across his chest, and watch me. Then I really showed off, and by the end of the song, everyone in the room formed a circle around me and cheered me on with screams and the ululations I had thought only women made. In those tiny, dimly lit, one-room student apartments, I did my best dancing and felt loved by each and every person there who treated me like a sister. I looked forward to my dates with Amin and the special bonding with others from my continent.

Cathy and I went to Amin's graduation from Dunwoody. At the celebration that evening, both Amin and I knew that with his return to Sudan in two weeks, everything would change. The familiar sadness of another farewell choked me, and I spoke in whispers so I wouldn't cry. Amin was the first one to weep. He said it would be a miracle if we ever saw each other again. He had hoped we'd be married here and then in another ceremony in Sudan, but as that hadn't happened, he sadly repeated, "All is lost."

It was then he told me he had been engaged to a girl since she was twelve, and now that she was eighteen, he'd have to marry her if he didn't bring a wife. He cried uncontrollably, and I found myself calmly wiping away his tears, even though the thought of Amin being someone else's husband hurt me and made me jealous. He said that if I ever changed my mind, he would take me as his second, third, or fourth wife.

I almost married Daudi, whom I met when I was a junior in college. He worked at the Tanzanian Embassy in Washington, D.C., and had come to Minneapolis to give a speech to the African Student Organization at the University of Minnesota. Right after the lecture, a Tanzanian friend handed me an invitation to a private party for Tanzanians. As I waited in the reception line, I noticed Daudi looking at me even as he greeted people in front of me. When I approached, he shook my hand firmly and asked me several questions in Swahili.

Three days later I received an invitation on impressive stationery from the Tanzanian Embassy, its beautiful emblem of two brightly dressed African women holding up the Shield of Independence with a burning flame in the center. I was invited to a reception in Washington for South African singer Miriam Makeba. Daudi had enclosed a round-trip ticket leaving the Minneapolis-St. Paul airport on Friday evening, the night of the reception, and returning late Sunday.

I didn't care what Cathy said—she was not going to deny me the opportunity of meeting South African singer Miriam Makeba. I'd collected all of Makeba's records and played them on the console turntable I'd won at a church raffle until I knew every song by heart. Never mind that the only ones I understood were the ones in English and an occasional Swahili tune like "Malaika," a love song I knew from childhood, or "Pole Mzee," about President Jomo Kenyatta and his struggles to gain independence for Kenya. I don't know whether Cathy was impressed by the invitation or hoped I'd find an important man to marry, but she let me go with only her customary objections about the "principle" of the whole thing.

Daudi sent two women to meet me at the airport, and we chatted in Swahili all the way to his apartment. He wasn't there, but they gave me a long silky, slinky red dress to wear, and they changed into similar fancy evening gowns. Seeing what they were wearing, I knew the woolen, double-breasted suit Cathy had decided was "appropriate" for the reception at the embassy would definitely put me in the *mshamba* (from the country) category at best. The red dress fit perfectly, and we drove to a hotel for the reception. Daudi met us at the door, kissed me on the cheek and took me straight to Miriam Makeba.

"My friend here says you're a great dancer," she said as we shook hands, "and you mix tribal and modern dance in a pleasing way."

"It's because I have your songs as inspiration," I managed to say.

"You must show me your dance."

"One of my fantasies in life is to sing like you."

I was pleased to carry on a conversation with Miriam Makeba without being intimidated by her. Smiling from ear to ear, Daudi brought me a glass of champagne, gave me a sip, then took me to the dance floor. For a big man, he moved well and he audibly approved of my dancing.

To my delight, Miriam Makeba sought me out, and we danced together, with her imitating my moves. Had Daudi told her to do that? Whether he did or not, I was touched and flattered beyond words.

When we got to Daudi's apartment that evening, there was a

maid ready to serve dinner even though it was 1:30 in the morning. After dinner I thanked Daudi for an exciting, wonderful evening. He kissed me nice and long on the mouth, saying, "Anything for my African queen."

We went sightseeing on Saturday, then out to dinner at an Ethiopian restaurant and to another embassy reception. "I could attend a reception every day if I cared to," Daudi told me. "Working at the embassy is synonymous with receptions. They become very ordinary after a while."

He sent me back to St. Paul with a small bottle of Je Reviens. Did he mean to tell me I would return, as the name of the French perfume suggested? He did. He invited me to visit him in Washington three more weekends before the semester was over, and on my last visit, he came to the airport himself rather than sending someone to pick me up. We went straight to his apartment, where he seemed agitated and uneasy. He didn't kiss me as passionately as usual, so I knew he had something on his mind.

He sat stiffly on the edge of the couch and began, "You see, my African queen, I've brought you here . . . I . . . want to . . . ah . . . I need to tell you something." I sat on a leather stool near him and gave him my attention. "I want to . . . I'll make it short and to the point. I'm looking for a wife. In my position, a wife is very important. I have made arrangements for you to finish college in New York, and then if you agree, we'll go to Tanzania to get married. I love you with all my heart. Will you be my wife? I will get you the most beautiful engagement diamond from South Africa if your answer is yes."

I knew he had feelings for me and I for him, but this I did not expect. Not so soon. I was becoming fond of him and of Washington, and I enjoyed his friends and high society life—a welcome break from my Catholic college life.

"You don't have to answer me today. I just want to know if you'd consider it, and I want you to know that my intentions are pure and very sincere. I'd like you to study in New York because we'd see each other often and you'd get to know me." When he said that, I realized I hardly knew him. How could he propose to someone he hardly knew?

"I'll think about it," I said.

"Tell me now that you love me. I need to hear it. I've looked for you for a very long time. Say you love me, come live near me, and I'll wait for you to finish school."

I sat on his lap and told him I loved him, which had the desired effect. He kissed me passionately and held me so tightly that several buttons from my blouse came undone. I felt his penis enlarge beneath my thighs, and I slowly got off him. I wasn't ready to make love. He grabbed me and put me back on his lap and began undoing the remaining buttons on my blouse. He kissed my breasts and buried his face in them. His skin was rough and sweaty, and he was panting and making strange noises as he continued to kiss and caress me.

"Please, Daudi," I said, "I don't want to go all the way."

"Okay, my African queen." He stopped abruptly. "Anything you say. If this doesn't prove my love and respect for you, nothing I do in the future will."

He let go of me. I stood up, kissed him on the forehead, and walked to the kitchen. I drank a glass of disgustingly cold water, which always had the power to bring me back to my senses. We both got dressed up and went out dancing until four in the morning.

Back in Minnesota my heart told me not to lead Daudi on. I really did not love him the way he loved me. Would I learn to love him more? I knew that in arranged marriages, couples often learned to love each other, even if they didn't love each other before their wedding night.

I'd always wondered if you could make love with someone you didn't really and truly love, but now I knew it was possible. Sex was only one way of expressing love. The feeling I had for Father Michael was different from what I felt for Father Antonio, and the love I felt for Amin was different from what I felt for Daudi. We wrote to each other and talked on the phone, but I didn't visit Daudi again. I finally had the courage to tell him I didn't want to marry him and had no good reason except that I knew it was the truth. I thanked him for introducing me to a life full of merriment and wonder. He understood, he said, and we corresponded until he married another Tanzanian two years later and became an ambassador for Tanzania.

After Amin left Minnesota to return home to Sudan, I compared every man I dated to him. Few came close to his spontaneity, charm, and handsomeness. I mentally superimposed his smooth black skin, his dancing hips, his no-nonsense thick lips, his short, kinky hair on any male who showed even the slightest interest in me.

Edward couldn't have been more different from Amin. I met him at the Chateau Frontenac one night when I was dancing up a storm and men were offering me drinks and promising me the time of my life. I was in Quebec taking a graduate course in French at the University of Laval. In Canada, just as in the United States, people on the dance floor watched me and asked if I was from New York. "Whoa! Where did you learn to dance like that?" "I love you, baby."

Edward was nothing like that. He waited until I sat down and then gingerly, almost inaudibly, asked, "Is this chair taken?"

"Have a seat," I said. I was a little surprised that he didn't want to dance because my attempts at taking a break from the dance floor were often met with "May I have this dance?"

I hadn't sat down for more than an hour and was eager to talk to this man who was obviously a gentleman. He was shy, and he stuttered at the beginning of every sentence until he warmed up. I was attracted to his soft voice and self-conscious mannerisms. His hairline formed the letter W, what we call in Africa "a genius's balding pattern."

After the usual introductions of name, home country, and field of study, he took me to the dance floor. I wasn't sure about dancing a slow dance as they seemed so useless and boring. I danced anyway, and I must admit that it was almost painless. Instead of my eyes wandering to watch anything in the room or my body fighting to keep a safe distance from my partner, this time I enjoyed his quivering, gentle embrace and discovered the pleasure in slow dancing. He moved effortlessly across the small dance floor, and I pretended I knew what I was doing.

I was displeased when someone tapped me on the shoulder in the middle of our third slow dance. After a few more dances, I refused additional offers and searched for Edward, who was waiting for me at our table. We decided to go to another nightclub, where we could talk and listen to jazz. We dated for the six weeks I was in Quebec, and when it was time to leave, I knew I had to see him again.

Edward's letters were pure poetry. I think I fell in love with them first. Despite being an early computer genius who had finished university at nineteen and was at work on his doctorate at twenty-two, Edward was a serious romantic. And he was disillusioned with the research projects he was conducting for the University of British Columbia in Vancouver. We communicated every week, and I was sure he was the man for me except for one little misgiving: he planned every detail about our relationship and our future.

I was worried because his plans were so meticulous. First, he would finish school, work a few months to afford my engagement ring, work some more, then finish his doctoral thesis, get married, travel, and enjoy married life for two years, buy a small house in Vancouver (he already knew which one), and have three children—two boys and a girl. Somewhere in his plans I was supposed to be free to pursue whatever career I wanted—so long as I stayed home after our first child was born. I admired a man who seemed to know exactly what he wanted and how to get it, but I also loved the excitement and anticipation of the unknown, and the challenge, confusion, and education of the unexpected. I felt a little uncomfortable having my life laid out in six-month increments. Edward was serious and unwavering about this matter, so I didn't discuss it with him either in letters or in our many phone conversations. He, who could account for every dime he spent, told me the precise minute he'd call me from Vancouver, and we'd talk for exactly five or sometimes seven minutes.

One day, a few weeks before graduation, Edward called me, said hello, and without further ado proceeded to tell me that it was over. He sounded like a total stranger. I was speechless. I couldn't even ask him why, what happened, or beg him not to leave me. "Good-bye. I will always love you." He hung up, and that was it. To this day I can hear his trembling voice letting me go.

I looked at the phone in my hand as if I didn't know what it was. I sat down still holding it, afraid that if I put it down, it would really be the end of our relationship. My heart ached. I tried to recall everything I'd said to him in the last few weeks and rewrote my most recent letters to him in my head. Could it be he was upset that I was applying to go to France with the NDEA Language Institute after my first year of teaching? Had I or Cathy or my friend Jackie been unkind to him when he came to visit me for Easter that year? Had he met someone else? I had to know. I called him back. He answered, but when he heard my voice, he hung up.

What was the matter with him? Why did he think he didn't owe me an explanation? Didn't he know that I had feelings too? How could he have sent me pictures of engagement rings in his last letter and in a few days called the whole thing off? Did he think—because he knew about some of my past—I was immune to rejection and didn't feel pain?

For the next few weeks, every free moment I had, I thought about him and cried when I was alone. Graduation activities distracted me a little, and securing a job as a French teacher for the fall lightened my heart a bit. When my depression turned to anger, I knew I was on the way to recovery. Who did he think he was anyway? How dare he play with my heart as if it were a computer program that he could write, rewrite, and delete as he pleased?

To console myself, I looked at some of the negative aspects of our relationship and his character. I was so intimidated by his brain that I had often needed to remind myself he was made of flesh and blood and not the computer chips he tried to explain to me. And really, who could live the predictable, organized life he'd laid out for us? Maybe I should have struck first and told him I preferred living lightheartedly in an unknown present rather than grimly programming and prearranging a predictable future.

I should have gone with Philippe, a man I met during the time Edward and I were dating. He was a *caleche* (two-wheeled horse carriage) driver in Quebec, who I knew loved me. We often wandered around town singing French songs and drinking French wine after dropping the last tourists of the evening at their hotels. Sometimes he was so wasted that neither he nor the horse could find the *caleche* shed. He loved to dance almost as much as I did, and we were so compatible on the dance floor you'd think we'd danced as a couple since we were born. He also told me that when I returned to the

States, he'd find another girl, because he would never leave Quebec City. We communicated for about a year, but he never wrote about my replacement. Maybe it wasn't easy for him to find another *Rose Noire* (Black Rose), the name he called me.

After Edward, I vowed never to date again and definitely never to tell any man I loved him unless he begged me on his knees, kissed my feet, brought me flowers and chocolates every day, and took me on trips around the world. He'd have to give me everything I wanted, do everything I told him to, and not question anything I did. He'd have to sign a contract saying he would not leave me without my permission. I felt better. Much better. Mother Rufina's constant warning that "All men are evil" played loudly in my head.

9

Becoming a Black American

In general, except for the occasional insensitive questions, everyone at St. Catherine's was kind and gentle with me. Students helped me in any way they could, and I felt I had come to the best college in America as far as being accepted, even though I was usually the only Black student in my classes.

Four months after I came to America, President John F. Kennedy was assassinated. We loved him in Africa because we associated the Peace Corps program with him. We called the flour in the white, red, and blue bags that America donated to Tanganyika, *kenedi*. "Two kilos of kenedi," you'd hear at the marketplace. "Before you fry the meat, roll it in kenedi."

That year race riots, civil rights marches and demonstrations were daily news, and we discussed the headlines in the Saint Paul Pioneer Press in school. We came to class ready to announce, "They did this, and they said that" and "They want this, and they stole that" as we tried to impress each other with how much we'd read. I joined in the "they" discussions until one day, a student in my history class looked at me and angrily demanded, "What do you people want anyway?" I turned my head along with the other students to see whom she was addressing.

"I know you people came here as slaves and everything, but you're not going to get anywhere by burning buildings and cities . . ."

"And looting and killing everybody," said another student, looking me squarely in the face. "What are we supposed to do? Hand over the country to you? Wouldn't you kill us all?"

A student in front of me broke in. "There's a reason why you're all so poor. You are lazy and ignorant. You drop out of school and terrorize the entire country, and then you expect us to calmly listen and fix the conditions you brought upon yourselves. I'm sick and tired of this whole racial nonsense."

"Why can't you be satisfied?" a student in the last row spoke up. "I think you're forgetting that you started out as slaves, and the more that's done for you, the more you want. You want more of everything. When are we supposed to know when you've had enough? I bet someday . . . someday . . ." For some reason, she shut herself up.

I realized that the students were directing their anger and frustration at me. Among them was a student I'd considered extra friendly and who had even invited me to meet her family. Now she glared at me with accusing eyes, suddenly seeing me as one of "them."

What's the matter with these students? Don't they know I'm from Africa, and just like them I have to learn what the riots are all about? Why do they think I'm supposed to know everything about American Blacks? I'd already realized that just because I was from Africa, I was supposed to know all about the entire African continent, while most of them couldn't even name the capitals of American states.

Many of the questions I'd been asked made sense to me now. They didn't see me as an African but as a person whose skin was black, and I was therefore supposed to be able to explain the actions of all Blacks to them. The fact that I was born and raised in Africa and that they knew more about American Blacks because they were compatriots, did not matter at all. To them I was first a Black, then a Black from another country, and then a person. To them, I was a flesh-and-blood representative of the Black race that they seldom had contact with—and at this stage they would not if they could help it.

Did they know what a miserable representative of the Blacks in America I'd be? Americans confused me when they said, "I'm Italian," "I'm Norwegian," "I'm Swedish," or "I'm German" when their ancestors had been born and raised in America as far back as they could remember. If they were Swedish, why didn't they speak Swedish or even know where in Europe Sweden was? I also wondered why, following that logic, Black Americans didn't simply call themselves "African." Was it because only they were forced to give up their African culture when they were uprooted from their mother country and left like cargo on the shores of a land already taken by others?

As puzzled as I was by my classmates' assumptions, their classification of me as a Black American nonetheless comforted me. Could it be that now, finally, I had my own group to belong to? Would Black Americans claim me just because the whites assigned me to them? It took only a short time, however, for me to realize that what we had in common was not only a pigment affinity but also a history of being treated as second-class citizens by the whites, which put us in the same condemned pool of inferior people. I'd finally found out firsthand from my classmates what I'd quietly observed—that being Black in America was not desirable. Still, I was thrilled to belong to this large American minority. I just wished the other students would give me a chance to learn about Black Americans first before designating me as their representative.

I knew Fat Mary could help me sort my worries and confusion, but I also knew my questions were brand new to her experience.

You know you can discuss anything with me. Whether I have answers or not doesn't matter. As always, I will keep what I cannot explain or understand and give it back to you at the right time.

"Fat Mary, I am feeling the weight of the whole Black race on my shoulders. It is particularly heavy because it's unfamiliar. Do my classmates know my heart has already endured much pain and sorrow and thus turn to me when they can't deal with their personal agonies? Do they really expect me to answer their questions? Does skin color define a person and their experience? Is that why they demand that I explain American Blacks? Do they think I'm faking it when I speak English with an accent or ask them to explain American life and customs? How could they seem so nice, then turn around and blame me for the injustices and unrest they fear will intrude on their happy and privileged lives? What are they so afraid of? Can't they look inside themselves first to understand what is happening in their country rather than unload their discontent on a student from Tanzania?"

All I know is that it's not about you. This revelation will open your mind and educate you in a way that no textbook can. You will now learn about Black American culture. When you were a child in Africa, one of your greatest desires was to belong. In America, your classmates see you as Black, and they believe they know your history based on that. Now you need to learn about Black Americans and embrace your new racial identity. In your heart, you will always be African, but in America you are a Black American. It is possible and desirable to be both.

I took Fat Mary's advice and spent hours in the library, reading and learning about the Africans who had become Americans. I was surprised at how little I knew. I was shocked by their history and shed tears as I read of the cruelty done to them when they were brought on ships to America. But how could I stand up to my classmates and to my future as a Black American when I hadn't lived their experience? Should I pretend to go along because I now understand what's expected of me? Should I forget my own unique African experience as they have had to?

And why were the Black Americans I met at school and parties not interested in learning about Africa? They knew even less about Africa than the *wazungu*. With a few exceptions, they changed the subject when I talked about our villages, our foods, our tribal dances, our clothing, our beads and basket weaving and marketplaces. They often were as condescending as the *wazungu*. How could I be comfortable with people who avoided or perhaps were ashamed of their roots?

I wanted to share with Black Americans beautiful and empowering aspects of Africa. Maybe the strengths and resources of African culture could counter the negative aspects of being Black in America.

At the same time, I did try to blend in and become more African American, but it didn't happen overnight. The most obvious distinction between us was highlighted in social settings. Each time I opened my mouth to speak, someone said, "You have an accent. Where are you from?"

My Swahili accent rendered my speech incomprehensible when I imitated Black American friends, who spoke differently from the whites when they wanted to. Having learned English from German, British, and American whites, I sounded outright ridiculous when I tried to speak what later I learned was "Ebonics." Although I now knew that in America anyone meeting me would consider me a Black

American, my efforts to become culturally Black consistently back-fired because of my accent. Wasn't my accent also a clue to white Americans that I wasn't a Black American? Why did they categorize me and think they knew everything about me based on the color of my skin? Americans in the 1960s looked at me in terms of my skin color first, then my nationality. It was evident to me that racial strife in America was a much deeper issue with different conditions and emphases from what I had known in Tanganyika.

Yet, just as I was comforted by the realization I belonged to a race or group of people in America, I was saddened that the simple and true way I had thought of myself in the past—as a racially mixed African—was disappearing as I learned to think of myself as a Black person. As much as I felt I wasn't part of any tribe in Tanganyika—and definitely wasn't a *mzungu*—I always felt I was an African first, then a mixed-race African.

10

Face under the Pillow

 In the summer of 1965, I participated in a program called Ambassadors for Friendship, sponsored by Reader's Digest through nearby Macalester College. Harry Morgan, who ran the International House at Macalester College, devised the program, which was funded by Dewitt Wallace and his wife, along with thousands of Americans who donated money and hospitality. The idea was to introduce foreign students to the rest of the United States and experience American hospitality firsthand. Two Americans (our leaders) and four foreign students traveled across the country in a donated American Motors Rambler station wagon for six weeks.

The other foreign students participating in this adventure were Yuna from Japan, Chantelle from France, and Lena from Sweden. Yuna and I had the darkest skin of the group, followed by our suntanned American drivers Deborah and Joan. With only a credit card for gas and three hundred dollars for the six of us, we drove from Minnesota to the Southern states of Mississippi and Alabama to New Orleans, through Texas, New Mexico, and Arizona, up along the coast of California to Washington State, then back to Minnesota. The intention was to foster goodwill and better understanding between our hosts and ourselves, wherever we found them.

Few stops were planned. We knocked on people's doors at night to ask for food and shelter. Imagine a motley crew of six strangers, each with a different accent, knocking on your door and asking to sleep "in your yard or the basement, and we would be most grateful for something to eat and maybe a shower."

We were received as guests and treated with kindness and interest about 80 percent of the time. We got a good sample of the diverse standards of living and dialects in the various American states. The murder of four civil rights workers in Mississippi a year earlier intensified the tense racial, political, and social atmosphere in the South.

I've often been asked if I've experienced racial discrimination in the United States, and I must say that early on I probably had, but didn't recognize it. Before realizing that I was seen by many as a Black person first and thus as a second-class citizen, a lot of intended discrimination likely went over my head. Ignorance is bliss—I didn't feel insulted. Still, one of the most painful incidents of discrimination occurred when I was an Ambassador for Friendship, driving across the South.

Early in the second week of our trip, we were in a peaceful park in New Orleans when one of our American drivers took me aside, interrupting my little game of finding and eating the last grain of sugar on my lap from a delicious donated donut. She suggested that during our trip through the next three states I should ride in the center of the back seat and keep my head on my lap whenever we passed a group of people along the road. I would also have to put a pillow over my head. Locals might stone the car, she warned, if they saw racially mixed passengers inside. I asked why only I had to do it when Yuna's skin was as dark as mine. She told me I was obviously Black and Yuna was not.

That night as I slept in my cold sleeping bag under a large oak tree, the intoxicatingly sweet fragrance from a nearby rose garden clashed with the disturbing emotions within me. Every fiber in my body said, "No! I won't ride across Mississippi with my head on my lap or under a pillow! Let them stone me!"

I woke Yuna, and we went for a short walk among the roses. I told her what I was supposed to do the next day.

"Don't do it!" she said.

The next day I refused to hide my head under the pillow on my lap. Our leader gave me a stern look, and I gave her a defiant look back.

"We're not going anywhere unless you do what we discussed," she demanded.

"I will not!"

"Don't you get it? We're not going to risk everybody's life because of your pride."

I didn't think protecting my dignity had anything to do with pride. I sat in the assigned middle seat in the back of the rambler looking straight ahead like a statue. The other three Ambassadors for Friendship started talking to our drivers. In short, they disapproved the plan and said that no matter what happened, they were on my side. We drove slowly and in complete silence for several miles.

I felt like a wounded animal. My wounds were serious and I'd take a long time to recover, but for the moment I couldn't dwell on them. Every cell in my body ached. I was back in the orphanage and Mhonda Middle School, where the nuns told me I was a child of sin and my parents didn't want me. What saved me as a child was that I instinctively knew I belonged to God.

In that car in the South, I reaffirmed my childhood's saving grace. I was a child of God, and in God's eyes and mine I was as precious as ever—every bit as precious as my drivers, the other Ambassadors for Friendship, and all the people who might want to stone me.

We drove the whole day through Mississippi with my head held high. Just after dusk, we passed a small town with only a few buildings and lights. As we entered it, we were congratulating ourselves on refusing to give in to prejudice when I heard our leader say, "Oh no, look behind us." She stepped on the gas. We were shocked into reality when we saw a group of about six or seven people, some of them women, heading towards us. I looked behind but couldn't decide whether the car was throwing up debris or the locals were hurling rocks in our direction. I instinctively ducked, resting my head on my lap, protecting it with my arms.

We got out of town safely, and a mile or two later we knocked on the door of a Catholic priest's house and asked for shelter. He offered us the carpeted basement of the church and phoned a woman parishioner, who came an hour later with peanut butter sandwiches and coffee.

We were all shaken by the intensity of our emotions and a fear of the hostility that might accompany us through the South. We hardly spoke as we drifted into sleep, hoping the morning would bring peace and relief.

Sleep seemed like an unattainable luxury. I wondered if I should have done as I was told. What if standing up for myself endangered the lives of my traveling companions? Yet, in my heart I knew that no matter how our American drivers interpreted my refusal to hide under a pillow, I was not being defiant. I was affirming my human dignity.

Standing up for your human rights is what you must always do. Fat Mary sat at the foot of my sleeping bag, cradling my feet in her soft, loving hands. *Your childhood has taught you that you will always encounter frightened, insecure people who do not think. They haven't learned to search in their hearts for solutions to their pain and sorrow. They blame others because it is easier than admitting they are prejudiced about race, religion, and culture. Family and society have influenced their beliefs. In their hearts, they know that we are all created equal in the eyes of God and the Universe. Whoever thinks otherwise will never be happy. You must try to understand them, forgive them, and you must show them the truth.*

For a very long time I had to deal with the pain in my heart, the anger in my chest, and the disappointment I felt every time I thought of that portion of my trip as an Ambassador for Friendship. It was one of the defining moments of my understanding of race relations in America. It felt like a baptism by fire, an initiation into Black American society. I finally understood the cross every American has to bear, because I now felt its weight bearing down on me. I am convinced that until America lives up to its promise of equality, the heavy cross of racial injustice will crush all Americans, regardless of color.

I learned from experience that some ingredients of the "melting pot" I was so eager to become a part of did not melt, even when stirred. Huge lumps of color, texture, belief, and culture refused or were unable to blend with other ingredients in the common pot. A better description would be "America—the multicultural, multiracial, and multicolored pot." Ideally, once in the pot called America, you'd be an American with all the privileges and burdens of claiming that nationality.

Traveling across the United States showed me the real America—definitely not the one of my childhood dreams. When I was a child, I thought as a child. Even this painful realization hasn't deterred me from believing that I am blessed and privileged to be living my adult life in my chosen promised land.

In June of 2010, I attended a reunion of participants in Macalester's Ambassador for Friendship Program that ran from 1960 into the late 1970s. About eighty people attended, including Yuna, the two leaders of our group, and me. Yuna stayed with me in my townhouse in Minneapolis, and we talked about everything—though neither of us brought up the incident of driving through the South.

One of our leaders, however, seemed preoccupied with making amends. She talked about how young and inexperienced we were and how if we had known then what we know now, it might have been quite a different trip. I told her that now we would never be able to so innocently pile into a car and drive for six weeks to nowhere in particular in search of American hospitality. Such a venture today would require waivers, insurance, lawyers, and who knows what else!

Could a group of young women ask total strangers to use their basements and facilities? Is it still possible to travel the way we did and not worry about safety? Furthermore, today everyone in the car would be on their cell phones texting family and friends and surfing the internet at every opportunity—and miss the whole point of the Ambassadors for Friendship experiment.

The driver who told me to hide under the pillow said she had been anxious to meet with me again after forty-five years. She was worried I wouldn't speak to her. I must admit that right after the incident I had little or no feeling for her one way or the other the rest of the trip. Every time I thought about it, I told myself she was doing her job of protecting everyone in the car the only way she knew how.

Sitting with her in my townhome, however, I felt bad that the memory of the incident was still so vivid for her. She apologized, saying she hoped I knew she never had anything against me. I told her, "I've moved on and do not now or ever did hold a grudge against you for doing your job. We were victims of our time in history." With that out of the way, the four of us had a great time tracing our 1965 trip on a huge road map of America.

11

My Ass

Anticipation and excitement grew as we neared the Grand Canyon. The Ambassadors for Friendship program had arranged a mule trip into the canyon for us. Everyone was looking forward to it—except me. As much as I can, I avoid being on or in close contact with any kind of animal, wild or domesticated. My traveling companions had no grasp of the terror I felt when the guides managed to put me, shaking and sweating, on a mule. They called the animal a mule, but that word was not in my vocabulary. To me it was an ass. That was the name I had learned from the British.

"You have to try it. You might never get the opportunity again. You'll love it. It will be so much fun," they each assured me.

I've always been skeptical of what Americans call fun—activities such as hiking on paths to nowhere or camping in the wild. I was miserable on the camping trips that I took with classmates. Why would I want to sleep on the ground in a constricting sleeping bag, argue with mosquitoes and other *dudus* (insects), listen to campers snore, and walk across the camp to use a primitive toilet—all in the name of fun? Why would I want to watch a pot boil over a smoky campfire when all I had to do in our apartment was turn on a burner, set the timer, and wait for it to buzz when my food was ready? Are my friends doing this for me because they think I'm homesick for the drudgery of daily survival in Africa?

I had the feeling that this trip into the Grand Canyon would be that kind of fun. Given my fear of heights and intense doubts about my ass's ability to descend the steep "white-knuckle" trail haphazardly cut into the very edge of the cliffs, I said all my prayers and put my life in the hands of God—and my ass. We started out in the center of our caravan of twelve, but eventually I ended up next to last, with only one rider and the guide's assistant behind me.

The smell must have triggered something because all the asses stopped at the same spot in the middle of the trail to relieve themselves. By the time my ass got to the designated dumping ground, a cloud of awful-smelling steam hovered over it, and the ground had become a pool of islands of mud and poop defined by steaming streams of urine. Riding slowly through the trail of thick dust clouds saturated with a pungent order of urea made me queasy. I felt like I was going to throw up. My eyes were burning, and because it was so dusty and smoky, I couldn't even see my ass beneath me. I was afraid to look down into the canyon, so I rode with my eyes almost closed. I was worried that my ass couldn't see clearly either.

In panic I yelled, "Help! I need someone to wipe my ass!" I began using my scarf to wipe the dust from his long lashes when I heard our trail assistant screaming angrily from behind, "What the hell's going on?"

I had no idea he was talking to me because I couldn't see him. "You there, what the fuck is going on? Look at the gap you've created between the riders. I've been very patient with you, but we're already fifteen minutes behind schedule. I'm going leave you and move on ahead." The rider in back of me agreed, and both of them passed me.

"And let me tell you, girlie, if you get lost, or if you fall into this hole, it'll be your own damn fault. Stop that! What the fuck are you doing?"

"I'm cleaning my ass."

He stopped dead in his tracks. "Whad'ya say?"

"I'm wiping my ass. There's so much dust, he can't see, and I'm afraid we'll fall into the canyon."

"What the fuck? Oh no! Don't tell me! You crapped all over your mule, and you're cleaning him up? Damn! I've seen throw-up, black-outs, and dizziness, but fuck, no one has ever crapped on me. There's always one, I tell you. I'm sick of this fucking job. We should've left you up on top like you wanted. I'm not cleaning your damn stinking animal when we get back, you hear?"

I had no idea why he was so angry just because we were a little behind. And what did he mean when he said I'd crapped on him? I decided that my ass understood me better than the assistant guide. I talked to my ass, assuring him I'd take good care of him as long as he didn't sit down and wiggle his buttocks in a communal toilet along the trail. I continued to wipe his eyelashes and his face, asking myself when the fun was supposed to begin.

My dusty, dirty ass and I were the last to arrive at the bottom of the canyon. Yuna came to meet me with a huge smile. She'd worn both a hat and a scarf for the descent, and when she removed them the white of her perfectly formed short teeth contrasted sharply with the jet black of her clean, shiny hair. Sitting on my animal with my curly, dusty hair tied back with a rubber band, my teeth clenched in dread of the same fun I'd have going back up the canyon, I must have looked as frustrated and disappointed as Yuna was happy.

"Wasn't this the most beautiful view you've ever seen?" She helped me get off my ass, and before she could ramble on, I asked, "What view?" I looked around me. "You mean the tiny stream running between the two walls over there?"

"No! The view coming down the canyon. I'll never forget this day as long as I live. It's the most beautiful thing I've experienced since coming to America. I can't wait to write in my journal tonight."

In my journal that night I wrote: "Today I was sure that my ass and I would go tumbling down into the Grand Canyon where we would die and no one would find us. We'd rot together and become part of the canyon, but at least I wouldn't die alone. Even though the guide didn't care whether I fell in or not, I knew that I'd have my ass to the bitter end! The Grand Canyon is the most frightening place I've ever been in America. All the way down, my ass' eyes were dusty and sad, and he didn't make any 'heeeeee haawwww' sounds going down or coming up. I'm sure he was just as afraid of the trip as I was and grateful that I wiped his eyes and stroked his back so often. The assistant guide was cruel and scolded me for no reason. Apart from being slow, I didn't understand what I'd done wrong. When he saw me in the bottom of the canyon, he looked at my ass and me and said, 'At least you cleaned up the crap before lunch. Idiot! It takes all kinds.'"

I still had no idea what he was talking about. My ass didn't look like an idiot. He took me down the canyon bravely and safely. The other Ambassadors for Friendship had huge smiles. Based on their happy faces and Yuna's comments, I knew I was the only one who saw the trip into the Grand Canyon as torture. In other words, fun the American way.

12

The New African

In Taos, New Mexico, our group wandered along the tiny streets leading to the artists' shacks, workshops, and art galleries throughout the downtown area. The feeling of peace, love, and life being lived was expressed in many ways. Every stone on the roughly paved and worn cobblestone paths glittered in the afternoon sun, reminding us of the thousands of footsteps they'd welcomed into this quaint town. We entered several galleries where I was pleasantly surprised to see the artists at work. Based on the art courses I had taken in college, I regarded artists as people who locked themselves, their hearts and minds, in an unknown realm where they could extract beauty from ordinary and extraordinary objects. They expressed their thoughts, visions, and images on canvas, wood, metal, stone, or clay for us mere mortals to glimpse their vision.

We entered a Western art gallery where A. Kelly Pruitt was putting finishing touches on a cowboy version of the Three Kings from the Christmas story. The six of us surrounded him, asking questions about Taos and his work. In return he asked us many questions about our respective countries. He wanted to know about art in Africa, and I was ashamed to admit that I knew very little. I suddenly realized that my college curriculum had not taught about or even exposed students to African art. I remembered how proud I felt when carvings by the Makonde tribe in Tanzania were mentioned as having influenced European artists like Picasso and Modigliani. I was lost in thought when Mr. Pruitt asked me my name, country of origin, and my opinion about his art. Imagine an artist asking me for my opinion! I believed that artists created what they wanted and weren't concerned about whether others understood or liked their work.

I wanted to tell him that the bold, thick strokes of multiple colors that were carefully blended, yet managed to retain their brilliance as they swept from the horses' circular rumps into the flowing robes of the Three Kings, transported me to ancient Jerusalem. But all I could say was, "I understand it." He looked at me critically, and I felt as I often did in college when my interpretation of a piece of literature did not match that of my teacher.

"Mary Rose Ryan—is that an African name?" he asked.

"I came with it from Africa."

"Would you do me a favor?"

"Of course," I said without having a clue what that favor might be.

"You'll be here for two more days, right?" I nodded and looked to the others to affirm it. "I'd be very honored if you'd let me paint you."

I thought he wanted to paint my face and skin with butterflies and balloons like I'd seen on children or with hearts and other designs permanently painted on adults. I didn't want to give him an outright "No," so I asked, "Will it come off?"

"Will what come off?'

"The paint."

"Sorry, I don't understand. Will what paint come off?"

Yuna came to the rescue. She and I had already discussed the awful drawings on adults that she'd told me were called tattoos. "He'd like to paint a picture of you? Am I right?" She looked at Mr. Pruitt. "Mary Rose thinks you want to paint a tattoo on her."

"Disfigure her glorious skin with a tattoo?" He laughed as he took my hand and looked me in the eye. "It's not very often that I have an African walk into my studio, and such a non-stereotypical one at that. I believe in your Ambassadors for Friendship program. We all have to learn to live together, don't we? You've inspired me to paint a portrait of you, which I'll call *The New African*. I'll present it to the United Nations to hang in the Hall of Nations. I have a commission and not until today could I think of an appropriate subject, but you've just solved my problem."

A wave of emotions, among them joy, awe, humility, fear, and gratitude, swept through my body as Mr. Pruitt stared at me. I'd been looked over from head to toe before but most often in ways that made me feel insecure and threatened.

Later that night Fat Mary jumped up and down with delight. It was so nice to have a joyous subject to discuss with her for a change. This time our roles were reversed and she asked me questions. *How does it feel to be an object of art? Don't you wish that those people who wanted to stone you in Mississippi could see you now? Haven't I always said that no amount of beating, ridicule, or degradation could change your beauty, inside or out?*

I agreed with Fat Mary that to be chosen by A. Kelly Pruitt for his vision of *The New African* proved he must know and appreciate his own uniqueness. I lived on that high for a long time. Anytime I read something negative about Blacks in the paper or heard about the problems we supposedly cause society, I relived that moment in Taos when an artist, one of those rare creatures who see reality with God's eyes, affirmed my precious human dignity.

A few weeks later when I was back in Minnesota, Mr. Pruitt sent me an article from the *Taos Sun* about our visit to his studio. His painting, *They Followed a Star*, was featured along with a lengthy account of our visit and the Ambassadors for Friendship program. It concluded with "World renowned Western artist A. Kelly Pruitt plans to present his painting, *The New African*, to the United Nations in New York." He also sent me a box of cards of the Three Kings painting he finished while we were there which I used for Christmas cards.

I've visited the United Nations several times, but it never occurred to me to look for the painting. I don't know whether it was ever delivered or whether it ever hung in the Hall of Nations.

13

The French Connection

Ballet was the only course I absolutely failed in college. My hips and butt refused to stay still while I performed my version of *plié* or stood *en pointe*. Loyce Houlton, my modern dance teacher at St. Catherine's who went on to create the Minnesota Dance Company, finally said, "Mary Rose, you are working very hard, but I must tell you that, even though you were born in Africa, you can't dance."

I didn't believe her! If there was one thing I knew I could do, it was dance. Having been brought up in a country where teachers were like gods, I didn't argue with her. I figured she had only her definition of dance. To console myself, at our apartment that evening I stacked three Hugh Masekela records on my stereo and danced nonstop for two hours.

Ballet could never have been invented in the tropics. I concluded that in response to frigid temperatures, people in the Northern Hemisphere forced their bodies to do unnatural movements requiring great efforts to learn and perfect. I put skiing and ice-skating in this category as well. Still, I love watching ballet performances despite failing it in college, and I admire the discipline it takes to make such unnatural, distorted, and exaggerated movements beautiful.

I decided to use my major in French to become a high school French teacher. Sister Marie Philip often commented that my accent was good, but she didn't know who taught me to put accent marks anywhere and everywhere, even on consonants. I told her I'd taught myself. I had no idea what those accent marks were for. But I'd seen them all over French texts, so after writing a paragraph of French,

I'd go back and indiscriminately put accent marks every few words or so.

Mrs. Reed generously helped me with my grammar even though she taught French conversation. The most originally dressed person on campus, she wore bright silk scarves, lace stockings, heels with floral designs, skirts with interesting colors and texture, dangling earrings, bright lipstick, and huge silver and gold rings on all her fingers. She was animated when she spoke—lively, positive, daring, and funny—and so beautiful in my eyes.

Sitting beside her one day, I recalled Cathy's suggestion, "You must always match your outfit if you can." No one must have informed Mrs. Reed of that rule. I looked at the multicolored, multi-textured, multi-jeweled, outrageously not-matching outfit Mrs. Reed wore and knew that if I had the variety of items she adorned herself with, I would dress just like her to remember how wonderful it felt to be near her.

Being with her I felt adored, not only because she often hugged me and said, *"Marie Rose, je t'adore, je t'adore!"* but also because she was the only teacher with whom I felt free to joke with as well as share a little about my life in Africa. Her accent when she spoke English was worse than mine, and I teased her about it. She wondered why Sister Marie Philip and my other teachers complained that I never said a word in class. "Why, *mon petit chou*, you're a chatter-box!" She encouraged me to speak up to give a needed international perspective to our small Catholic college.

When I graduated from high school, the Maryknoll nuns had us wear those awful caps and gowns. I decided it was an American thing because four years later I was wearing the same getup! While families and friends roamed the campus with cameras and class-mates hugged each other goodbye, I quietly savored having achieved my dream of further education. The struggle was worth it. Cathy, who made it possible, was with me at her beloved college campus greeting teachers and friends.

During the long ceremony, I kept thinking of Mr. Murray, who had died the year before. I missed him terribly, and Onamia wasn't the same without him. Although we'd never verbalized our love and admiration for each other, my heart always knew he loved me. The night of his funeral I cried the same kind of tears I had shed when I learned about the death of Rosa, the big girl at Kifungilo who had always been kind to me.

Right after graduation, I received a scholarship for a summer graduate course in French at the University of Laval in Quebec, Canada. My roommate Jenny was from Fort Lauderdale, Florida. At first I was leery of her as a Southern white because of my experience traveling in the South with Ambassadors for Friendship, but she reminded me a lot of my friend Jackie in her sincerity, warmth, and beauty. When we went out in the evenings, she said she couldn't stay out late, dance, or drink wine because she was a Christian. I reminded her that I, too, was baptized and assured her that if I arrived in heaven before she did, I'd dance for her in front of God when she came.

14

Dancing for Dollars

I read and re-read my contract to teach French at Regina Catholic High School in Minneapolis for three thousand dollars a year—my first job and my ticket to financial independence. Until then I had depended on Cathy for everything. My roommate Barbara and I split the rent, utilities, and food. Although I had very little after taxes, I was able to open a savings account and make a small deposit each month.

At Goodwill and Salvation Army stores, Barbara and I bought outrageously low-priced items for our apartment, furnishing the two bedrooms, large kitchen, living room, and bathroom with necessary and unnecessary items, including a wrought iron cat as a doorstop. I treasured my top quality but faded, damaged but mended, wobbly but functional antique and wicker "finds," as Cathy called them. They matched the architecture of our 1920s building, which originally must have been the residence of a wealthy family. Subsequent residents stripped it of stained-glass windows and ornamentation, leaving gaping holes in otherwise exquisitely carved built-in buffets, armoires, and bookcases. The "early Salvation Army" decor of my first apartment offered me a particular satisfaction and pride during that time in my life.

Other satisfactions included the joy of not making my bed in the morning, not having to give an account of everyone who walked through my door, and not waiting for a "decent hour" to use the phone. At last, the tangible benefits and rewards of my struggle for an education came pouring into my daily life. I appreciated and understood the meaning of "Home Sweet Home."

After moving in, I went door to door in the neighborhood to introduce myself. I admired the exterior of apartment buildings and houses that once must have been well-kept mansions and wondered about the trash, including rusted cars, that littered the unkempt yards. Most residents were not home, others were still sleeping mid-Saturday afternoon, and the three women who came to their doors looked confused and skeptical. One of them said, "So what?" when I introduced myself as her new neighbor. I didn't feel very welcome, so I didn't visit anyone else.

I found out later that we were living in one of the most crime-infested neighborhoods in Minneapolis. I took the bus back and forth to work, but never once did I witness any of the acts of violence reported on my street. One night I heard what sounded like the voice of a young man screaming and pleading with an angry woman. She cursed and swore, using words I'd never heard before. I wrote the words down so I could find out what they meant. One sentence was repeated over and over again: "Did you screw the motherfucker?" I figured "motherfucker" was someone's name, but the word "screw" threw me off. People were always yelling on my street, but it never once entered my mind to move or be afraid of the neighborhood.

Barbara insisted that I end my self-imposed exile from men and accompany her to a club she'd heard about. One of many here-to-day-gone-tomorrow operations from California at that time, Never On Friday International met only on Fridays. Its mission was to entice singles to pay high cover charges and buy overpriced drinks for the privilege of dancing to live bands and watching scantily dressed go-go dancers in cages. On a cold Friday evening in December, I ventured out again into the world of evil, manipulative, unpredictable men.

A handsome, tanned man with very dark eyes and a perpetual smile greeted us at the door. Hanging on his arm was a tall, shapely blonde, half his age, with a prefabricated smile.

"Welcome to Never On Friday," he said. "It's going to be a great evening. I'm Andre, your host, and my ravishing hostess is Marina." He looked only at me as he greeted us.

Marina smiled, saying, "Here are tickets for two free drinks each. You girls disappear and enjoy yourselves."

What did she mean by "disappear"? I felt Andre follow me with his eyes as I went to the far side of the half-filled hall of a downtown hotel. As soon as we got to our table, the band started up and someone asked me to dance. I hadn't danced in a while, so I danced long and hard, prompting the usual comments from the crowd.

Whenever I returned to our table, there was a fresh bourbon and soda, courtesy of Andre. At the end of the evening, he came over to me. "Whoa! You can dance, Baby! I knew you'd liven up the party the minute I saw you. Will you be a go-go dancer with us next week?"

"Okay," I said right away, ignoring the funny feeling in my stomach as I gave him my phone number. The next week he took me to a downtown hotel for dinner. After dinner, he handed me a black leather bag and said I could go up to his room to change into the dancing costume for the evening. I went to the restroom instead and examined the outfit. What in the world? Was I supposed to wear this red-sequined, thong-like bottom with the two-sizes too-big, matching minimal top, the fishnet hose, and silvery four-inch spike heels? I put them right back in the bag. He was happy to see me return so quickly and must have assumed I had on the outfit beneath my miniskirt and sparkly top. We drove to the dance hall where Marina, his hostess, was waiting at the door. "Look who's our featured dancer tonight," Andre announced.

Marina, with her plastic smile, gave me my dance schedule, then informed me, "You can't drink tonight. You're working."

"How much will I make?" I joked, never expecting to be paid for what I enjoyed doing more than anything else in the world.

"A hundred dollars now, and if you stay with us, three hundred dollars a night."

What? I could make as much money dancing for three hours a night as I did teaching five hours a day, five days a week! I tried not to think about the money as I looked around the room and spotted a decorated glass box with psychedelic lights circling inside. Three more such cages were suspended from the ceiling in the corners.

Andre announced that we were going to be treated to "raw, sensual, exotic dancing. Our dancer comes from Africa, where this dancing is part of daily life." He was trying to quote what I'd told him about African dance, but in this setting what he said seemed all wrong.

He scowled when I climbed into my dancing cage without the costume he'd given me, but after my first half hour of nonstop dancing to boisterous applause, I saw him cheering with the rest of the crowd. I finished my first shift and descended as the spotlight went to the next dancer's cage.

Andre met me with a hug and kiss. "You're just great!" He was so excited he couldn't speak fast enough. "Baby, you're the greatest! I've never seen such abandon and bliss on a dancer's face! I tell you, you're the best I've seen. You should teach the others."

I heard the compliments, but his words didn't impress me. I was busy looking at the other dancer moving her hips in slow motion and making suggestive movements. She shimmied and shook until her sequined top almost fell off. I didn't fully understand why everyone liked my dancing so much. I danced nothing like her.

Suddenly the lights in the dancers' cages went off and despite electricians' efforts, wouldn't come back on. I could hear the crowd's disappointment. Guests were still arriving—but no dance show. Andre's face was troubled. I spotted a wide, wooden staircase with large flat-topped supporting pillars at the second landing, about ten feet above the floor. As the band played, I slowly walked up the steps and onto the one-foot-square platform on top of the pillar and started to dance. I danced for an hour nonstop amidst cheers, blown kisses, and flying dollar bills. Dancing while perched on the pillar's tiny surface was easier than I thought. I couldn't move my feet and legs too much, but that didn't stop the rest of my body! I loved the attention and decided I would do it again if I had the opportunity.

I got the opportunity when Barbara and I went back to another Never On Friday singles party. Andre and Marina begged me to dance on top of the pillar when the go-go dancers took a break. It was fun and I got the same enthusiastic reaction from the partygoers as I had when I danced before.

"You are so refreshing" I heard again and again when I got off the platform. "Where did you learn to dance like that?" Men were waiting for me and offering me drinks.

"No, no, you can't have alcohol." I heard Andre's voice behind me as he handed me a fruit punch. "Let's talk. I have a proposition for you."

"I'm not working today, just having fun, and I want a drink." I accepted a drink from the man nearest me and turned back to Andre, who offered me a job traveling around the United States with Never On Friday International. Five hundred dollars for performing one day a week plus all expenses paid meant I'd make over two thousand dollars a month, compared to three hundred dollars a month before taxes I made as a teacher. And I'd be doing what I'd never considered work! In addition, he'd pay me for each dancer I trained to perform my "natural technique." Andre said he'd call me in a few days for my decision.

I tried not to think about the money, but it was very tempting. Because of my teaching contract, I couldn't accept his offer at the time, but I could when the school year ended. I was on my own and didn't have to ask permission. I'd simply tell Cathy about my good fortune in getting this work. I'd be making more money than she was, and I could help her.

I had dinner with Andre and Marina to discuss the job offer. I told Andre I could begin when school was out in June. Marina, who had been cautious but cordial towards me since we'd met, was quiet and sullen. When we arrived back at my apartment, Marina got out to let me out of the backseat of the two-door car. I started to say thanks and goodbye when she cut me short, pulled me out of earshot of Andre, and told me in no uncertain terms, "I don't give a fuck what you do, Nigger, just stay clear of Andre!"

I was dumbfounded. Hearing the word "nigger" made me ache with anger. The only way I could express how I felt was to spit on her. Andre got out of the car and came over to us.

"You bitch!" She dug into the curls on my head with her sharp nails. "I'll fix you!"

Andre grabbed her and pulled her away from me. "Cut it out! What happened?"

"Your son-of-a-bitch jungle bunny spat on me. I told you she was a primitive slut!"

Andre slapped her and, covering her cursing mouth with his hand, shoved her into the car. To me he said, "I'm sorry, I'm really sorry." He shouted toward the car, "What's the matter with you? Do you know what you've done? You've insulted the person who could train our dancers and make money for us!"

"You're on her side? Look at my face! A fucking nigger spat on me. Can you get that into your lusting head? I bet you fucked her too." I heard her sob loudly as I walked into my apartment without saying goodbye to Andre. I was really confused. How could such a beautiful girl use such ugly, hurtful words? No money, nothing was worth being around her and her filthy, abusive language!

Inside, my roommate greeted me and went back to reading her book. I loved Barbara, but at that moment, I wondered if she also thought I was a nigger and if one day I aggravated her enough, she'd use that word on me.

I had felt the same pain when I rode in the car with my head under a pillow. The pain constricted my chest and refused to let me sleep. Even remembering the joy of feeling unique and beautiful that I'd experienced with the artist in Taos could not stop the hurt. I realized that just as you can recall and reexperience the blessings in your life, so too can you relive the hurt of every insult and abuse you've accumulated over the years. There is no such thing as immunity from the joy or pain of the past, especially from the pain.

I asked Fat Mary if my life would ever change.

You cannot change the fact of people feeling uncomfortable and threatened by you. Be steadfast in your childhood love and belief in yourself. You planted the seed of self-worth when you were five years old. You're now very strong and powerful. Don't give that power away.

15

The Statue

On one hand, Andre gave me the chance to dance freely, to dance my heart out, and to be recognized and praised for what to me was natural behavior! On the other, the crude blow delivered by his girlfriend was painful and hurt me deeply. But one thing I know about is pain—intentional or unintentional—caused by others. Oddly enough, the brief dealings I had with them and the opportunity to dance were the occasion of a major shift in my life.

My last night of dancing on the platform before splitting with Andre and Marina, I noticed a young man staring at me intently for so long that, except for the ice cubes in his drink shifting every so often, I thought he might be a statue or even a store mannequin. I could hear the ice in his glass clinking between songs, but I didn't see him drink, and he didn't move from his spot. Most men there were dressed casually, so the statue's sports coat distinguished him from the frenzied crowd. When I came down from the platform, the statue moved toward me.

"May I have this dance, madam?"

We danced several dances. By then I wanted to sit down, but he refused and continued to do what he called dancing until I was called back to the platform.

When the evening was over, Andre proudly wrapped his arms around me, paying no attention to my dripping, sweaty body and clothes. Marina joined us to say goodbye to people as they left. Down the line, I saw the statue again. He approached me and stretched out his hand, saying, "It's a pleasure to make your acquaintance, madam." Where could he be from with his textbook British English?

He seemed nervous but determined to speak to me. My next action was a surprise to me, and it proved my dislike of men was taking a back seat. With one arm snugly linked to Andre, who was busy saying goodbye to everyone, I reached into my purse, ripped the address and phone number from a check, and slipped it into the statue's handkerchief pocket.

The next morning when I opened the door to get the newspaper, I found a long, narrow purple box. Oh no, I thought, I'm not touching that. I woke up Barbara and told her something suspicious was at our front door. Nothing but nothing rattled my roommate.

"I'll check it out," she said. "Well, your suspicious box contains a dozen red roses addressed to Miss Mary Rose Ryan." She handed me a little green envelope attached to the box.

"Roses? Who would send me roses?"

"Read the note!"

I ripped the card open. *The language of flowers expresses what I cannot express. It was a pleasure to make your acquaintance last night. —Kjell Bergh.*

I had no idea who Kjell Bergh was and didn't recognize the phone number written on the card. After reading the note again, I guessed from its proper English that the roses must be from the statue. I told Barbara about the strange man who didn't take his eyes off me the whole night and who learned his English from Queen Elizabeth herself.

Barbara hadn't seen the statue because she was dancing with a guy who turned out to be Kjell's friend Steve. Barbara wanted to know more. "Is he good looking? Tall?" She was placing the roses in an apple juice bottle, since we hadn't found the right vase to complement our Goodwill/Salvation Army decor. "Oh look! Here's a letter!" she said, pulling an envelope from under the roses and handing it to me.

January 26, 1968

Dear Mary Rose,

Flowers speak their own language—and in themselves constitute the ideals of Man: filled with beauty, overwhelmed by quietness and still so ultimately full of life as they are.

Unfortunately, man does not live up to his ideals. And thus the promise of the flowers seldom reaches beyond the stage of symbolism of what Man could and should have been.

And then, as a refreshing breath of spring, comes the rare exception to the paradoxical rules of life, every bit as refreshing as a flower, proudly raising its neck in defiance of devastating winds and yet so very much full of life, joy—and quiet wisdom.

My words will never equal the beautiful language of the flowers. Accordingly, I shall let this modest bouquet express my feelings in its own words.

Brief meetings seldom leave deep impressions in my mind. If you will listen to the language of the flowers, you will know their interpretation in my mind.

It gave me a deep pleasure to meet you—and I am deeply impressed with your very natural and honest way of being.

På gjensyn! (Until we meet again!)

Kjell Bergh

Was this some kind of subliminal love letter, open to several interpretations, or was this Kjell guy a poet? I've always been leery of poets who complicate life and emotions with verses and rhymes that give me a hard time figuring out what they are really saying.

I gently felt the velvet crimson petals of the roses between my fingers as I counted them. "Why would anyone buy twelve roses when one's enough?"

"Roses are usually sold by the dozen," Barbara answered.

I remembered that the flowers I received in Africa were always picked from a garden, the roadside, or a forest. These roses in their apple juice bottle were store-bought. Just like a store-bought dress was a status symbol in Africa, the roses had more mystery than beauty for me. I went to the telephone.

"Hello, may I speak to Mr. Bergh?

"Yus a minuut," a male voice answered. The heavy accent reminded me of the nuns in Kifungilo, and I was grateful that my spoken English had improved thanks to the American Maryknoll sisters in Africa and my years in America.

"Hello!"

"Hi Kay-jell. This is Mary Rose. We met last night and you sent me roses and a letter this morning," I said matter-of-factly.

"Yes. Thank you for calling. It was a pleasure to meet you. Did you like them?"

"I was very surprised, but they are pretty. And thank you for the letter."

"Did you like it?'

"I think so."

"Good."

"Okay."

"Okay."

"Goodbye."

"Goodbye."

"I can't believe that you're not more excited about the roses," Barbara commented.

"You know I don't trust men . . . but this one is different. He seems to—" The phone rang and I grabbed it. "Hello."

"Hello! Would you come driving around the lakes with me?"

"Today?" I wondered who in their right mind would go outside for no reason in the middle of winter, much less drive around frozen lakes.

"There's fresh snow, and I heard another snowstorm is coming." Was this Kay-jell guy crazy? "I like to drive in snowstorms. I'm from Norway, you know."

"So?"

"You don't want to come?"

"No!"

"Would you go to the cinema with me?"

"But it's winter, and I don't go out unless it's necessary."

"It's necessary!" he whispered.

I didn't know what to say, so I said, "Okay."

"I'll be there at six."

When I opened the door for him, I was shocked. I didn't remember him being so good-looking. I did remember his deep blue eyes, but hadn't seen or felt their softness; the blond hair, but hadn't noticed it was almost shoulder length; his slim body, now outlined by

Levi jeans, wasn't visible under his sport coat the night before, and he was taller than I recalled.

One thing I got right from the night before was how proper he was. I wanted to initiate the conversation, but a quick "hello" was all I managed.

"Hello, Mary Rose, I'm glad you decided to come with me. The car is warm and I see you have good Norwegian mittens on."

"They were a Christmas present. What did you get for Christmas?" I asked.

"A few presents, but Christmas is not too important to me."

"It's not?" I wondered what kind of person didn't like Christmas, but I said no more. He took my hand and led me across the street to a light blue car.

"I left the engine running." He opened the door for me, ran around the back of the car, and jumped in, saying, "I thought it would be better to take you to a movie instead of driving outside in the winter when there is snow on the ground."

"Don't make fun of me. I feel the cold more than most people. See?" I removed my mitten and touched his forehead.

"You are ice-cold. Don't you have heat in your apartment?"

I was wearing most of the warm clothes I owned, from a knee-length wool coat with a hood that covered my wool stocking cap to long johns, wool knee-high socks, and fur-lined kickerino boots. He wore jeans, loafers with socks, and a well-worn bomber jacket. If our dressing styles were any indication, we were as different from each other as winter and summer. I was a little irritated that he wasn't taking my feelings about the weather seriously.

When we came out of the movie, the car had been towed away, and we had to walk halfway across Minneapolis and pay a fine to reclaim it. To say the least, it was not a very exciting first date.

The first thing he did was to correct my pronunciation of his name. The proper Norwegian way was beyond me, so I settled on calling him "Shell" as most Americans did. Kjell was telling me a lot about himself as we walked, but I was too busy protecting myself from the cold to pay much attention or ask questions and make polite remarks. He said he'd just arrived from Norway the week before.

He mentioned his family, who had names that sounded strange to me except for Ellen, and he was renting a room from a Norwegian family from his home town of Kristiansund, Norway. One thing I understood beyond a shadow of a doubt that night was that Kjell was a Norwegian and, if I saw him again, I'd better not confuse him with a generic white person born and raised in America.

He said he was studying at Macalester College and working for a car dealership.

"Do you like your work?"

"Yes, and I especially like the owner of the company—he's Norwegian, too. They're the best tribe in the world."

I wondered if he was making fun of African tribes, but then I remembered I had told him nothing about myself so far, but also realized he hadn't asked. We rescued the car and I got in. My teeth chattered as if they were going to jump from my mouth, and I was figuring out whether or not I should forgive him for exposing me to the cold for over an hour, and I decided I couldn't. He took me to the door and asked to see me the next day.

"Could you call me tomorrow? I can't think well when I'm this cold."

"It isn't so cold."

That did it. How could he tell me what I was feeling "wasn't so cold"? Did he think the whole world measured temperature with a Norwegian thermometer?

"No, it's not cold at all," I said. "It's actually 90 degrees out, and I was afraid my woolen clothes and fur-lined boots would be stolen if I left them in the apartment, so I wore them all."

"I'll call you."

I wanted to say, "Don't bother," but I didn't.

16

Little Monkey

Kjell and I dated at least three times a week from then on. After we'd gone out for two months, something struck me about him. He had asked me very little about myself apart from questions such as when did I get home from work and what foods did I like. He had never asked me the questions I dreaded most—about my family. I thought again and decided he wanted to establish his Norwegian-ness and that my "whatever-ness" didn't matter much to him.

Like my college classmates, almost all the men I'd dated wanted to know what my father did, how many brothers and sisters I had, what they did, where they lived, could they speak English, and were they coming to America to see me. I usually told as much of the truth as I could: I was brought up in an orphanage, I didn't know my parents, and Cathy had adopted me.

To my surprise, almost everyone continued to interrogate me. How come I was taken to an orphanage? What happened to my parents, and why did Cathy decide to adopt me? I couldn't answer those questions. I knew that here in America, as in many other countries, my identity was wrapped up for the most part with who my parents were and what they did. Because of Cathy's love, I was slowly learning to be more self-confident, only to fall hard every time I had to face those simple, mostly innocent questions. Often I found out my answers really didn't matter, as my friend Jackie had told me in college. I wished I could learn not to feel so uncomfortable every time I faced those basic questions.

Was it true that Kjell liked me for me and who my parents were didn't make any difference to him? I decided to discuss this with him, and depending on his answer, I would or would not marry him—though he hadn't even asked.

One day I posed the question, "How come you've never asked me about my family?"

"I'm not interested in your family. It's you I love."

I didn't know how to interpret his reply, so I said nothing. Already on our third date, he had told me he loved me. From the way he kissed me and treated me and how he always said, "I'll never hurt you. I just want to make you feel good," and how patient he was each time we were together, I felt he was different from the other men I'd dated.

"But you must wonder what kind of family I'm from."

"I already know all I need to know about you. Your family in Africa can't change anything."

"Do you want to know something?"

"What?"

"I have no family."

"Hallelujah! That must be why it was love at first sight the night I saw you dancing at the top of the stairs. You moved like you owned the world and everything in it, and I tell you, this Norwegian boy wished you belonged to him. I planned to marry you the moment I saw you."

"Isn't that a little presumptuous? How did you know I didn't have a boyfriend?"

"I saw the guy with you, and I watched you all night. You weren't in love with him, and he was flirting with other girls while you were dancing. I can still remember what you were wearing and how I told Steve, 'She's the one! I'm going to get that girl.' I was lucky that you paid some attention to me, because I'm very shy. I had seen you with that guy a week before, but I hate to dance, mostly because I can't dance. The second time I saw you, I asked Steve to dance with your roommate so you'd be left alone and I could ask you. I'm still not sure what I did on that dance floor, but I was not going to let you slip away again." Steve had been an American Field Service student in Norway and stayed with Kjell's family.

"You—shy? Tell me another story!"

"There was a Norwegian boy who loved an African girl. He married her, and they had two children, and they lived happily ever after. End of story."

I was sure he was proposing to me, but who proposes to someone after only three months of dating? I decided that if and when he proposed, he'd have to do it clearly and simply.

To tell the truth, I knew then that I would marry Kjell. He easily dismissed all my fears about being undesirable because I had no family and no wealth, yet it took time for me to believe he loved me for me and nothing else. I had to marry him. Who else had sent me a dozen roses every week for three months straight?

Despite my relief when I realized Kjell didn't care about my past or parentage, it was unsettling that he didn't want to know more about me. Could it be that the only thing that mattered to him was what he wanted? If I had a family, would they not matter to him at all? In Africa, when you marry someone, you marry their family too. How could he pretend family didn't matter? Did anything else about me matter?

Perhaps he had faked his proper English the night we met or was tongue-tied and remembered only the textbook English he learned, because three months later he was using American slang just as I was. He liked to tease and joke with me even though I seldom got his jokes. I didn't mind his teasing, but one day he called me his "little monkey."

I had visions of *wazungu* in Africa shooting at Africans climbing trees and getting away with it because they "thought they were monkeys." The *wazungu*, and sometimes even the nuns, often called Africans "monkeys." I told Kjell that this had better be the first and last time he called me his "little monkey," otherwise his little monkey was going to return to the jungle. He couldn't understand why I was upset, so he tried to explain saying he liked monkeys because they were cute and clever, cunning, quick, and cuddly. The more he explained, the angrier I got. Needless to say, "little monkey" was deleted from his terms of endearment.

17

Mrs. Reed

 Five months after meeting Kjell, I got a National Defense Education Act Institute scholarship for teachers of French to study in Rennes, France, for the summer of 1968. Though I wanted to go, I hated to leave Kjell. My last words to him as I left for Europe were "Wait for me."
"You too," he answered.

The dormitory room I was assigned in Rennes was small and bare. The first thing I did was to put a 5x7 black-and-white framed photo of Kjell on the dresser and talk to him. "You're so handsome!" I told him. I heard him answer, "I know!"

While I was still conversing with him, Mrs. Reed, my French professor at St. Catherine's and now a professor for the NDEA Institute, burst into my room and danced towards the window.

"Who izz zis man to send you flowers all zhe way to France! Sit down, Marie Rose, and tell me all about him. I am your French mother, and I must approve anyone who wants you. Imageeeeen, sending roses across continents! How rich izz ee?"

"His name in Kjell Bergh, and he's even poorer than I am, if that is possible!"

"*Mon petit chou*, you're not poor! Well, maybe so, but you're zhe most beautiful and best dressed poor student I ever had. I couldn't wait to meet zhe woman who brought you to America because I thought for sure she must be as chic and classy as zhe models in *Vogue* magazine. Can you imageeeeen my surr-prrrize when she came to an event at the college in a high-waisted, green pleated dress and grandmother shoes!

Now, Marie Rose, I know for sure your German nuns didn't teach you how to dress. Where did you learn such style?"

Dear Mrs. Reed. I loved her to death, and I usually laughed so hard at her vivid, colorful language, but I didn't know how to react when she made fun of my Cathy. "From Goodwill stores, J. C. Penney's basement, and from donations brought by the students. Cathy buys my new clothes, and I just wear them the way I want. And I sew some of my clothes too."

"Really?" Then she pointed to Kjell's photo. "And zis man sends you roses?"

"Isn't he handsome?"

"Oo la la! Zhat izz true! Ee must love you verrrry much. But I want you to marry a Frenchman."

"Maybe I'll find one here."

"You better not. If you don't marry zis one who sends you roses, you're an idiot!"

"He hasn't asked me officially, but I'm planning to marry him anyway. He's so different from other men I've known. Imagine— he doesn't care at all about my past or my family! Remember we discussed that many American men are shallow, conceited, and prejudiced? I guess prejudice exists everywhere. And from what I've gathered so far, Norwegians are prejudiced because they believe Norway is the best, most civilized, and least racist country in the world—and don't you dare question it."

"So ee izz Norvegian?"

"And how! Sometimes I wish I felt that strongly about America. As Africa's child, I will always have an allegiance to Africa, and now I'm grateful for the opportunity to live in America and to say that it's now my country too. Yet so much reminds me that I'm not from there."

"My children are American, my husband izz American, but I am French and I will always be French."

I had to laugh. There could be no doubt in anyone's mind the moment they met Mrs. Reed that she was French—with a more sophisticated version of Kjell's "Norway is the greatest country" mantra. I so enjoyed her style. From rings on every finger and bright purple opaque tights worn with black and yellow polka-dot heels to the multicolored scarf thrown across her chest and secured with a huge rhinestone pin—no matter what she wore, it suited her.

I gave her a single red rose from my bouquet and told her it was from Kjell. "I know he'll like you when you meet."

"Merci, mon petit chou."

At that moment, a dark, smiling Frenchman knocked at my door and conversed in French with Mrs. Reed. Was I supposed to understand French spoken at that speed? Mrs. Reed introduced me to Xavier, an assistant at the institute. Xavier, who looked like a brooding fifteen-year-old, took my hand and kissed it. *"Enchanté, Marie Rose."* He took a quick glance at the photo on my dresser, winked at me, and left.

"Xavier izz the nicest boy you will ever meet, and I want him to show you Rennes. We are both from here. Forget Mr. Norvegian meanwhile and have a good time. Tonight we're going to La Cave. Xavier dances too—maybe not as good as you, but who can compete with an African when it comes to dancing?"

Oh Mrs. Reed! First she tells me that if I don't marry Mr. Norwegian, I'm an idiot, and then she tells me to forget him and have fun with Xavier. It must be the French way.

La Cave was a disco and nightclub built underground and originally used by Franciscan monks, probably for brewing beer and wine. Maybe they hid there during the Second World War when Germans bombed the nearby city of Brest, made famous by Jacques Prévert's poem with the haunting, melancholy phrase, *"Il pleuvait sans cesse sur Brest"* (It was raining on Brest unceasingly) which we had to memorize and recite in class. I had a wonderful time with Xavier and his friends whenever we went to La Cave. I had no idea there were so many kinds of wine. We had wine with every meal, and Mrs. Reed led the toasts that began and ended with *"Vive la France!"*

The coursework wasn't too hard except for the compositions and the hated *explications de textes*, the painstaking analysis of a literary work required to prove we understood it. Without Xavier's help, I would have flunked that course. Baudelaire, with his somber, macabre poems, was the only poet I enjoyed. No matter that I didn't understand even my own *explications de textes*, Xavier congratulated me on my oral interpretations and said I had a perfect French accent.

After the six-week course, our group traveled the Loire Valley to visit the chateaux along its banks, complete with *Son et Lumiére* performances. We visited several cities including Paris where friends of Sister Marie Philip and Mrs. Reed welcomed us into their magnificent homes and treated us to wine and cheese parties, though we must have tortured them with our prepared speeches of gratitude in French.

One weekend while we were still at Rennes, Mrs. Reed took me to the island of Noirmoutier, to the house where she was born, to meet her delightful mother. I felt like she was my long-lost grandmother. She hugged and kissed me as if she'd known me all her life and begged me to dance for her. When I did, she joined in and danced with everything she had, shouting at the top of her voice, *"Je suis Africaine! J'aime les Africains! Je danserais toujours á l'Africaine!"* (I am African. I love Africans! I will always dance the African way!) The visit to Noirmoutier was one highlight of my trip to France. The other was the weekly arrival of roses and multi-page letters from Kjell. Mrs. Reed demanded her one rose each time. It had to be the biggest and most beautiful one from the dozen. She then proceeded to kiss me the French way on both cheeks and lecture me about marrying Mr. Norvegian.

18

Wedding Plans

Coming off the plane into the Minneapolis-St. Paul airport, I spotted a long white box. My heart beat faster and faster as I ran to Kjell, and we embraced and kissed. Neither of us could talk much except to say how much we missed each other. We stopped several times on our way to the car to look at each other and kiss. Just before we got to the car, he pulled something out of his pocket.

"Mary Rose, will you please marry me?"

He put a thin yellow band on my finger, saying it would have to do until he could afford a proper diamond engagement ring. I didn't jump up and down with joy and excitement because I already knew I was going to marry him. I simply said, "Yes!"

"From now on I'm going to call you Maria Rosa. It suits your personality better than Mary Rose."

"As long as you marry me, you can call me anything you want!"

"Except 'my little monkey'!"

While I was in France, Barbara had moved out of our apartment and Kjell had moved in. It already felt like the home I was going to make for myself, even though by now I knew it wasn't in the best neighborhood. I noticed how neat Kjell was. Everything was in its place, and it was spotless. I remembered once I'd visited him when he was sick. He could hardly lift the bowl of soup I brought, and his hand shook as he raised the spoon to his mouth. I wanted to feed him, but he insisted he could do it. Well, he couldn't. He dropped the soup bowl, making the bed a wet mess. As sick as he was, he insisted on cleaning it himself and begged me to leave.

"I don't like people around me when I'm sick," he said.

"But I'm not 'people.' I'm the one you send flowers to every week."

"Roses!" he corrected me. He was pale and thin and obviously wanted me to leave him alone. Although I was a little hurt, I left.

When we were sick at the orphanage, we were always well taken care of and paid attention to, so when the feeling of being unloved and unwanted became too heavy to bear, we sometimes faked illness.

I imagined us already married. One evening as we lay in each other's arms, it dawned on me that my longing to belong to and have a family of my own could now be fulfilled. Kjell was the first man I wanted to have a family with. When he asked me to marry him, did he realize he would mean more to me than just a husband? Did he understand I'd also place the whole meaning of family on his shoulders? Should I ask him if he could carry that load? Maybe it was unfair to expect so much from him just because he loved me and would marry me. He was signing on only to be my husband and the father of my children, nothing else. No, I wouldn't burden him with the whole weight of what family meant for me. I promised myself to ask him only to be my loving husband, the father of my children, and to grow old together.

Cathy had married the year before. I was her maid of honor, and I made her wedding dress, along with the gowns of her three bridesmaids. As my new American father, her husband John felt it was his duty to have a heart-to-heart talk with Kjell before he consented to our marriage. I have always been amazed at how Cathy and then John took on the parent role with no hesitation. Kjell described their hour-long walk along the Mississippi River as "scary." I was used to Kjell's exaggerated and dramatic terminology, so I concluded that everything went well.

"Why would he ask me so many questions about my intentions with you when he knows that I want to marry you?"

"That's John." There were many things about John I didn't fully understand, but I supported him and said, "John is fascinated with details. Your impatience with him doesn't bother him. He's also interested in the process of communication."

"He talked as if he's your father."

"He is. He's married to my mother."

"No way! Cathy is not your mother, no matter how she tries to act the part."

"But she's not acting. Cathy feels that she's my mother."

"Weird."

Kjell never fully understood my relationship with Cathy. Knowing how he felt about having family living in the same city with him, I could understand his denial. But little did I know that his attitude toward Cathy and John and my relationship with them would never change. He would laugh when I told him that Cathy, as my mother, meant more to me than anyone else in the world.

"I don't think you will ever know what she means to me," I protested. "Maybe you refuse to understand."

"There's nothing to understand. She isn't your mother, and I hate it when she pretends to be."

"One more time—she's not pretending! Have you ever heard of adoption?"

"She acts as if she carried you for nine months, nursed you, and brought you up, when all she did was convince herself you needed a mother. She needs to be needed, that's all."

I hated it when Kjell dismissed my truth with his "logical" arguments about emotions he was ignorant of. "Let me tell you one thing. I need Cathy more than I need you. And don't you ever forget that. I can always find someone else to marry, but I can never find another Cathy."

"That's where you're so wrong! You could never find another man like me, and don't you forget it!"

His smug self-righteousness angered me, but because I was in love with him, I let it go. We often argued about Cathy and John, even though they were the only family either of us had in Minneapolis. His parents and two sisters were far away in Norway. His older brother, who was married to an American, was studying in Arizona.

We had no money, but that fall I had exchanged my three-thousand-dollar-a-year teaching position at a private Catholic school for a job at Washburn Public High School that paid eight thousand.

"Are you sure you'll be happy in a public school?" Cathy asked.

"I don't know. But I need the money." I could see the pained look on Cathy's face. She was worried because I had stopped going to church regularly when I moved out on my own, and now she was sure I was losing my allegiance to Catholic schools.

"Don't worry!" I assured her as I always did. "If I die before you, I'll welcome you to heaven, and if you precede me, please organize a surprise party for me."

We had no place for our wedding ceremony. I had stopped going to church, and Kjell outright despised organized religion. I don't know what the Norwegian requirement to be members of the state-run Lutheran Church did to him, but he told me about getting his tonsils removed at a hospital run by nuns when he was nine years old. He insisted they stop the prayers coming through the P.A. system into his room.

We also had no place to hold our wedding reception. But the biggest disappointment for me was not being able to afford a photographer. I've always had a thing about photos. I was fifteen years old the first time I saw myself in a black-and-white group picture of the Kifungilo children. Once I figured out which one I was, I stared at myself for a long time. It showed me from the waist up with two long braids tied in little bows resting on my shoulders. I was smiling. I couldn't understand why the big girls had said I was ugly. I told myself to remember how happy I felt looking at the photo and promised that when I left Kifungilo, I would go to a studio and have a photo taken of myself, no matter how expensive. Then whenever I felt sad and unwanted, I'd look at it and love myself in the picture. Maybe that would help erase the childhood image of ugly "Piggy," as I was called. I would tell the person in the photo that she was beautiful, and one day others might see it too.

Kjell and I were perfect candidates for elopement, but then we thought about getting married in our new efficiency apartment on Bryant Avenue. I planned to ask Patrick Dinya, my Tanzanian priest friend, to perform the ceremony, and Jackie, my beloved friend from college, to be the witness. We'd store the Murphy bed in its hole in the wall and hope it wouldn't fall down during the ceremony.

"I'll sew my dress and the bridesmaids' dresses," I told Kjell.

"But you won't need bridesmaids if we're getting married in our apartment."

A wedding without bridesmaids—what kind of wedding is that? Was it even legal? I remembered being a flower girl at Rosa's wedding when I was six and a bridesmaid at the wedding of a college friend. "The bridesmaids will wear African dresses. I'll make them from the kitenge fabric I saw at a fabric store. The panels are cream-colored with a deep red-and-green starfish design. They'll look so pretty coming down the aisle!"

"Is somebody in there listening to me?"

"I can have only two bridesmaids because the panels are eight dollars each and the material for my wedding dress is about twenty. Shoes will be twenty-five dollars. I can sew a veil too. I'll be so pretty!" Kjell and I looked at each other in silence for a few moments. "I don't want to get married if I can't have bridesmaids."

"Okay, don't get upset. You can have all the bridesmaids you want."

"I won't get married if I can't walk down the aisle with my bridesmaids."

"You pick the aisle and we'll walk down it."

"I want Cathy to be there!"

"Cathy will be there."

"And Mrs. Reed."

"Mrs. Reed will be there. Is there any particular aisle you prefer?"

"A church aisle, of course."

"Wait! That was not in the bargain." He stood up abruptly and threw himself on the bed.

"Kjell, I am a Catholic no matter what it looks like from the outside, and I'd like to get married in a church."

"Now that's a problem. What happened to having the ceremony in our apartment?"

"I want a proper wedding. I want my friends from all over the world to know and to come if they can."

"There goes the money for your ring."

"This ring will do." I took the ring he gave me the day I returned from France from my finger and noticed that the skin beneath it was green and sickly looking. "Does the church part scare you?"

"It's the only thing I'm not prepared to do." He paused. "But if that's what you want, I mean if you want an aisle, an aisle in a church, I guess that's what I'll have to do. What church do you propose we get married in?"

"I have no idea, but Cathy can help us."

"Don't let Cathy plan our wedding. We'll have a choir singing and guitarists from some Catholic church playing like they're at an amateur country music festival. Overweight grandmothers in awful hats will bring tuna hot dishes. The men will be Guindon cartoon characters with fishing poles and rusted tackle on their caps and—"

I went to the bathroom and closed the door. I didn't want him to see me laughing at how funny he was, but I knew he meant it. I dismissed his exaggerated fears about Cathy as our wedding planner, pulled myself together, put on my annoyed face, went back into the room, and told him he was a ranting and raving, crude, ignorant, pompous and demeaning, ungrateful and clueless pagan Viking!

By the way he smiled back at me, I'm sure the only word that registered was "Viking."

19

Our Wedding

We got married a year after we met, in December of 1968. Cathy and John did plan our wedding. A guitar ensemble did play at the ceremony, and there were several overweight grandmothers with net hats at St. Leo's Church in St. Paul, a newly built church with contemporary architecture that John and Cathy attended. Father Patrick Dinya from Tanzania officiated along with the pastor who made Kjell sign a document promising that any children would be baptized in the Catholic faith. The pastor seemed to be in uncharted territory. A Catholic marrying a Lutheran was bad enough, but a Norwegian marrying an African was unheard of in his parish.

I made my simple, cream satin sheath with a full-length woolen dress coat and cloth-covered buttons from neck to hem. My veil was an exquisite handmade mantilla that Cathy had bought in Spain. I had practical cream pumps on my feet with hose that Cathy insisted I wear. Even in the dead of winter I hated to wear pantyhose.

Kjell refused to wear a formal suit (probably because he didn't own one and didn't have money to rent one), so he wore a white turtleneck shirt that I made for him and his old ocean-blue blazer with navy slacks. He grew a handsome mustache for the occasion, which saddened Cathy. My two bridesmaids, Jackie and Jenny, wore the dresses I made from a single panel of African kitenge cloth with a bold center design running down the front. Wide headbands made from kitenge scraps called attention to their fancy hairdos and accentuated their beautiful faces and long, elegant necks. My dress and shoes, the two bridesmaids' dresses, and Kjell's turtleneck shirt cost ninety-five dollars.

The finished basement of the house that Cathy and John had just purchased in Golden Valley was the site of a cozy, catered reception with a lovely wedding cake and—to Kjell's chagrin—no tuna hot dishes! A young Norwegian girl from Macalester College played the *langeleik*, a traditional stringed instrument that suited Kjell. She sang while most of the Norwegian students we invited got drunk.

We did have a few snapshots of the wedding. We asked friends with cameras to take pictures, none of which were posed, and we selected about ten for our five-page wedding book.

I was glad we didn't elope because we wouldn't have received the many wonderful gifts that made us feel outright rich. Apart from the reception, Cathy and John gave us a set of Mikasa china for eight with wine and water glasses. Since Cathy was familiar with my mostly absent cooking skills, she gave us a seven-piece set of flaming orange, cast-iron Le Creuset cookware in hopes the bright color would entice me to cook.

"Now these are your 'good dishes' to use only for special occasions," she warned.

"Yes," I said, "but what are the special occasions?"

"When you have special people come for dinner."

"Do you really think I'll ever have anybody over for a meal I have to cook?"

"Looks like you'll have to. I won't be cooking for you."

"You'll have to come to make sure I'm using the good dishes for the special people."

"Sorry, but you're on your own." From the way she looked at me and stressed "on your own," I realized she had mixed feelings about my belonging to someone else. Before Kjell, she knew she was the most important person in my life, and I wondered if she felt things would change drastically for her now.

I put my arms around her and said, "You've been married for a year now, and that hasn't stopped you from being my American mother. Why should my being married change anything about our relationship? In case you're worried, let me tell you once and for all that the way I feel about you will never, ever change."

A lot of the gifts we received were the kind I'd seen displayed in fancy cabinets in people's houses. I never dreamt that one day I too would have a silver tray like the one I received from my students at Washburn High School, the Quimper pottery bowls from Mrs. Reed, or the beautiful Juvel sterling silverware we received from Kjell's parents and his relatives in Norway.

We received five fondue sets, which were popular at the time. I was glad because I liked fondue cooking—it encouraged coziness and conversation.

The gifts that made me really feel rich because I used them every day were bed sheets, towels, knives, toaster, a can opener from Father Patrick, pot holders and dish cloths (from Cathy, of course), everyday glasses from Target, plastic placemats, and a dual-control electric blanket. Imagine an electric blanket! Whoever invented them had me in mind. I'd turn on the blanket a few minutes before I got into bed, and to Kjell's delight, my flannel bunny suit was no longer needed.

One night, no matter how high I turned the controls, I was still freezing. I turned the controls up another notch and another half a notch, higher and higher. Nothing happened. I looked over at my husband, and his naked body was dripping wet.

"Something is definitely wrong with this magnificent invention. Please fix it, or I might not survive till morning, I'm so chilled!"

"We can't let that happen, now can we?" he said as he pulled me over to his side of our king-size bed. He let go of me in alarm. "Jesus Christ! What happened to you? Are you okay? You're frozen while I'm melting."

"It must be your superior Viking blood. By the way, for someone who hates religion, you always call on Jesus Christ when you need him."

Liquid clung to his densely hairy chest as if someone had spilled a bucket of water on a shag carpet. Tiny water rivulets running down his body soaked the bed and now dripped on me like a warm shower.

"Something is really wrong," he said, throwing the covers off the bed. He reached over me, trying to find the cause of the problem. "The controls got switched! You turn your side up and I roast. I try to turn my side down and you freeze. Am I brilliant or what!"

He turned on the light. Sure enough, as we untangled the wires, I remembered that when I made the bed that morning I couldn't get rid of an odd bump under the covers at the foot of the bed, but I had let it go, hoping my fastidious, neat husband wouldn't notice.

20

Up in Smoke

Marriage gave me the unexpected gift of a new name—a surname.

Fat Mary wanted to talk to me: *I know you are happy and proud to have a last name you didn't have to make up. The names you gave yourself in the past are every bit as important as your legal name now. Your names might have changed, but you have not changed. Your married name will not change the fact that you still have the need to know about your parents. Your new legal name does not erase your history. A name is useful for others, but how you see and love yourself is more important than your husband's name. Don't forget that.*

I had given myself various last names: Rygne, Ryne, Ryme, and finally Ryan. When I went to middle school in Mhonda without a last name. The nun in charge said "Two" would be my last name to make an example of me as a "child of sin."

Now I had a name. I was Mrs. Bergh! I liked it when my students called me Mrs. Bergh, but I didn't like being called Mrs. Kjell Bergh. It was one thing to acquire a legitimate last name and quite another to lose the comfort and familiarity of my first name. Whenever someone introduced me as Mrs. Kjell Bergh, I smiled and said, "My name is Maria Bergh."

Teaching French at a public school was quite different from teaching it at Regina High School. The teachers weren't nuns, and we didn't pray at the start of each of my five classes of thirty-six students. Harold Dunn, the head of the French Department with whom I shared a classroom, was a gentleman who stood out among the truly dedicated teachers and the burnt-out ones who were simply putting in time until retirement. The few teachers I had gotten to know well at Regina genuinely liked their work and their students. Here male teachers busied themselves checking out young female teachers and making lewd comments about them in front of me. Because Blacks in this school were few and far between, I thought I would stand out, but I often felt invisible.

While extremely outnumbered, Black students demanded to be treated with respect. I got to know a senior named Kenneth Jones who said that one day he was going to take an African name. He had formed a club with other students and asked me to teach them African dance. I stayed in touch with him through the years and learned that he later went to West Africa and changed his name to Seitu Jones. He's now an internationally acclaimed artist and activist.

I loved teaching. I was only a few years older than my students, but I often felt it was the other way around. I knew nothing about being a teenager in America or what kind of life awaited them after they left my classroom. At the end of every class we'd take ten minutes to discuss life and issues in America and Tanzania. We listened to French records of Edith Piaf, Yves Montand, Mireille Mathieu, Françoise Hardy, Soeur Souririe and discussed them. It was a painless way to learn a language that they would seldom hear spoken outside my classroom.

My teaching style reflected how I had learned English in Tanzania, where we acted out the words and phrases. In Tanzania we happily jumped on our desks as we proclaimed, "I am jumping on the desk!" My students, however, would not go to the big windows along one side of the room and say, *"J'ouvre la fenêtre."* (I am opening the window.)

What was wrong with these American students? Didn't they know I was the teacher and they had to do as I said? I learned quickly that my authority meant little, if anything, to them. I was not the all-powerful and feared *mwalimu* of Africa. Many students were just putting in mandatory time. But all through my childhood, I had envied anyone who had the golden privilege of going to school. Being guaranteed an education was something most Africans could only dream about.

I insisted on teaching by action. Students memorized French dialogues at the beginning of each chapter and then had to recite them in front of the class. They laughed when I got carried away with the dialogues, especially when I acted out what I expected them to do. Eventually they became creative with their dialogues, and then it was my turn to laugh and enjoy myself. My classroom was loud with discussion and laughter. But I knew I was being watched for any subversive teaching methods I might introduce into this homogenous, white, regimented school.

One day, to recreate Jacques Cocteau's poem "Déjeuner du Matin," I lit a cigarette (not the forbidden act then that it would be today). I'd noticed a teacher walking back and forth outside of my classroom. He finally got what he was looking for—he saw me smoke in class. He reported me to the principal, who called me out of the classroom to reprimand me. He warned me that if I continued with my unorthodox teaching methods, I'd have to be transferred to "one of those modular schools where teachers do whatever they want."

I apologized and then asked the principal why the teacher who reported me wasn't in his classroom. I knew he had a class that hour. The principal simply motioned me back to my classroom. After I was inside, I picked up the poem where I had left off, without smoking this time, and told my students why we had been interrupted. They were furious! They started telling me all sorts of things that other teachers did and didn't do and that they couldn't believe I would be singled out for caring enough to make the poem come alive for them. One of them said, "Don't worry, Mrs. Bergh, we'll take care of you!"

When the bell rang to end class, they rushed out to see the principal. I received a note of apology from him in my mailbox the next morning, saying, "You're one of the most exciting teachers we have here. I am sorry for the misunderstanding."

After all, I was only trying to make the study of a foreign language a little more palatable to bored students who'd rather be anywhere but in school. Students were not allowed to smoke in the building, and faculty members could smoke only in the teachers' lounge. One student informed the principal that I didn't know how to smoke and that she had given me a smoking lesson. I flunked it because I couldn't inhale, much less make smoke rings as described in the poem! With the racial tension going on at school, I wondered if he was afraid he'd be accused of harassing a Black teacher.

Whenever I entered the teachers' lounge, I had the sensation that something was spoiling, even dying. By the end of the year I figured it out. That something was me. I had compromised my love of teaching and my commitment to making the French language relevant to the students. I had been acquiescing to the school's demands and forgetting to teach with joy and spontaneity. For the most part, I felt like an outsider. I made up my mind to switch to another school the first opportunity I had.

21

Norwegian Family

With both of us working, Kjell and I managed to save enough money for our first trip to Norway. This was supposed to be our honeymoon trip. By this time, he had brainwashed me into believing there couldn't be a better place for a honeymoon than Norway in the summer. I was a little apprehensive about meeting my in-laws because most parents of the white boys I'd dated had made me feel very unwelcome.

I remember the good Catholic family from Minneapolis who invited me to go to church with them. After Mass, I overhead the mother say, "She's very nice and really quite pretty, but she'll never fit in. She's not our kind." The irony was that when it came time to meet their parents, every last one of my white boyfriends assured me, "My parents will love you!"

Kjell hadn't said much about his parents other than that they were happy for us. I couldn't have prayed for better in-laws! Kristian and Liv Bergh accepted me and loved me from day one. There was nothing fake about how they related to me and, like their son, they seemed to be thrilled I had no family for them to bother with.

The first evening we met, Kjell's father said, "Vee your family now. Me, *Far, og det er Mor.*" (We are your family now. I am Father and she is Mother.)

"*God natt, sov godt, takk for i dag, Maria,*" Liv said. (Good night, sleep well. Thank you for the day, Maria.)

"*God natt, Mor,*" I answered.

Mor and *Far* gave us their room, which had two wooden twin beds pushed together, with huge fluffy pillows and a lightweight cover, which I assumed was what Kjell had described to me as a *dyne* when I wanted to take my electric blanket to Norway.

"First of all, the electric current is different in Europe and second, in Norway everyone sleeps with a *dyne*." The lightweight goose-down covers they used were warm and more comfortable. After one night with a *dyne*, I knew I had to sleep with one forever!

The Berghs lived in a townhouse in a development called Veitvet, just outside of Oslo. The rooms were small but well decorated with lace curtains, embroidered pillows and tablecloths. Lots of pewter and crystal bowls, candleholders, and several vases filled with fresh flowers sat on tables and shelves. Black-and-white photos and more recent family photos in color glared or smiled at me on the way up the stairs to the bedrooms. I stared at a photo of the Bergh children—Einar, Kjell, and Berit before their sister Ellen was born. Kjell must have been four years old.

Talk about a stereotypical Norwegian child! He had powder-white hair spilling onto his forehead, a perfectly serious face looking straight ahead, and both hands clutching his suspenders. I saw the same intensity in the grown man I'd married and felt proud. *Mor*, who spoke more English than *Far*, told me that "Kjell was a fine boy," as she stroked his face on the photo. "Everybody wanted to look at my pretty boy. And he had a smile for all."

We spent most of the time in Norway visiting Kjell's family in Oslo and in Kristiansund on the West coast. Compared to the quaint little towns we passed on the two-hundred-fifty-mile drive from Oslo, modern Kristiansund had contemporary architecture.

"Most of the town was destroyed by German bombs during the war. We'll see the old German bunkers," his father said. I finally understood why Kjell was obsessed with the Second World War, and why, whenever I talked about the German nuns who raised me, his only comment was "Damn Nazis!" German bombs had flattened the town where he was born.

Kjell had good-natured aunts who lived with their husbands on farms and worked as hard as the Kifungilo nuns. At every home we visited, we were fed a thousand variations on *smørbrød*—open-faced sandwiches. They made the sandwiches with two hundred varieties of fish from delicious to dubious, cold cuts from smoked ham to smoked tongue, vegetables from radish to kohlrabi, and cheese from Jarlsberg to the soapy-tasting, brown gjetost goat cheese. My favorite was the shrimp sandwich, made with a thin slice of white bread smothered with unsalted butter, topped by a lettuce leaf full of slightly salted baby shrimp, and then, just in case there wasn't enough cholesterol to burst your arteries, a spoonful of mayonnaise was piled on the shrimp and crowned by a thin slice of lemon and a sprig of dill.

To celebrate our marriage, our hosts brought out cognac or brandy, which was stashed away for special occasions. I really liked Kjell's aunt Anna, who was interchangeably called Fat Aunt or the Hippie Aunt. Her son, Robert, a sailor, had spent much time in India. When he visited us in Minneapolis, he had us in stitches with his impressions of Asian Indians and their accents. Fat Aunt smiled all the time, perhaps because she couldn't speak English, or maybe like her son, she was a jolly person who loved life. We'd be canoeing the fjord by their farm and without any announcement, she'd strip down to her bra and plunge her overweight self into the icy water, flapping her arms, laughing and singing like a grandmother mermaid.

Though I assumed that her family called her "Fat Aunt" lovingly, I knew that if I spoke Norwegian, I would have discussed with her how much I hated being called "Fat Mary" as a child. I had already observed that my Norwegian family often ridiculed fat people.

We often went fishing in Batnfjord with Karl Karlsen, Kjell's grandfather, and Uncle Bjarne, both on his mother's side. I had never fished in my life. Just to humor my bragging relatives who had regaled me with impossible and outrageous fish stories, I caught an eleven-pound cod the very first time I threw in the line. Though the relatives praised me as if I knew what I was doing, fishing was not for me.

Kjell's brother Einar, I was told, was addicted to fishing. "He is perfectly happy sitting in his boat, hanging on to his line for hours on end, waiting for the fish to bite before realizing there's no bait on his line." Later, when I heard my Norwegian relatives recount the story of that first fishing trip, the fish I caught had grown to twenty pounds, and I had struggled to pull it in, almost tipping the boat!

The only thing I dreaded about the farm relatives was the

obligatory showing off of the library. I think they mostly preyed on newcomers to the family like me. Fat Aunt took my hand and led me to a room under lock and key. She kept me in that chilly room for hours telling me (in Norwegian) everything she felt I needed to know about the multitude of relatives whose pictures covered the four walls. I nodded and smiled a lot and yawned, hoping she would realize I didn't understand a word. It didn't work.

"When does the honeymoon begin?" I asked Kjell after a week had gone by.

"Tomorrow."

"And what will we do during this honeymoon surrounded by relatives?"

"First, we'll visit my grandparents and Uncle Bjarne, and on the following day the honeymoon begins."

Kjell's grandparents on his mother's side had a farm on beautiful Batnfjord, at what seemed the end of the world. They lived the old-fashioned way, growing and processing a lot of their food and walking everywhere. Kjell had told me he spent many happy summer months working with his grandparents on this farm, and I could see there was a loving bond between him and his grandfather. Sitting in their small living room, I watched eighty-year-old *Bestemor* (Grandmother), who was bent over and lame after being kicked in the ribs by a cow several years earlier, slowly climb a steep staircase that led to the attic where they slept. When she got back down, she motioned me to approach her. We went outside, and with great effort she sat on the step by the door and motioned for me to sit down next to her. Turning to me, she reached for the collar of my blouse and pinned something heavy on it, then held out a tiny silver mirror, which she had also brought from the attic. The mirror reflected a silver and porcelain pin of the breathtaking Norwegian countryside, painted in pink, blue and gray.

"For you," she said. *Mor* later told me the pin had belonged to *Bestemor's* mother and it was her wedding gift to me. *Mor* had sent us a place setting in our silver pattern from them all, but *Bestemor* said this was only for me, not for Kjell. It was a memorable moment of my honeymoon trip. Apart from this little ceremony, she didn't fuss over me like the other relatives.

22

Boathouse Honeymoon

 The long-awaited honeymoon began at eight o'clock the next day as promised. We put on knee-high rubber boots and carried food and drink in a backpack. That should have told me we were not heading to a Four Seasons Hotel! Kjell said we were going to hike to a cabin up in the mountains where he'd spent some of the most peaceful moments of his youth among beautiful, trout-filled lakes and bushes with every kind of edible berry, including cloudberries. I hoped he wasn't taking me fishing and berry picking.

The sun accompanied us to the first lake but played hide and seek all the way to the second lake, where the famed honeymoon cabin awaited us. Sheep as big as cows surrounded what looked like a boulder by a small lake. The sheep were leery but curious as they stared at us.

"There's the cabin!" exclaimed Kjell, quickening his steps.

The boulder was the cabin! Kjell was so excited, and I struggled to hide my disappointment. He unlocked the huge padlock and tugged to open the rusted squeaking door. He squeezed himself inside, then announced he had to take the boat out of the hut so there'd be room for us.

I said nothing. I was already cold. An old, heavy boat with oars filled the cabin. I turned to the sheep and pouted, refusing to help. I heard Kjell fuss inside the cabin after he pulled the boat out. As I had no choice, I decided to be a good sport. I went to the door where I saw a big, old-fashioned, four-burner, cast-iron stove filling almost a quarter of the space inside the cabin.

"It's a little smaller than I remember, and this stove wasn't here before."

"Where do we sleep?"

"We didn't bring sleeping bags, but here's a mattress." Kjell pulled out an awful looking, smelly bag from a corner of the cabin and threw it on the floor. It was a primitive, twin-sized burlap mattress, roughly held together by straw stitching and filled with what seemed to be chopped cornhusks. The only way we could fit on the miserable mattress inside the tiny cabin was if I slept with my head tucked under the stove. I volunteered because I thought it would be warmer there. It wasn't. I fell asleep counting the sheep breathing noisily outside the cabin's thin walls but woke up every time I turned, because the stove knocked me down, scratching my face and dumping velvety soot over me. By morning I couldn't move. My whole body ached and refused to straighten out of its frozen fetal position.

"What happened to you?" my husband asked when he woke up.

"Just be quiet!"

"Are you okay?"

"Oh, shut up! How can anybody trying to sleep under a cast iron stove in a godforsaken cabin in the Norwegian wilderness on their honeymoon be okay?"

I touched my face and realized that my lip was swollen and I had a huge bump in the middle of my forehead. I was getting angrier by the minute. Why did I believe that anywhere in frozen Norway could be ideal for the honeymoon I had imagined? Really, love is blind. You just don't question the obvious when you're with someone you love.

"I'll make a fire. That will put you in a better mood."

I pouted and went outside, resigning myself to my misery. The sheep, with their black watery muzzles pointing toward us, stood guard in a circle around what Kjell called a cabin but to me didn't even qualify as an African hut. As I pondered my future life with Kjell, I made up my mind to never again take anything for granted. After all, a Norwegian and an African are bound to interpret words differently.

In the midst of my self-pity, I heard Kjell shout, "Jesus Christ! What in the world?" as he bolted out of the cabin. He was covered with feathers and soot and looked only a little better than I did. Kjell's attempt to make a fire in the pre-World War I stove had disturbed a family of squawking geese, who called the cast-iron stove home. I was angry to the point of tears. I never got over my disbelief and utter disappointment about our attempted honeymoon at the dilapidated boathouse by the freezing shores of a forlorn lake near the most mediocre mountains in Norway.

We secured all the cabin valuables including the boat, which by this time was covered with icicles, and headed down the mountain to the next level of civilization.

I must not have gotten all the soot off my face when I washed in the frigid lake that morning because on the way, we met three very fair, very Norwegian children aged five or six, who greeted Kjell with glee, but when they saw me, took off screaming and yelling. When I caught up with Kjell, he was laughing so hard he couldn't talk. I ignored him. I knew what was going on. It was probably the first time these farm children in this remote region of Norway had come face to face with a Black person.

"You scared the living daylights out of the children. They thought you were a real live troll!" Kjell resumed laughing as he put his arm around me. I removed his arm from my shoulders. The honeymoon night we'd just spent rendered his embrace painful.

"They know a troll when they see one. You've got to agree, it's funny!"

I didn't agree. "Will your grandparents be expecting us?"

"I told them we'd be spending a few nights at the cabin, but they always have room."

"Did you really think we could have stayed at the cabin? Did you enjoy the night?"

"I would have enjoyed it more if you weren't so miserable. I remember how much I loved spending the night up there as a child. I wanted to share the peace, tranquility, and beauty of my favorite childhood spot with you."

"Was it as tranquil and beautiful as you remember?"

"Yes. You've got to admit that."

"Kjell, I don't know about you, but I can't appreciate beauty and tranquility when I'm cold and miserable. To appreciate nature, you have to be aware of how and what you're feeling inside. You have to be in the present moment. My present moment up there was miserable! From the little I've told you about my childhood, you've overestimated my pain threshold."

"Compared to what you must have gone through with those German nuns, this was a picnic."

"First of all, this was supposed to be a honeymoon. And second, precisely because of my childhood, I will never, ever, knowingly and willfully choose to rough it out when there's an alternative. For that reason, let me tell you right now that I will never settle for anything less than the best, materially or otherwise, if it's available and I can afford it."

"As long as we can afford it."

"From now on I'll call the shots. We could afford a better place for our honeymoon."

"You're missing the point."

"There's no point to get or miss. I refuse to suffer for the sake of suffering."

On the way back to Oslo, Kjell saw an ad for a cabin in Hokksund, a tiny village near Drammen, about an hour's drive from Oslo. "How would you like to own a cabin in Norway?" he asked.

"Please define cabin. If it's your honeymoon boathouse, no way!"

"There's a cabin for only three thousand dollars that's fully furnished, from beds to dishes, on a lake where we can go fishing and swimming."

"If all the lakes in Norway are as cold as our honeymoon lake, no thank you!"

"Let's just look at it. I've always wanted to own a little cabin in the woods. It will be our first investment together, and in a few years, we could sell it at a profit."

"Okay, let's look at it," I said, pretending he made sense. I couldn't see investing the money I saved from my teaching job in a cabin halfway around the world. The only way we'd get to use it would be by working our butts off for the money to travel to it.

"The good thing about having a cabin so close to Oslo is that my parents and family will be able to take care of it and use it. Kristiansund is too far for them to travel just for a weekend, but they can get to Hokksund in an hour."

"Are we buying a cabin for your family or for us?"

"We're buying it for ourselves, but for all practical purposes, my parents and my sisters would be using it more than we would."

Kjell's parents met us at the realtor's office in Drammen, and the realtor drove us about twenty minutes to Hokksund. From there he took us through an alpine forest, whose branches formed a canopy above our heads, leaving the ground underneath light and soft, cushioned by pine needles.

"There it is," said the realtor. "Isn't it charming? The owners called it Tussebo—home of the female trolls." Tussebo was across a small lake, and we had to take a rickety-looking wooden structure that looked suspiciously like the boat stored in our honeymoon cabin to get there.

With apprehension and fear, I reluctantly came to accept the love affair Norwegians have with their homemade boats and remote, rough-hewn *hytter*—cabins. I realized we inherit the burdens and blessings of the culture we are born into, and I convinced myself that Kjell would be just as perplexed by Africa and Africans as I was by Norway and Norwegians.

Kjell and his parents loved the cabin. *"Det var hyggelig,"* (That is nice.) they kept saying. I could tell by their exuberance that they had found the cabin of their dreams. Since I'd never been in their dreams, they completely forgot about me. I really didn't care one way or the other, because I knew I'd get little use out of it. *Mor* was going to make new curtains and bring sheets for the narrow wooden bunk beds in the tiny bedroom. It didn't matter that there was only one bedroom as there was a guesthouse near the outhouse a couple could use, and the living room had plenty of space to extend the homemade wood sofa. Firewood around the cabin could keep a fire going all day, and the four-burner, cast-iron cooking stove in the tiny kitchen was a little rusted but otherwise suited them fine.

"Look, here's the refrigerator!" *Mor* pulled open a heavy wooden door in the kitchen floor that covered a three-by-three-foot cement-lined hole in the ground.

The entire cabin was of wood, its insides of natural varnished pinewood, its outside stained red. Rosemalled plates and cups hung on a ledge above the homemade wooden dining table with its hand-woven wool runner. A pewter vase with dried wild flowers, leaves, and weeds brought softness to the place. On either side of the table stood roughly cut, narrow wood benches that reminded me of the refectory in Kifungilo. The clearing immediately outside the cabin had sparse grass and Norwegian pines within the warped wood fence. Rocks, carefully picked and placed for their size and function, invited us to sit and visit or to stand on them to see the edge of the lake or gaze at the surrounding hills and valleys.

We bought the cabin on the spot, and the laughter and animated chatter in Norwegian from my husband and in-laws all the way to Oslo told me they were very happy indeed. Kjell's family did take good care of Tussebo. Every letter from Norway that he translated described the improvements we'd find on our return. His sister Berit did most of the curtain sewing and wall painting when she stayed there with her son. Several guests brought useful and needed items from cut-up newspaper for the outhouse to kerosene for the lamps. Tussebo was the first house we owned, and we both felt a sense of accomplishment. Kjell announced that we'd go to Norway every summer, if for no other reason than to admire our minute piece of property.

23

Pregnant Thoughts

The next time we went to Norway was to show off our daughter Katarina. She was born on an unbearably hot, ninety-seven-degree July day in 1970. My pregnancy was a confusing time for me, but having a child was the next step toward my goal of creating a family of my own. While carrying Katarina, the longing for my mother that I'd thought had vanished with Cathy came back with a vengeance. I wished she were around to answer my many questions and help me become a good mother, though I wasn't so sure what good mother would give up her child to nuns to raise unless there were extenuating circumstances. Cathy and John were thrilled for us, but Cathy had never borne a child so she couldn't fill that role.

I was sometimes elated with the prospect of having a child and sometimes terrified. Kjell was thrilled to become a father, and I took great comfort in the knowledge that my child was wanted by both of us.

For the first time in my life it occurred to me that I must have had a father, and he must not have wanted me either. Fat Mary, who always knew when I needed her, showed up with a smile on her face.

You don't know that. Maybe they thought the orphanage would give you what you needed when they couldn't. It's a higher form of love that is impossible for a child to understand. You decided very early to love yourself and be responsible for your happiness. You might never have done that if your parents had raised you.

"But I still believe that children belong with their parents," I told her. "Children shouldn't have to carry the weight of their existence without help from the people who brought them into this world."

You are a deep thinker, a steadfast believer in your innate goodness, a hard worker, and you're filled with gratitude, empathy, and love. These are your childhood blessings and lessons that will now guide you into motherhood.

Yes, I'm grateful for all that I have and all that I've become, but I still wouldn't wish my childhood on anyone. The lessons were too hard to learn and not everyone who was in my situation had the ability to learn them. I was very grateful for my beloved Fat Mary. I wished everyone at the orphanage could have found her like I did if they needed her. She saved me then, and she was showing me now that all that I endured was not in vain.

But did my father even know about me? And if he did, what did he feel when he let me be raised by nuns in Kifungilo? Try as I might, I couldn't imagine Kjell not wanting his child. Every day he'd feel my growing stomach and talk to the baby. "You're going to be the most beautiful child in the world, with the most beautiful mother and a so-so father. Look, the baby's already dancing!" he'd announce with excitement as he felt movement.

"Better not be skiing," I teased, referencing my inherent distrust of the sport. I dislike anything that prevents me from walking, running, or acting in a natural manner. Why attach those long sticks to your feet that make it impossible to walk, then wear an expensive, bulky *dyne* suit—and this is where I absolutely don't get it—go out in the cold and pretend you're having fun sliding down a snow-covered hill? I can't believe people do this on purpose. Even if we had snow in Africa, we would never invent such a sport.

As the school year came to an end, I found it harder and harder to teach and climb the two, long flights of cement steps to my third-floor classroom. I sewed most of my maternity dresses and didn't need much material because minis were the style in 1970. I must have been quite a sight to someone coming up the steps when I was descending. I had gained fifty pounds and could feel every ounce of it. Carletta, a friend I'd met teaching at Washburn and who lived in our apartment building, took me aside one day. "I like those bright green panties you're wearing, but they clash with the African print that's desperately trying to cover your belly."

When it came to clothes, no one, but no one could tell me how to dress. Like Mrs. Reed, I wore whatever I wanted and however I wanted. Most of the time I kept up with the fashions, but dressing like everybody else was boring, so I added little touches that made me stand out as original or gaudy. I'd vowed while in high school that if I could afford it, I'd never dress in beige or gray with matching purse, shoes, and lipstick like our American lay teachers and the other *wazungu*.

Our baby was two weeks overdue. Someone had told us that if we drove very fast down a steep, rugged road several times, we might induce labor. I think it was the only time in my life I actually relished a fast ride. The next morning my water broke, and Kjell took me to the hospital. My gynecologist came right away, examined me, and announced that everything was fine, but I might have a long labor since it was my first baby. "Practice your Lamaze breathing techniques and the nurse will call me when it's time."

Mr. Eugene Murray, pharmacist,
Cathy's father.

Maria during her
college years
(1966).

Ambassadors for Friendship travelers with host.

1967 Graduation picture –
"Mary Rose Ryan."

Maria and Cathy at 1967
graduation from the
College of St. Catherine.

Maria with Afro.

Cathy's wedding.

Einar, Jackie, Kjell, Maria, Jenny, and Steve
at Maria's wedding.

Bridesmaids Jenny and Jackie at Maria's wedding.

John and Cathy at Maria's wedding.

Cathy and Maria at her wedding.

Mrs. Reed with Maria at her wedding.

Kjell's parents, Liv and Kristian Bergh.

Kjell and Maria in Norway.

The Tussebo cabin in Norway.

Young Audiences presentation with grade school children.

African dance performance with the Minnesota Orchestra.

24

Katarina

Kjell and I had faithfully practiced the breathing exercises during our Lamaze classes and felt we were quite the team. We were ready to spring into action. Unfortunately, my delivery didn't go according to plan. Katarina came quickly and with her, a major gush of blood. The bright red blood pulsated to the rhythm of my heartbeat. Blood spattered everywhere, including on the mirror strategically placed for us to witness the birth of our daughter. Instead, it magnified the truth about the drama and trauma of childbirth. I was hemorrhaging severely, and my doctor had to order several units of blood to be given to me intravenously. I realized with a shock how serious this was.

Am I dying? Why so much pain? "It's all right. You'll be all right," a nurse murmured, wiping my soaking wet forehead. I got a brief glimpse of our wondrous but strange-looking baby before she was whisked away to an incubator.

Kjell was in the waiting room, ready to be called to assist with his part of the delivery—the Lamaze breathing exercises during labor. He witnessed the commotion in the hallway, but it never occurred to him that his wife and firstborn might be in trouble. He told me later he thought it was a normal delivery until he saw me with bags, tubes, and needles jutting out from my body. I was in so much pain I couldn't even nod at him. He turned pale and staggered out of the room, holding on to the wall to keep from fainting. He fainted anyway.

When the pain subsided, I found myself thinking about my mother. I wondered whether my birth was as traumatic for her as Katarina's was for me and if that influenced her to give me away.

But how could anybody part with someone who gave you life's most painful yet most beautiful and holy moment? I felt I was indispensable to God at the moment he chose to deliver this miracle to the world.

When we talked about her birth to family and friends, Kjell summed up his experience saying, "To think I dutifully attended those miserable Lamaze classes, practiced those breathing exercises, and was ready to act, only to find out the birth had taken place without me—and my wife and child could have died."

Katarina was a good baby. As she was growing up, my life with the nuns at the orphanage was constantly on my mind. I wondered how often the nuns kissed and hugged me as I was now kissing and hugging my daughter. It must have been Sister Theonesta who nurtured the feelings of tenderness, love, and bliss I now felt for my daughter. I wondered if they were adequate or, because I was deprived of them, I couldn't love her enough. Was there a book to teach me how to give my daughter what she needed? Was it irresponsible to have a child when I didn't know how to love? Or was mother love instinctive? Thoughts of inadequacy as a mother bothered me off and on for a long time until one day I decided that a mother's love had to be instinctive and unconditional, and I couldn't help but love her even though I didn't know how to measure it. I knew that no one could love a daughter more than I loved her. I realized my mother couldn't have felt about me the way I felt about Kata (her nickname), and I agreed with Fat Mary that she might have thought the nuns were better equipped than she to give me what I needed.

I knew next to nothing about child rearing. I don't think I'd ever held such a small baby before. Soon after coming home from the hospital, I was giving her a bath in the kitchen sink when I noticed her face slowly turning deep purple. I realized I was gripping her neck tightly. I let go and quickly checked to see if the rest of her was changing color too. No, and the color in her face gradually returned to normal. Then I panicked. I had almost strangled my daughter.

Crying and trembling, I picked up the dripping Kata, held her high above my head, and offered her to God. "You know, God, if you want this little child you created to grow up and become whom you intend her to be, you have to help me. You're just as responsible for her as I am. You must know that I am afraid of motherhood. Please, God, send someone to take care of her because I don't know how. Keep her guardian angel on duty around the clock. Would I inadvertently kill her someday? Lord have mercy on me!"

My prayers were answered because the desperation and fear I felt that day about motherhood never returned. Sticking to our promise to the pastor who had married us, we baptized her a week later, and my college friend Jackie became her godmother.

We bought our first house when Kata was a year old. It was a small two-story contemporary "box house" with a tuck-under garage in southwest Minneapolis. The previous Christmas, Kjell, who was now working full time at the car dealership, had given me my first car. I was very impressed with my big material possessions: a house and a car. Whoever thought that one day I would have a house of my own? This wasn't just any old house. This was my house. I sat in the middle of all the boxes of stuff I'd accumulated and wondered how I could have fit the possessions of my entire life of nineteen years in Africa into one small suitcase when I came to America seven years earlier. I counted my blessings.

"*Asante sana*," (Thank you) I said to God. I begged him to never let me take anything for granted or forget that nothing in the world could replace the important people in my life. I thanked him for Rosa, Sister Theonesta, Elizabeth, Sister Silvestris, Lizzy, Paulina, *Mwalimu* Haule, the Maryknoll Sisters, Sister Martin Corde, Father Antonio, Father Michael, Cathy, Mr. Murray, Jackie, Sister Marie Philip, and Mrs. Reed. Since my marriage, I'd thanked God every day for Kjell, and now for Katarina too.

As soon as we settled into the house, I called my good friend Doris and invited her to see my new home. Doris, an artist from Kenya, painted, did macramé and pottery, carved wood, and made jewelry. She was also handy at painting walls, wallpapering, and refinishing furniture. Together we wallpapered the kitchen and bedrooms with bright flowered paper and painted the living room a soft yellow.

I sensed we might not stay long in this house because several incidents reminded me that no matter how well I did or how grateful I was for my good fortune, I was a Black woman—a rarity in the neighborhood. During the first week after we moved in, the doorbell rang almost every hour as my neighbors came supposedly to welcome me to the neighborhood, though I knew they just wanted a peek at me.

My next-door neighbor was an admitted and proud clone of Archie Bunker, the patriarch from the TV show *All in the Family*. I didn't mind him, though, because he was openly racist and I stayed away from him. Exactly like on TV, his wife was constantly trying to explain and apologize for his language and remarks. Kjell and he had heated discussions about every topic he considered un-American: foreigners, communists, Negroes (Blacks was too mild, he said), Jane Fonda, Vietnam, welfare, Native Americans, and all the "damned minorities." He didn't mind me, he said, even though I was from that "God-forsaken, primitive and poverty-stricken continent." I turned out okay because I was "saved by white missionaries and a white husband."

That first summer in our new house, I took Kata down the street to the community center and park where there was a swimming pool. She loved water. She played in the tiny puddles of rainwater on the patch of grass in front of our house and asked me to fill the potholes on the driveway with water so she could play in them. I often packed sandwiches for us to eat in the park. One day she got into a fight with another little girl at the pool. I was told that she pulled the girl's hair and the girl hit her in the face. We talked about fighting and playing with others.

"I don't have to do what you say! You're not my mom!" Kata said to me. I cursed the fact that Kata spoke in full sentences before she was two years old.

"What? I'm not your mama?"

"No, you aren't. You're my nanny."

"Nanny? Who told you I was your nanny?"

"Susan's mom. She said you're Black, and that my mom is white." I held her close, and she hugged me as if her life depended on it. She cried some, then said, "I know you're my mama and Dad is my daddy."

I knew she would suffer because of my color, but I had no idea it would happen so soon. I wondered if or how I could insulate and protect her from the kind of hurt and inner turmoil I had grown up with.

We lived only a year in my dream house because we spotted a charming Japanese-style house in the Kenwood neighborhood where we had rented before. We'd asked the owners to let us know if they wanted to sell, and sure enough one day the call came. Without hesitation, we begged, borrowed, and bartered to move back to Kenwood, a neighborhood known as progressive, intellectual, and academic. I hadn't appreciated that until I moved next door to Archie Bunker in South Minneapolis.

We became good friends with the neighbors behind us, with whom we had an easement for the driveway. Kata was two and a half when we moved. When she met our neighbor, big, six-foot-four Charles, she rested her tiny hands on her hips and said, "Hi, my name is Katarina Bergh. I live in the Japanese house. My daddy is from Norway, and my mom is from Africa. I am from America. Where are you from?"

All Charles could do was laugh. He was stunned that such a small child could speak so well and wasn't afraid of his size or height as other children were. Kata, small for her age, saved us a lot of money by wearing size four clothes until she was almost six years old.

We became good friends with Charles and his wife. They had five children, and the youngest was Kata's age. I was relieved that Kata finally had a playmate next door. Charles worked for the FBI, and after he retired he mentioned that he was told to keep an eye on us because we were foreigners who traveled a lot and had visitors from all over the world.

25

Taking Steps

Although Doris had no children, she was wonderful with Katarina. She babysat often, and the three of us went to garage sales every Saturday. Only now do I understand the definition of a garage sale—someone's junk becomes someone else's treasure. I don't know which I enjoyed more—finding incredible deals that two weeks later I didn't know what to do with or trying to see who could spot a garage sale sign first. During one of those Saturday morning garage sale forays into our Kenwood neighborhood I almost got killed.

I cheated. I got a babysitter for Kata and went out very early, without Doris, to case the streets. I wrote down the location of the best garage sales based on the size of the house and its surroundings and peeped over fences and driveways for a look at the quality of the stuff for sale. I noticed a small yellow cardboard sign on a hedge around a small, immaculately kept house. Figuring it was the carriage house for one of the mansions that made Kenwood an aristocratic neighborhood, I drove Kjell's new orange sports car up what I assumed was the driveway and made a sharp right turn.

Before I realized it, my car was thumping down a series of small concrete steps covered by weeds and moss. I screeched to a halt an inch from a side door to the house. Stunned, I sat in the car trying to figure out what had happened and what to do. It took me several minutes to squeeze out of the car because the door was jammed by the concrete steps.

"Thief! We're calling the police." A voice belonging to a woman between ninety and death shrieked at me from behind her lace-curtained window.

"I'm sorry. I just had an accident. I'm not a thief."

"Nigger, don't you come a step closer!"

I froze. My head started reeling, my heart started pounding, and my temperature rose as it always does when I hear that word. I looked up at the old woman. She seemed more scared of me than I was of the situation.

"You don't have to call me nigger just because I got into an accident. May I please use your phone to call my husband?"

"Not a step closer!"

"Okay, I'm going next door to see if I can use your neighbor's phone." I didn't have to go anywhere. My car was already surrounded by a group of neighbors.

"How on earth did you drive the car down the steps? Look, not a scratch on it," said one.

"Where were you going?" another asked.

"I was following that garage sale sign." We all looked at the sign on the hedge.

"That sale," someone volunteered, "is two blocks away."

The woman behind the curtain shrieked again, "She's lying! She's a burglar. We've called the police."

"If I were a burglar, would I drive down your steps at nine o'clock in the morning?"

"Jesus Christ!" a neighbor angrily said to the woman. "The poor girl had an accident. The least we can do is help her." He and several other men pushed, tugged, lifted, groaned, and swore, but the car did not budge.

"Jesus Christ!" the man said again. "The car is built like a tank. I've never seen this model."

"My husband works for a car dealership. It's the new sport model."

They tried again, but it wouldn't move, so I went to a neighbor's house to call Kjell. I did not want to make that call. I didn't know what would be worse—having to explain to Kjell that I drove down somebody's steps or hearing about it for the rest of my life. I told Kjell I'd been in a car accident, that I wasn't hurt and the car seemed okay, but he had to come right away with a tow truck.

By then a policeman had arrived. I couldn't believe my luck! I knew him. He lived in the neighborhood, and I had always greeted him with respect because I was instinctively afraid of the police. He turned out to be a nice man who was interested in Africa and hoped to go there.

"Now, Maria, only you could mistake steps for a driveway. I realize you have no cars and maybe even no drivable roads in Africa, but aren't you carrying this Africa bit a too far?" he joked.

Everybody laughed with me, and the woman whose husband was the first to help told me to forget about the accident and "come on over for breakfast."

"No one is hurt, and the tow truck is on the way, so I'll be going," the policeman said.

I told the woman I would take a rain check on the breakfast invitation. When I went two weeks later, she asked me when and where I had learned to drive.

26

The Norwegian Way

I loved my Norwegian family, and we all got along very well. They had warmed my heart the day we met when they told me to call them *Mor* and *Far*—Mother and Father. I especially got along well with *Far*, but I think that quite often *Mor* didn't know what to do with me because I was not the wife she had envisioned for her son. The first few times I visited them, they took me to see all the tourist attractions in Oslo. My favorites were the Viking Museum, the Norway Folk Museum, the National Gallery, Oslo City Hall, and Vigeland Sculpture Park.

I had been warned that my personality and culture might clash with that of the Norwegians, and it didn't take long for me to figure out why. We differed mostly because the Norwegian psyche was foreign to me. I realized that Norwegians don't like to ruffle feathers and will avoid confrontation at any cost. They do not want to be different from others. They try to blend in with the people around them and, if possible, with their surroundings too. Don't do anything that will call attention to yourself. Above all, don't show your emotions, especially in public. If something unpleasant comes up in a conversation, ignore it, push it under the rug, change the subject, and pretend nothing happened.

After Katarina was born, we went to Norway every summer. I started getting bored with the trips because I knew exactly how our vacation would go. The first evening after we arrived, we usually had a beautiful welcoming dinner. The next day everyone went about their business as if we lived with them all year. *Far* was busy with his youth sports club activities, and *Mor* worked long hours in the flower shop at the local shopping center. Kjell spent most of his time visiting his childhood friends and business acquaintances. After spending four days alone in the apartment, I let my frustration out during the obligatory after-dinner *kaffe*, served at 10 PM.

"I'm sick and tired of sitting alone in the apartment all day. I'm afraid to venture out to do things by myself because I have no sense of direction, and I don't speak your language. What's the use of making the long trip from America to see you when it's obvious that no one has time for us? I'm done spending my precious summer in this far away, cold, and indifferent country!"

No reaction. I knew they'd heard me because they averted their gaze, stopped sipping their coffee for a moment, and glared into their cups. On cue, the drinking continued, with six dainty coffee cups nervously rattling on their saucers. A minute or two passed before *Mor* put her cup on the table, slowly stood up, rearranged her skirt, gently lifted the coffee pot from the table, turned to me and said, "Maria, would you like more coffee?" and the conversation picked up where it had left off. My rant was shoved under the rug.

The next time I was in Norway, I was pleasantly surprised to find that my little tantrum produced some results after all. Berit, Kjell's sister who was working full time, took a few days off to go shopping and anywhere else I wanted to visit. We got to know and love each other because we spent quality time together each subsequent visit.

Valuable insight into the family's reaction came from Elsebeth, the Danish wife of Steinar, Kjell's best childhood friend. When I told her about the incident, she said that not all Scandinavians are like the Norwegians. "We Danes are different," she said. "We don't pay attention to *Janteloven*."

"What's that?"

"It's difficult to describe, but Janteloven, or the Law of Jante, is a set of social rules about how to behave. It's from a novel, but it's based on how people used to act. For example, you should never stand out, never believe you are anyone special, and certainly not more special than the group."

"That sounds like the opposite of American individualism and keeping up with the Joneses."

"Janteloven covers a multitude of behaviors, and the incident with your in-laws is part of that same mindset."

"I wonder if that's why Kjell left. He said he loved Norway but could never live here." I was grateful to Elsebeth for the insight. She promised to take time off from work so we could do things together. We shared a love of dance and were kindred spirits in many other ways. She and Steiner became my lifelong friends, and they were a big reason why, from then on, I couldn't wait to visit Norway.

Kjell and I worked hard those first years of our marriage to afford our trips to Norway and other luxuries. For short trips, we left Katarina with Grandma Cathy or with our good friend Margaret or other friends. For longer trips, we took her with us or arranged for friends to stay with her in our home. When he was home, Kjell dropped Kata off at Montessori preschool on his way to work, and I picked her up after teaching. Kjell traveled extensively every month, and we really missed him when he was away. After dinner, Kata and I would go to the calendar and count out loud the days before his return. His hard work eventually paid off, and he provided us with a lifestyle I could only dream of. We literally traveled the world for his business conventions, staying at high-end resorts and hotels whose restaurants had place settings with five wine glasses and four knives. We took yearly family vacations to Norway, the Caribbean, and other parts of the world. We wined and dined with national and international dignitaries from kings and presidents to actors and recording artists.

Soon after the movie *The Emigrants* was released in 1971, Kjell and I were invited to a private reception in the Twin Cities for Liv Ullmann, the Norwegian actor who starred in the film. Liv stayed with us, and we talked into the night. I remember her intelligence, compassion, and love for me and the world. She couldn't hear enough about Africa and told me she had been to several countries on the continent.

The reception was held at the palatial residence of a local Swedish-American businessman on Lake Minnetonka. During dinner, the host acknowledged Kjell for his business success and his service and promotion of all things Scandinavian in Minnesota. I was proud of my husband and his accomplishments and clapped along with the others when the host referred to me. "And," he said to sum up, "I have to tell you, Kjell, how I admire you for marrying Maria—seeing that she's Black and everything."

I was not expecting that. The other guests around the table laughed nervously, nodded, or stared into space, but Liv Ullmann looked at me and rolled her eyes in disbelief.

Someone quickly changed the subject, asking Kjell if he had ever been to Africa.

"Not yet," he said, "but it's a priority, and now I will have a personal guide."

On the way home, Liv hugged me and said, "I apologize for my race."

27

Africa after Ten Years

As he skied through the frozen Norwegian terrain, Kjell dreamed of warm tropical lands and vowed to visit Africa someday. The few physical descriptions of Kifungilo and the Usambara mountains I had given him made him long to see for himself. His enthusiasm convinced me I should go back to Africa as a tourist too.

When I left Africa, I never dreamed I'd want to return. I hid the apprehension I felt about taking my first trip back to Tanzania after ten years in America. Who or what was I going to visit? The land? The orphanage? My childhood friends with whom I hadn't stayed in touch? Though I had tried to forget the pain of the orphanage, I really hadn't. I needed to talk to Fat Mary.

"My husband will never understand why this trip back to the orphanage is so difficult for me," I began. "You safeguarded many painful memories for me. Please give them back to me in small doses."

A lot has changed since you left. Not only at the orphanage but also with you. You are not the same lost and lonely child. You have a mother in your new country. You have a husband who loves you, and now you are a mother. This visit to Kifungilo will anchor you in the truth about the loves and relationships that give meaning to life. Don't fear that those familiar surroundings will resurrect the ghosts of your past. Remember they are just that—ghosts! Yet they are the elements in the tapestry of your life that you have been weaving since the day you were born. When you look at your tapestry from a distance, you will discover that all the threads, colors, and stitches have blended and were necessary to give substance and texture to the beautiful work of art that is your life. One

*day your tapestry will be finished and you will share your masterpiece
with the world.*

Talking about my childhood even with Fat Mary was still painful. Returning to Tanzania meant agreeing to open my Pandora's
box. I knew I couldn't pick and choose what would face me once the
lid was open. I'd spent years relegating the unpleasant memories to
the back burner, but there was no way I could avoid facing them and
looking at them up close if they appeared during the trip.

Kjell, I knew, did not understand. He was never one to talk
about my past. He seldom asked me what my childhood was like. As
close as I was to him, he was the last person on earth I could open
up to, because whenever I tried to go deeper into my orphanage life,
he'd tell me to let bygones be bygones. Yet it was okay for him to hate
the Germans forever because of what they did to his hometown of
Kristiansund.

After a while I figured out that Kjell could express his feelings
only in the abstract. He was not comfortable with emotions. Hadn't
he said one of the best things about me was that I had no family?
How could having no family be a plus? Did he truly believe growing
up without a family would not affect a person's life?

We flew from New York to Oslo, where we left Katarina with
her grandparents. I hardly spoke during the long trip from Copen-
hagen to Dar-es-Salaam on the cramped plane. I didn't believe I was
actually going to a place that everyone, except me, thought was my
beloved home. Is home the place of your birth? Is it a house with
parents and relatives? Could it be a place like Kifungilo, made up
of many brick buildings built by Germans at the end of the Second
World War, high up in the mountains of northeastern Tanzania? Is
there a universal definition of home? Why did I love Mama Africa so
much without feeling Africa was home?

In Dar we were to be the guests of the Swedish ambassador to
Tanzania. In Minneapolis, we had become good friends with Swedish Consul General Knut Granstedt and his wife, Alie, whom I had
tutored in Swahili before they left for their new post as ambassadors
to Tanzania. We were frequent dinner guests at the Swedish consul-

ate. Every time I saw them, I dreaded they might mention my awful faux pas at one such formal dinner.

Kjell and I had been invited to their home along with several local dignitaries and various European consuls. Kjell was seated at the far end of the table. To my right was a distinguished gentleman who said he was from Poland. We exchanged stories and customs from our countries, and I told him that I was a language and dance instructor. I asked him what his profession was.

"I'm a conductor," he said.

"What train?" I asked.

"I beg your pardon?"

"I've seen the Burlington Northern passing by my friend's house."

"I beg your pardon?" he said again.

"It must be a difficult and maybe boring job, but at least you get to see a lot of American landscape."

"I beg your pardon?" he said for the third time. I wondered if he was getting progressively deaf, and if I should speak louder, but then he turned to face me, took my hand, and said, "I should have introduced myself properly. My name is Stanislaw Skrowaczewski, and I am the conductor of the Minnesota Orchestra."

I wanted to dive under the table. Instead I reached for the wine with the intention of downing the entire glass in one gulp but missed my mouth and splashed red wine all over my African dress. I put the glass down, looked him in the eye and said sheepishly, "Really?"

"Really!" he said.

With my napkin, I wiped the wine from my face and neck, thankful that my multicolored African kitenge outfit absorbed the wine with no trace. I changed the subject and started talking about the delicious dinner we were having. I joked about the Swedes' toasting ritual of saying *skål* a hundred times during the meal. To my relief, the orchestra conductor continued our conversation as if nothing had happened. After dinner, we went to the living room for coffee and liqueurs. I barely listened to the conversation because I was busy composing my apology.

When it was time to leave, I turned to apologize as the conductor approached the door. Before I could speak, he shook my hand

and said, "It is with humility and gratitude that I say goodbye. It took an African princess to put things in perspective and keep it real for me. Thank you!" He then hugged and kissed me on both cheeks.

In the car, Kjell asked me how I enjoyed the dinner. I skipped the details and told him I enjoyed my conversation with the Stanislaw guy (I didn't even try to pronounce his last name) and was impressed by his intelligence and class. If Kjell knew what had happened, he might never take me out in public again!

So here we were in Dar-es-Salaam, guests of the same hosts. No one mentioned my faux pas. They treated us royally, and helped us get seats on a plane to the island of Zanzibar.

On the plane, the stewardess, a well-groomed young woman, who had boarded the plane wearing a khanga tied around her waist, removed it, switched her plastic beach shoes to black patent-leather high heels, and put on crimson lipstick. The miniskirted African stewardess meant business as she served colorfully wrapped, home-made taffy to the passengers. She reprimanded an African gentleman who, we guessed from the broad grin on his face, was flying for the first time. "Put one back!" she said, slapping the man's hand for taking two pieces. "Do you think this is First Class?" We didn't dare take more than one piece each.

The minute we got off the plane in Zanzibar, everyone was herded to the immunization corner of the tiny airport and force-fed an antimalarial prophylactic with the same spoon for all and no water to wash it down.

Upon leaving the arrival area, an airport official arrested me for wearing a knee-length skirt. It was against the law for even women tourists to expose their legs and ankles on this predominantly Muslim island. The official took me to a waiting merchant, who sold me the only khanga available to cover my ankles. Printed on it in ugly green, yellow, and black was a proclamation of the merits of Zanzibar's Afro-Shirazi political party.

With my ankles duly covered, we emerged from the tiny *duka* (shop) to be greeted by a blue-black Swahili man who said his name was George Washington. He was our tour guide for the afternoon, and we were to follow only him and look only at what he showed us.

What I remember most about our tour with George Washington was the Anglican Cathedral, built on the site of the old slave market where, from as early as the seventh century, Africans were sold during the East African slave trade. Slaves were captured on the mainland of Tanganyika and other parts of Africa and sent on Arab *dhows* (ships) to Zanzibar, where they were held in moldy, dark, underground chambers with little ventilation as they awaited shipment. For centuries, enslaved Africans were taken to the Middle East, North Africa, India, and beyond. This Eastern slave trade was different from the slave trade across the Atlantic Ocean, which brought Africans to the Americas and the Caribbean. In the early transatlantic slave trade, the demand was for male laborers to work on plantations and in mines. In the East African trade, the main demand was for domestic servants. The sight and smell of these chambers was a sobering reminder of the appalling realities of the slave trade.

After our tour ended, we watched as George Washington greeted a new group of tourists: *"Bonjour, mes amies. Je m'appelle Charles de Gaulle, et je suis vos guide cette après-midi."* (Hello, my friends. My name is Charles de Gaulle, and I am your guide this afternoon.) Instead of the red, white, and blue top hat he had worn for us, he was now wearing a black beret.

Back on the mainland, the buzz and confusion of passengers bickering for tickets outside the tiny rectangular slit of a sales window came to a sudden hush as the Swedish ambassador's Mercedes Benz dropped us at the bus station in Dar-es-Salaam the next morning. The ticket salesman shouted insistently at us, "What—are you *wazungu* crazy? You will not ride this bus! It is harmful! Only Africans, because they are used to it, can ride it. I have never seen a *mzungu* on any bus here. Go away!"

Since it was the only way to Marian College in Morogoro, where I had gone to high school and where I wanted to visit friends from Kifungilo, we begged him to sell us tickets. He finally gave in, telling us we were stupid and had been forewarned.

After we had waited about an hour during which several other Africans cautioned us to be careful of our possessions and our lives, the driver showed up. Once we were all on board, he slammed the door of the driver's compartment and roared out of the potholed parking lot. Scenes from my bus trips to Mhonda and Marian College flashed before me. I wondered if the required ritual for bus drivers to obtain their licenses was blowing out of the station, driving like a maniac, coming to a screeching halt, violently turning the bus around, going back to the station, filling the gas tank, and starting out again!

We sat two rows behind the back wheel, where we rocked and rolled so much we had trouble staying put! A nice young man, who felt sorry for Kjell, offered him the English *Tanzania Standard* newspaper and tried to carry on a conversation. He understood how I might ride on a Tanzanian bus, but why would a *mzungu* do such a thing?

A troop of baboons sauntered across the road and were in no hurry to make way for us. The driver waited until he was almost on top of them before hitting the brakes. They were not afraid and sat nonchalantly on the road until several passengers got out and shooed them away with rocks and sticks.

In Morogoro, my friends Mariana and Simon looked the same as they had ten years earlier. Their son, Eddie, whom they had adopted from Kifungilo when I was still there, had left home to be a car mechanic.

I was eager to see Marian College, my high school, so Simon drove us there and waited for us. We entered through a gate made of a single roughly hewn log that I didn't remember from before. I was amazed at how small the buildings looked and how short the distances were from classrooms to dormitories to the church, which was being built next to the convent the year I left Africa.

The place had deteriorated from when it was run by the Maryknoll Sisters. The African headmistress was a former student who had been two years ahead of me in school. She wasn't there, and the office workers refused to let me show Kjell the records of my graduation in 1962.

I rang the door of the convent several times before it was opened by a barefooted African girl wearing a tattered orange blouse with a bright green, worn-out khanga tied around her waist.

"Is Sister Martin Corde here?" I asked.

"Geneva?"

"I was told Sister Martin Corde is here. I was in the pioneer classes at Marian College."

"What's your name?"

"Maria Bergh—I mean, Mary Rose Ryan."

"Wait here," she said. Almost immediately she returned and asked us to follow her.

I couldn't hide my surprise when I saw Sister Martin Corde—whom I remembered sashaying around the school grounds in her long white habit, playing with her crucifix, and nodding her pointed headpiece encouragingly to students—now dressed in a khanga tied over a short, flowered dress. Just as we students had done ten years earlier, she sat on the cement steps having her hair braided.

She jumped up, gave me a long hug, and shook Kjell's hand. "It's so nice to see you, Mary, and I'm pleased you've found the love and happiness you deserve in America," she said, nodding at Kjell.

If it hadn't been for her heartwarming smile and soothing voice, I would not have recognized her!

"I'll never forget your kindness to me while I was here. You were the only Sister who really understood me and took the time to talk to me. You told me to believe in miracles."

She smiled warmly at me, then asked, "You must be shocked by the many changes you see here now, but I believe it's all for the best. Are you surprised to see me like this?"

Looking at her sitting on the steps with her nappy hair three-quarters braided and her sandaled feet, I gave an exaggerated nod. We talked about the many changes at school, in the government, and the church.

"I'm so glad you don't have to wear those weird habits, and your new name is beautiful."

"Geneva is the name my parents gave me. Can you and your husband stay for supper?"

"We're having supper with Mariana and Simon. Do you remember them?"

"Of course, I do. They helped me take care of you and the other girls from Kifungilo. You all needed some extra love. Say hello to them for me."

Our visit to Marian College was brief. Sister Martin Corde—Geneva—was the only nun there. The other nuns had returned to the United States when the government took over the school or gone to other missions.

Back with Mariana and Simon we continued our visit, joking about Africans and Americans and laughing and crying about our life in Kifungilo. They also plied me with questions about the gadgets we used in America.

"Is it true," Simon asked, "that in America a machine washes and dries your dirty clothes? And your bread comes already sliced? I remember when President Kennedy was alive. He cared about us and sent us the Peace Corps and the bags of kenedi flour. Do you see on TV that we are poor here in Tanzania?"

"I heard that American housewives spend hours watching the telly and cry because the rich and beautiful people on TV have sad lives," added Mariana, "and that housewives don't have to cook because they can buy already cooked food in frozen packages."

I enjoyed my friends' curiosity about my life in America, and almost everywhere I went I was asked similar questions. For the most part, people living in villages had no electricity, yet they were fascinated by the technological side of American life. The next day at the Morogoro market, Mariana urged me to describe a washing machine to a group of Luguru women selling fruits and vegetables.

I recalled my first awed encounter with a washing machine at the apartment I shared with Cathy as I began talking to the women. "A washing machine is a square metal box with a stick in the center," I explained. "You put dirty clothes in the box and add soap bars that have been ground into a powder like cornmeal. Then you push buttons on the box to make hot and cold water pour into it. The stick swishes the clothes slowly, scrubbing them gently instead of beating them on the rocks like you do here." The women stared at me spellbound, some with incredulous looks and furrowed brows.

"The box knows when the clothes are clean, and it stops, and the dirty water goes out. More water comes into the box and rinses the clothes. Then the inside of the box spins very fast, squeezing the water out. It stops when the water is gone. The clothes you put in are all washed at the same time and come out clean."

Then they fired practical questions at me: "How does water get in the box? Do you make several trips to the river to fetch water? Where do you put in the firewood? How does the water get hot? How does the machine know when the clothes are clean?"

I decided that no matter how much I tried, I couldn't explain what I didn't fully understand myself but now took for granted. No use describing a dryer, or soap operas to people who had never seen a TV, or frozen food to people who had never seen a refrigerator, or ice for that matter, or an electric stove—or a vacuum cleaner.

By the end of the visit, I was looking forward to my journey to Kifungilo. The next morning, having obtained front seats with Simon's help, Kjell and I settled into our second suicidal bus trip with another maniacal driver who handled the huge bus like a toy.

28

Kifungilo

We returned to Dar-es-Salaam from Morogoro, and after another comfortable stay with the Granstedts, we rented a sedan from a reluctant Asian Tanzanian, who repeated as often as possible during the negotiations, "The road to Lushoto is suicidal for both passengers and car!"

We had requested a Land Rover, but he wouldn't even consider it. "I have only three Land Rovers, and they are in great demand for tourist safaris to the national parks. I make more money with them. Very few people rent a car to go to Lushoto." We wanted reliable transportation but realized he was right.

The car dealer had every reason to worry about his car. The tarmac that once covered the road was now reduced to sharp, slate-like slivers jutting from pool-sized potholes filled with debris. It took us two hours to drive thirty miles. Even Kjell, who usually liked road challenges, was speechless. We stopped in Korogwe, and I showed him the Rosminian priests' mission where Father Michael lived and where I had first seen a telephone.

Despite the long drive, Kjell insisted on going straight to Mombo and then on to Lushoto. The road between the two, which had the reputation of being the worst in the country before I left in 1963, hadn't seen a road crew since! The car crawled up the mountain, hugging the slopes, while the engine screamed with effort as we slip-slided over what was once a road. We were much better off driving along the pedestrian *shoti-katis* (shortcuts), which were even steeper, but we could at least see a path. Waiting for us in Lushoto were Sister Nerea, who founded the dentistry there, and Sister Eileen, formerly Lizzy, one of the older girls from my time in the orphanage. She had gone to Germany to become a nun and a dentist. The delicious German supper recalled my visits to the dentistry as a child. Sister Eileen looked, talked, joked, and laughed exactly as I remembered, and I knew she was happy to see me.

"Sister Silvestris is delighted to see you. She's been telling everyone you are coming ten thousand miles to visit her, while other Kifungilo girls who live only a few miles away never come."

I had been writing to Sister Silvestris and Mother Rufina from America, and they always wrote back. That night at the dentistry with the Sisters seemed surreal. It was as if I'd never left Kifungilo. I couldn't sleep. My feelings about the orphanage and the nuns had changed little over the years, and now I was willingly returning to the source of my childhood misery. Of course, no one, not even Sister Eileen, fully knew how tormented I was over not having a family. Neither did they know about Fat Mary, my soul friend and guardian angel, without whom I could not have survived Kifungilo.

I hoped that after this trip the Sisters would know I was ever grateful to them for raising me, and that I am happy with the person I have become. Although I didn't dare, I wanted to ask the Sisters why they often were mean to us and why everyone called me stupid. I was also eager to find out whether Sister Silvestris would still call me Fat Mary and whether I would know any of the girls there now.

I am very proud of you for going back to Kifungilo, Fat Mary whispered when all was quiet that evening. *You will see that in many ways, you haven't left. Your actions have always been guided by your past. You now realize that your childhood gave you the tools you would need to live a life of purpose and meaning. This visit will reveal the importance of never denying your past. You must look at it without judgment, because it is the truest basis of your present self.*

Morning brought its own surprises. To my relief, Sister Eileen decided to ride with us to Kifungilo. She had us laughing till we cried. She and Kjell joked and carried on about Africa and Kifungilo as if it were Kjell who'd been at the orphanage instead of me! Very little about the road and terrain came back to me until we reached the tall, slender cypress trees lining the one-mile entrance to Kifungilo.

How different everything looked! The long, narrow road I had once dreaded walking was now short, even, and wide. The two fish-ponds in the bottom of the valley seemed tiny compared to how I remembered them. Sister Eileen and I broke into the walking safari songs we used to sing: "The children of Don Bosco Home, they have a little Benga" and "Do you know the way to Sakarani?"

Sister Silvestris and Mother Rufina were waiting for us in the same room at the convent where I had been shown for adoption. Mother Rufina seemed shorter and Sister Silvestris seemed subdued. Obviously happy to see us, they greeted us with hearty handshakes.

Sister Silvestris noticed the Playboy bunny logo on Kjell's shirt. "What a nice rabbit that is. Mother Rufina, look at the rabbit." The three nuns agreed that Kjell had a very nice rabbit on his shirt! I pinched Kjell hard, so he managed to control his laughter.

One of the many stories Sister Silvestris told Kjell about me was how I visited the children with mumps in the infirmary and begged them for the bacon she had heated, wrapped in a cloth, and tied around their cheeks to reduce the swelling. "But she was not the only child who did that. They all did! The children were always hungry! They used to steal and steal. Even Fat Mary stole food. She was so fat! My Fat Mary, you're not so fat anymore. Is American food bad? They don't have good German food, ya?"

We all laughed, and Mother Rufina, who always wanted everyone to know that she was knowledgeable and read widely, turned to Sister Silvestris and said, "No, no, Sister. In America, one must not be fat. Everybody wants to be thin. Our little Mary is an American girl now."

"Do you remember how you answered the priests when they asked your name?" Sister Eileen cocked her head, raised her eyes, and said, "I'm an Amelican gal!"

Mother Rufina laughed nervously, but Sister Silvestris said, "My Fat Mary always wanted to be like the Americans, her best friend Elizabeth wanted to be like the English, but no one wanted to be like the Germans." I gave Kjell a stern look before he opened his mouth to make one of his pointed remarks about Germans and Nazis.

The nuns walked us to the priests' retreat house, showed us our room, and announced that lunch would be right after the Angelus.

Then we could rest, after which Sister Silvestris would take us on a tour of the entire mission compound and the former Don Bosco Children's Home. Afternoon coffee would be at 4 pm, more rest, dinner at 6 pm, then in the evening the Sisters would come to the retreat house to show us old photo albums of Kifungilo.

"Now I know where you got your organizational skills and discipline," Kjell told me as we settled in.

Our beds were homemade, of wood, with no headboards; huge soft pillows were tucked inside embroidered cases of crisp white linen. On the wood nightstand stood a ceramic washbasin and jug, a piece of Lux soap, a candle, and some matches. The towels were of heavy, loosely woven cotton, beautifully embroidered with scenes of German castles. Kjell disapprovingly pointed to the crucifix and various pictures of the Virgin Mary and other saints that hung on the walls.

"Did you really expect to stay in a Catholic mission, in the priests' retreat house no less, with no reminder of where you are? This is the Convent of the German Precious Blood Sisters! Keep that in mind." Although I found comfort in the surroundings, it was obvious Kjell was bothered. "I can't wait to see the rest of the compound this afternoon," he said. "So far this place looks like a miniature Germany."

"Having been raised by them, I see Germans in a category by themselves. They are self-sufficient, brilliant, ingenious at adapting, hardworking, aggressive, and industrious." I shouldn't have started talking about the Germans. Whenever I tried to see the positive side of my life with German nuns, Kjell reminded me not to be so forgiving.

"They're also intolerant, ruthless, and cruel racists."

"You can't blame the Kifungilo nuns for the Germans bombing your Kristiansund."

"Germans are known racists, and no amount of missionary work could redeem them from what they have done to the world."

"You are now a guest of the Kifungilo nuns, who happen to be German and who would never hurt you. Could you accept that hospitality graciously for my sake?"

"You're right. These nuns couldn't hurt a fly. Are you sure they're the same ones who beat you and put you in the pigsty?" He started to tease me, but I wouldn't bite.

"This is 1974, and times have changed."

Indeed, times had changed since I'd left in 1963. Tanganyika gained its independence in December of that year and was now Tanzania, after the union of the mainland with the island of Zanzibar in 1964. The country had embarked on a system of government called *Ujamaa*. Loosely based on the ideology of Chinese communes, *Ujamaa* means "familyhood," or extended family. During my visit, not only did I see for myself the results of Ujamaa but also the countless conversations with friends and acquaintances about this social and political experiment revealed the complexities and problems facing the country after the British left.

I never found out what happened to most of the remaining orphans, now grown, for whom Kifungilo was built. On our tour of the mission grounds, Sister Silvestris' voice and choice of words made it apparent that things had changed a great deal. Previously, the people who lived in the Usambara Mountains were referred to as the Wasambaa or the *washenzi* (pagans). Now they were "our comrades" and *wenyeji* (locals). Previously, orders came from the British governor; now they came from *Mheshimiwa Rais Nyerere*—the Honorable President Nyerere. It was obvious the nuns were afraid that what had happened after Congo gained its independence from Belgium—white people including missionaries were tortured, raped, and deported en masse—might also happen here. Sister Silvestris prefaced most of her sentences with *zamani* (long ago).

"*Zamani* we paid the workers what we thought was fair, but now there is a fixed salary, and even when they don't work, we can't fire them. You know, Mr. Bergh, they have become so lazy, because they are guaranteed their *mshahara* (salary), and some even talk back to us. We must be very careful about what we say to the Wasambaa nowadays, because they can report us to their district commissioner in Lushoto and we can be deported. But in spite of these difficult changes, I love Kifungilo and always will. This has been my home for many years. This is where I want to die."

At that moment, I realized that no matter what Sister Silvestris did to us children—the physical and verbal abuse and severe punishments, the strict rules she enforced—I had never hated her like many of the other children did. I could always talk to her about what was on my childish mind. She beat me as much as she beat every other child, but she often showed her love for us too.

While I was deep in thought, a plump cat came meowing towards Sister Silvestris. "Here pussy, pussy, come pussy." She reached into the deep pocket that had contained treats when I was a child and produced a dry piece of bread. She leaned down to pet the cat, then picked it up and held it.

"Mr. Bergh, come and see my pussy," she said. "Isn't it the nicest pussy you've ever seen? We have other wild pussies in Kifungilo, but this one is clean and always knows where to find me. Yes, what a good pussy!" Kjell was laughing so hard that I had to stand in front of him and pet the cat. Sister joined Kjell's laughter, saying, "I can see that Mr. Bergh likes my pussy too!"

We covered lots of territory as Sister briefly explained the history of Kifungilo to Kjell. She told him about the hardships endured by the first nuns, who had a difficult time finding land for their mission and had to manage without a priest for several years. Mother Ancilla had decided to build the Don Bosco home for the many children who were the offspring of *wazungu* and Africans because mixed-race children were often hidden by their mothers and shunned by villagers. Once the children were in their care, the Sisters started a school for them. Sister Theonesta, a teacher for the primary grades, had taken care of me as a baby. Sister Silvestris recalled how they had to find appropriate places for the half-caste boys to live as well as further schooling, jobs, and husbands for the girls as they grew up. She had recently started a health clinic for "her Wasambaa" on the mission grounds rather than continue walking to nearby villages to bring medicine to the sick.

I was hearing most of this for the first time. Kjell didn't seem to be paying much attention to what Sister Silvestris was saying, but he was visibly moved by the exquisite beauty and tranquility of the place. By now I was used to his avoidance of deep topics that might force him to show emotion. He spoke little during our afternoon coffee as we enjoyed several kinds of fresh baked pastries and pound cakes, strong café au lait from coffee grown, roasted, and ground in Kifungilo, and fresh milk from the cows we had seen grazing in the meadow during our tour. We realized we would again be hungry and almost unable to wait for supper just two hours later! Our typical German dinner, which we devoured, consisted of pork flanks, sweet red cabbage, homemade noodles, and a dessert compote made from canned peaches just as we had prepared for the priests' retreats when I was a child.

29

Revelations

Mother Rufina, Sisters Silvestris, Eileen, and Jacinta came down after supper and spent two hours with us going through three photo albums that Mother Rufina carried under her arm like the treasured keepsakes they were.

With them I saw a side of Kifungilo that I had not known existed. From the way they referred to us children—their little girls and boys—I felt how much they had cared for us, and I was surprised. Someone had painstakingly written in calligraphy the first names of the children who were at the orphanage on the first three pages of one of the albums. I found my name three-quarters of the way down the third page: "Little Mary, January, 1944."

The nuns told stories about many of us. Sister Silvestris insisted on holding the heavy black construction-paper pages with pictures held in place by black photo mounting corners, so no one would turn the page before she finished her story. It was her night since she was our mother and she had all the stories. Most of them were so funny that we laughed until we cried. But occasionally Mother Rufina would turn the page before Sister Silvestris finished.

Once they discovered that Kjell understood and spoke German, the nuns ignored me and carried on the rest of the evening in German. I was pleased at how much I understood. These were the same voices that had scolded me in German when I was a child. It was a revelation to discover that they were human after all. To me as a child they seemed so different from regular people, not only because of their frightening nun habits but also because I never saw them together in a cozy group, carrying on an easy conversation, laughing, joking, even touching each other. Had they been like this when I was little?

All the nuns in the album looked the same, but most of the children looked different from what I remembered. I lingered over the photos of Sister Theonesta, of Rosa, my first big girl caregiver, and of my friend Elizabeth and me with huge yellow bows on top of our heads, matching our yellow dresses. We must have been four or five years old in the picture taken after Sunday Mass.

As we looked at the picture, Sister Silvestris said to Kjell, "Your Fat Mary was very clever, but she was afraid of everyone and cried a lot. Yet I always knew she would be one of our best. Her friend Elizabeth was very clever too, but she was clever in the wrong way." Sister reached over and pinched my cheeks.

I looked at the few pictures of me again and again. As a child, I had longed to have a picture of myself. The very first photo I had of myself to keep had come from Cathy. It was of the two of us when she visited Kifungilo to ask permission to take me to America. I treasured that photo and mainly looked at myself in it. That image proclaimed my hopes about the new life that awaited me in America with a mother who loved me. Despite everything, I had lived, grown, and attained the best education available to me. Holding the photo made me so happy and proud.

I love to look at photos of people I know and love. There is something about a photo that is magical. I wonder if what I see in a friend's photo now is what I will see after that person dies. Our photos capture our being. Many Africans believe that when someone takes your picture, they take an image of your sacred and invisible essence. I find that fascinating and true.

The nuns left, chatting and chuckling all the way to their convent. Kjell and I went outdoors to use the modern toilet before bed, but the black night studded with a trillion brilliant stars made us stop in awe. We held each other without saying a word. Sitting down on the cement steps, we silently experienced the African night. It was as if a canopy of fire sparks intentionally engulfed us and we dissolved into it. Being there with the one I loved, who loved me, I realized that the child who walked and lived surrounded by this intoxicating beauty of Kifungilo had been unable to see it then but could see it now because at last she knew love.

"Never in my wildest dreams did I imagine Kifungilo to be so beautiful," Kjell began as we settled into bed. "I have never, ever seen such a sky, such a night! Never have I experienced such an intense awareness of nature. Here you have apples, pears, bananas, and pineapples growing side by side with Norwegian pines and jacaranda trees. Did you see the size of the calla lilies lining the irrigation canals, and did you feel the soft velvet moss clinging to the twigs that formed bridges across the canals? How could there be so many different kinds and colors of roses? Those Norwegian pines! And the vegetable fields with big cauliflowers, fat kohlrabi, and huge leeks. Everywhere I looked I was surrounded with nature at its best—high mountains with clouds halfway down the slopes and in the valley near the convent, the villages with their clumps of huts and worn footpaths that looked like pieces of a jigsaw puzzle. The wonderful perfumes in the air—I tell you, Maria, there was a moment when I had sensory overload. I couldn't absorb any more. Damn! This place is beautiful."

Before this visit, I would not have agreed with Kjell's evaluation of Kifungilo, though I'd heard it described similarly by *wazungu* when I was small. Were my senses dead to the beauty of the place? Back then, my experience of the physical setting of Kifungilo had mostly been harsh. The bitter cold cutting my bones and the ferocious wind bending me like a green twig in the mornings as I walked from the girls' quarters to church, were my most vivid recollection of nature at Kifungilo. Kjell's pleasant, sensual overload did not correspond to the agony that my whole body had felt every Saturday evening after spending the entire day stooped over a broom, sweeping a week's accumulation of pebbles, dust, and leaves from the paths. The unbelievably huge snow-white calla lilies lining the clear irrigation canals that he admired reminded me of my fear of falling into the canals as I inched my bare feet across the little wooden bridges covered with slippery moss.

The impressive and graceful aromatic cypress trees along the path of the outdoor Stations of the Cross leading to the cemetery brought back a dreaded ritual. During the forty long days of Lent before Easter, all of us children stopped at each of the fourteen stations commemorating the passion and death of Jesus. We knelt on the cold, rough, uneven ground at each station, listening to readings and prayers that seemed to last forever.

"Kifungilo has some of the most beautiful natural surroundings and well-planned landscaping in the world," Kjell had remarked when we were in the lush garden by the pond.

"Quite an admission coming from the son of a landscape artist in Norway and from someone who dislikes Germans so much."

"I don't dislike Germans—we have several German friends. I've never held anything against Germans as individuals, but I do have a hard time forgiving them for what they have done to other humans."

"For me, Kifungilo has shrunk. The buildings aren't as dispersed as I remember, and they're not nearly as large. The pigsty where I was locked up with a pig as punishment doesn't seem as menacing. I now understand the difference between a child's and an adult's point of view."

"You never told me about the beauty of this place. Granted it's at the end of the world, but if I'd known, I'd have come sooner."

"When I lived here, I hated it most of the time. I never thought of Kifungilo's beauty. As a child, did you appreciate the beauty of Norway—its fjords and waterfalls, dramatic mountain ranges, serene lakes and valleys—like you do now?"

"I did."

The many positive things that happened to me in America seemed to have opened my eyes to what I was too blind to see before. Minnesota, with its miserably cold winters when trees lose their leaves and plants wither and die, with its towering cold concrete buildings and bundled-up people, was a stark contrast to Kifungilo. Now, Kifungilo stood out to me as a jewel—cut, carved, and polished by human hands without modern technology. For the rest of our stay in Kifungilo, I knew I would dwell on its beauty. Had the sadness of my childhood prevented this beauty from revealing itself to me when I was growing up here? Maybe absorbing this beauty now would help balance my childhood memories.

I can explain, Fat Mary assured me. *This beauty has always been here. You saw it with your eyes, but not with your heart. What you do not feel in your heart does not leave a lasting impression in your mind. When you were here, you needed to cultivate an inner beauty that sustained you—the beauty of your spirit.*

The Precious Blood Sisters realized that with Tanzania's independence and the government taking over the schools, they and other missionaries might no longer be needed and might even be expelled from the country. To preserve and perpetuate their work, they decided to accept Africans into the order and train them as nuns at the convent in Kifungilo to continue the work of education. We met some of the young African Sisters-in-training when they brought us breakfast.

After breakfast, Sister Jacinta came running down the path. Shooing me out of the dining area, she motioned to Kjell. She was hiding something under her full-length, blue-and-white pinstriped apron. I left them alone despite knowing Kjell was uncomfortable with missionaries and even more uncomfortable with nuns. After a few minutes, he came into the bedroom laughing so hard I had to join in. When he tried to talk, he laughed even more.

"You won't believe this crazy Sister Jacinta!" he finally managed to say. "She came right up to me, pulled my ear down, and whispered, 'Mr. Bergh, I have a gift for you!'"

"'Thank you, Sister,' I told her, 'but it isn't necessary.' She pulled out three huge bottles of Safari beer from under her apron and stacked them in my arms. I didn't have the heart to tell her that I don't drink. I thanked her very much, and she roughly pulled my head down towards her again and whispered loudly, 'Mr. Bergh, I doo zis only for you—und ze bishop!'"

I remembered that Sister Jacinta was always up to mischief. She had the roundest rosy cheeks, often stretched out in a smile, and her deep blue eyes seemed to dance to the rhythm of her quick thoughts. Long before this she had pulled off some pretty unorthodox activities for a Precious Blood nun!

We walked up to the convent together because she was going to take us to Gare.

30

And Somebody Else

We started our walk to Gare, another mission in the valley also serviced by the Precious Blood Sisters. There was a road, but it cut through hills and valleys and took three hours compared to half an hour on foot, following the beaten track that must have been carved into the steep mountains by goats.

Sister Jacinta, who was Austrian, yodeled loudly as she ran down the valleys and scampered up the *shoti-kati* trails like a goat. She told us stories and pointed at trees and caves where such-and-such a Kifungilo girl sinfully lay with a Wasambaa. It was obvious how much she liked being in the outdoors rather than the kitchen, preparing meals for the perpetually hungry nuns.

Approaching Gare, we ran into a funeral procession headed by Father Kennedy, the senior priest at the mission. The official, professional mourners and relatives of the deceased, dressed in dark *kaniki*, led the procession. Behind them came the narrow wood coffin made just that morning and carried on the heads of four elderly men. Village people followed. The women were dressed in their brightly colored khangas, with one piece carefully draped over the head to signal a solemn occasion. As we approached the procession, we noticed the women semi-genuflecting as they passed Kjell, saying, *"Tumsifu Yesu Kristu!"* (Praise be to Jesus Christ!) and waiting until Kjell finally mumbled something back to them. The men wouldn't let him off so easily. They wanted him to bless them and knelt at his feet, repeating, *"Tumsifu Yesu Kristu!"* Kjell quickly figured out what was required. He had seen Father Kennedy blessing the locals with the sign of the cross as he walked at the end of the procession. Kjell sacrilegiously gave the suppliant mourners his best karate chop and muttered, "Milelelelelelel amen," trying to imitate Father Kennedy, who replied to the mourners in front of him with *"Milele na milele, amina!"* (Now and forever, amen.)

In Gare, we visited with Father Kennedy and Father Spillane, who were just as I remembered them. After lunch, Father Kennedy, a good friend of the family of Heini (the contractor who helped the nuns build most of Kifungilo), accompanied us to the nearby village of Kivumbi to visit them. Heini's five children attended Kifungilo, and one of the girls who bullied and tormented me during my childhood had married into the family.

She must have known we were coming because she emerged from her house with her four children neatly groomed, their black hair slicked against their heads with the unmistakable scent of English lavender Vaseline. She looked old, haggard, and burned out. Did she remember how much she had tortured me? Of course not. She was happy to see me, to meet Kjell, to ask about America, and tell me about her hopeless life with her alcoholic husband. She was a schoolteacher in Gare Middle School, but she said the salary was so low that her life was only a little bit better than that of the Wasambaa around her.

It was good to see her. Strangely enough, except for an occasional nightmare, I had forgotten her role in my childhood misery. Hadn't she also been working through her own demons? Didn't she just do to us what the big girls did to her? And didn't I—without thinking—try to do the same to little Monika, who was temporarily put in my care just before I left for Marian College?

I didn't really know about her life in Kifungilo, just as I knew little about anyone's true inner feelings. We didn't discuss them, and when I tried to I was labeled stupid, so I kept it all inside and in the care of my Fat Mary. I had been jealous of her because she was thin. I wanted to be her friend because she had a sister, and I hoped to be included in their extended family.

We also visited her two sisters-in-law, who had been at the orphanage as well. We talked only about the good times and the fun we had when we were naughty. I think we secretly knew, even back then, that no matter what hardships we endured, we were still better off than our African half-sisters and half-brothers who were reared in the villages. As we left, I felt a slight sense of satisfaction seeing that what goes around comes around.

We started our climb up the treacherous footpaths, this time with walking canes and taking only the *shoti-katis* back to Kifungilo. Halfway up the mountain, we heard a man who was intoxicated, singing at the top of his lungs in a mixture of Kisambaa, Swahili, Latin, and English. He bellowed, "*Gloria in Excelsis Deo. Gadi sevi awa glatesti qwini.*" (Glory to God in the highest. God save our greatest queen.)

"Stay avay from zhat Rashidi," Sister Jacinta warned. "He'z very troublesome. He doesn't know zhe difference between a Sister und ozer vemen. He haz no manners. Und he iz even more drunker zan usual!"

We tried to take another *shoti-kati* that Sister Jacinta knew, but it was too late. The drunkard had already seen us, changed his path, and somehow staggered very quickly to the top of our path. There was no avoiding him now. He looked first at Sister, then at Kjell, then at me, as he stroked his chin and scratched his head. Suddenly he threw himself onto his knees, blocking our path, and screamed at the top of his lungs, "*Mungu wangu weeeee! Sasa nitakwenda mbinguni. Nimetokewa na Bikira Maria, Yesu Kristu—na mtu mwingine!*" (Oh my God! I'm going straight to heaven. I've had a vision of the Virgin Mary, Jesus Christ—and somebody else.)

He continued this litany, repeating it again and again while trying to hang on to Sister's skirt. She hit him with her hand and shoved him with her foot, yelling, "Go avay, dirty man! Go avay! God vill send you to hell for zhis!"

The drunkard wrapped his hands around her legs as she made her way up the slope, forcing her to drag him along. She turned bright red with exasperation.

Meanwhile, Kjell was enjoying every minute of this. Sister begged the drunken man to let her go, but he wouldn't. Reluctantly, Kjell approached to help, but now the drunkard, still clutching Sister's legs, looked at him and declared that Jesus Christ had ants on his chest. He let go of the nun and began pulling at the hair on Kjell's chest. Kjell broke free of the drunken man, who then went tumbling into the bushes and shrubs still singing, "I'm a saint! I've seen the Virgin Mary, Jesus Christ, and somebody else!"

When his incantations became just an echo, we sat on a rock to have some coffee. Sister elaborated about the problem of alcohol in the villages. "You see, Mr. Bergh, zhis is alvays zhe problem vit zhe Vasambaa. Zhey drink und drink und drink. Ze vemen in zhe village make beer out of bananas or millet so zhey're drunk most of zheir lives. Zis is a real problem. Zhey can't tell vhen zhey are drunk! Zhey sink zhat because ve are vemen, zhey can take us to zhe village like a cow. Zhey can't understand zhat ve are vemen of God."

We talked and laughed about our encounter with the drunkard and his vision of the Virgin Mary and Jesus Christ. But until Kjell addressed me as "Hey, Somebody Else," Sister hadn't realized that the drunkard called me "somebody else." For my part, I was a little disappointed. Couldn't I have been a saint or an angel and not just "somebody else"?

After a well-earned restful night, we walked up to the convent where Sister Silvestris and Mother Rufina were waiting outside our car for that day's excursions. We went to Rangwe, where old Father Benedict was still living. He had always been kind and gentle to the Kifungilo children whenever we showed up in our lorry for a picnic at his mission station.

We also went to Sakarani Mission where Brother Fortunate remembered me. Sakarani was another little paradise, too beautiful for words. It was a miniature Kifungilo. Unfortunately, it was so isolated that the priests and brothers who worked there suffered extreme loneliness and depression. It wasn't any different now. The overweight priest who greeted us seemed to exist in a permanent state of alcohol intoxication.

"Now, Mr. Bergh, we're going to take you to the end of the world," said Mother Rufina. The "end of the world" was located high in the misty mountains of the Usambara rain forests. We parked the car a distance from the edge of the precipice, and were impressed by how Mother Rufina at age eighty shuffled along way ahead of us. On a clear day, which was rare at this altitude, the promontory gave a breathtaking view of the valley beneath, reaching from the Usambara region to Tanga on the Indian Ocean, past Handeni, Korogwe, and the Pare Mountains to the Uluguru Mountains in Morogoro. The scene below and around us was as dramatic as the mountains along the fjords of Norway with their hundred-foot drops into the ocean, except that here there were no waterfalls or snow—only a patchwork of cultivated plots with a maze of paths leading to villages big and small that peeked at us through the mist.

We visited the graves of old missionaries and the ruins of a church built by Germans. Mother Rufina said that a priest still came once a week for the Catholics to say Mass, baptize and hear confessions. Then we returned to Kifungilo via the Lushoto dentistry, where we had a late lunch. While the nuns rested, Sister Eileen took Kjell and me to see the only person from my childhood who still lived nearby. She was someone I needed to see.

31

Zami

"Why are you wasting your and Mr. Bergh's time going to see Zami?" Sister Eileen asked when I said I wanted to go to Zami's farm. She didn't seem too keen about our trip there.

"I need to see her again. She was my big girl."

"*Pole sana!*" (I'm sorry!) she said, shaking her head. "I was told that Zami was one of the cruelest big girls at Kifungilo. She's lucky I didn't know that—I would have beaten her up. When I was ten, I beat up my big girl so bad she never touched me again. I wasn't afraid of anyone."

"I was afraid of everyone! You worked with Sister Nerea at the dentistry and didn't spend time with the other big girls. But I remember you often came to our rescue."

"Once I saved you from Sister Clotilda. *Yule alikuwa shetani kabisa!* (She was a devil!) The time she beat your hands with her stick, your fingers were so swollen I couldn't separate them as I bandaged them. Another mean nun I'll never forget is Sister Theonesta. She made my life miserable."

"Sister Theonesta?" I gulped. I couldn't believe what I was hearing. "My Sister Theonesta?"

"Yes, your Sister Theonesta. I know she loved and cared for you as if you were her child, and you slept in her bed when you were a baby, but she was mean to the rest of us."

I was too shocked to continue the conversation. I decided to visit her grave the next day and have a talk with her.

On our way, Sister Eileen told me that Zami had married the old German farmer who lived near Kifungilo. "Her husband has died and she runs the huge farm alone now. We buy fruits and vegetables from her. In the orphanage, we called her *Mchoyo*—Greedy, remember? She hasn't changed."

Kjell knew bits and pieces of my life in Kifungilo, but I rarely spoke about Zami. I had been able to face a lot of the pain and suffering of my childhood, however when I mentioned Zami or even thought about her, tears filled my eyes.

My heart pounded as we approached her farm with the tile-roofed, three-story red brick house set on a hillside. She had married the old German owner of this farm who was kind to us when we arrived each year in a lorry for a picnic, but we were afraid of him because his face was red and we thought he was a hundred years old. The place was as remarkable now as it had been then. The large mullioned windows were like the windows in Kifungilo that we cleaned every Saturday with old German newspapers.

As soon as we got out of the car near the house, I heard a door creak on rusty hinges. Zami came out smiling to greet Sister Eileen. She squinted as she tried to remember me.

"*Unamkumbuka Mary mdogo siyo?*" Sister Eileen asked. (You remember Little Mary, don't you?)

"*Mungu wangu, singemtambua kama usingenikumbusha!*" (My God, I'd never have recognized her!) Zami said. "Why are you so thin? Don't they feed you in America?"

Just that morning Sister Silvestris had asked whether Kjell was too poor to provide food for me. Judging from everyone's response to me, I no longer looked like the Fat Mary who had left Kifungilo ten years ago. I shook Zami's hand without saying a word. I tried to speak but had no words, no thoughts, no emotions. We went inside to her receiving room. She told her house servant to bring tea, pastries, and the best fruit from the garden. "*Wageni hawa wametoka Amerika!*" (These guests come from America!)

The servant shook my hand firmly and curtsied to Kjell, saying, "*Karibuni sana!*" (A hearty welcome to you!)

I couldn't swallow the sandwiches and biscuits we were offered, so I only sipped the tea.

"Looking at you, I now believe what I heard—that everyone in America is on a diet to get thin," Zami said.

"Maria didn't diet," Kjell volunteered. "American life and culture shock did it for her. I'm glad she's thin. I hate fat women."

"Please don't hate me!" Sister Eileen scolded him. "I don't know how I got fat. Before I went to Germany, I was thin and had a wonderful figure that was a shame to hide under a nun's habit so early in my life."

"My wife adores you, so I couldn't hate you—and nuns aren't interested in attracting men anyway."

"Don't be so sure!" Sister Eileen said mischievously. "Zami is the opposite of me, Mary. Remember how big she was at the orphanage?"

"Don't remind me," Zami laughed. "Those days are gone!"

No, those days will never be gone, I thought. If she thinks those days are gone, then she must not remember how she mistreated me and the other little girls. Her formerly tall, imposing figure and youthful, smooth, tight skin, which had glistened from frequent applications of Vaseline, now resembled the shriveled, gray folds of an old female elephant's underside. She had lost so much weight since Kifungilo. With her hanging skin and thinning hair, she had the gaunt look of a famine victim. Her large protruding eyes, which had petrified me as a child, looked like bloodshot marbles. The big wart under her nose was no longer there. In its place was a circle of scar tissue she tried to cover with makeup. She still had her menacing teeth, but her lips were reduced to slivers of cracked skin that sucked up the orange lipstick she wore.

"Let me tell you, Mr. Bergh, Mary was very fat. She loved to eat so much that I called her 'Piggy.' And she was lazy. She would stop in the middle of washing clothes or ironing to daydream! I had to beat her to get her to work," Zami explained.

I had no emotional reaction to Zami. Though I could never forget her role in my life, I felt detached from her. The entire night before the visit I wondered how I could face her—the source of so much childhood grief—and not feel like a helpless child again. It never occurred to me to confront her or ask why she had been so mean. I had confided my fear and hatred for Zami to Fat Mary in my childhood, and we decided that the big girls who were mean to the little girls didn't know better. They were repeating and perpetuating what had been done to them.

I also knew that some big girls were worse than Zami. As a child, whenever I felt sorry for myself, I thanked God for that. In my nightmares over the years, I often dreamed of big girls beating children with a thick iron rod for not stealing enough fruit from the Sisters' garden. Zami never used an iron rod on me. Instead she pinched, hit, kicked, and stepped on me. She never beat the other children she took care of because they had parents who visited often, and she would get into trouble if they reported her.

We walked around the farm as Zami showed off her property with its many fruit trees, vegetable gardens, flowers, and plants fed by an elaborate irrigation system. Unlikely as it was for a Kifungilo girl to make something big of her life, she had succeeded. She had married, had a son whom she was educating in Nairobi, and lived a life of plenty. Besides being self-sufficient, she was the manager of the spacious, luxuriously landscaped former governor's lodge in Magamba.

Under British colonial rule the estate had been the private retreat residence for Governor and Lady Twinning. After Independence, it became the vacation residence of President Julius Nyerere and other African government officials. With her private keys and acknowledgment by the guards, she gave us a tour. What opulence the British had created for themselves in Africa! The estate and house came with horse stables, polo and cricket grounds, imported Spode china, crystal glasses, Victorian style furniture, intricately carved armoires, embroidered dining room chairs and love seats, canopy beds flowing with lace, hot and cold running water, fireplaces, and carpets and Persian rugs so exquisite you felt you needed permission to walk on them. I never knew such European comforts and wealth existed anywhere in Tanzania.

Here I came to understand a major difference between the Germans and the British. The Germans who migrated to Africa worked and produced what they needed themselves or with the help of the locals while the British imported their luxuries or took them from others. Germans built their little Germanys by hand in the regions of Tanzania where they settled, while the British looked at Africa as a place to reign over with pomp and circumstance and live a lifestyle they could not afford in England.

We thanked Zami and returned to Kifungilo, tired and happy to see our just-changed beds with hot-water bottles under the fluffy covers at the priests' retreat house.

That night I wondered why I had no reaction one way or the other to Zami. I also wondered why I never felt bitter or wanted to get even with any of my childhood tormentors. I had hated them at the time and avoided them. No matter how I questioned what I had suffered at their hands, subconsciously I understood that the abuse we endured from the big girls at the orphanage stemmed from their own pain.

I understood that Sister Silvestris thought her strict ways were necessary. When I was a child, I could describe physical pain but had no words for what I now know was psychological and emotional pain. My conversations with Fat Mary truly saved me! She helped me analyze my life, and she remained true to our agreement to save what I couldn't understand or articulate and give it back to me at a time when I could as she was doing now. Did Fat Mary take such good care of me that today I harbor no anger or bitterness towards my childhood tormentors?

I knew Fat Mary approved of my first trip back to Kifungilo because she was totally absent. She must have known that maturity and compassion had replaced my confusion and pain, even though the memories remained fresh. Time and America had given me perspective.

I looked for her after I visited Sister Theonesta's grave. "Fat Mary, don't hide, I still need you. Please help me understand how Sister Theonesta could love me like a mother, yet be so cruel to the other children."

Sometimes there is no answer. Could it be because she knew you as a tiny, helpless baby? Maybe she always wanted to be a mother, and you fulfilled that longing. All people have within them the ability to be both good and evil. While it's hard to understand why someone would choose to be evil, it is a choice.

My dear Fat Mary, she did explain it after all.

32

"Pancha"

We left Kifungilo loaded down with food and drink for our safari, along with holy cards and promises of prayers from the nuns. We gave Sister Silvestris a donation, which she vowed to use for her Wasambaa, and Mother Rufina promised to pray for Kjell's conversion so we would all meet one day in heaven. Kjell was not impressed.

As we drove off, I looked back to see the Sisters waving so hard that their silver crucifixes danced on their bosoms. Despite the wonderful visit, I felt just as happy as I had the last time I said goodbye to Kifungilo.

It was hard to believe that the wide, smooth roads of just ten years ago were now cavernous ditches surrounded by jagged slabs of tarmac. When our second flat tire occurred on the road from Mombo to Korogwe, I asked God to drop the spare tire we needed from heaven! After lots of swearing, Kjell pushed the car off the road, and a group of African men and children from a nearby village appeared and surrounded the car. One by one they showed off their rudimentary knowledge of English, volunteering their best guesses as to how the car could be fixed.

"*Festi, Godi will geti the spare det have no pancha!*" (First, God will bring a spare with no puncture!)

"*No, the gari will geti api itselfi.*" (No, the car will get up by itself.)

"*Very big ploblem. No spare! Koli bwana Karabu. He go to car shule.*" (Very big problem. No spare! Call Mr. Karabu. He went to car school.)

Kjell took the jack from the trunk and went to work. The African observers came closer to watch the operation. As Kjell slowly jacked up the car, the children screamed with delight.

"*Eet is goingi! Eet is goingi up, up, up!*" They clapped every time Kjell lifted it another inch. The man who had been to "car school" came running toward us carrying a large wooden suitcase that I presumed was his toolbox. The villagers completely ignored us and explained to the *fundi* (expert) that we had no spare tire, and it looked like the *mzungu* couldn't do anything because his face had already turned red. They got so involved and were having such a good time singing and commenting about the proceedings that they decided Kjell was too slow. They would have to take matters into their own hands.

One of them shouted, "Hip! Hip! Hurrah!" assuming Kjell was British, and together they lifted the car high enough for the fundi to put a metal contraption beneath it to hold it up. In a short time he fixed the tire with some goo from his toolbox and assured us that it would "never pancha again!" With little faith, Kjell lowered the car as the singing began again, and one of the men gestured broadly as if directing the progress of the descending car.

As soon as the car was down and we started to get in, the little children tugged on my sleeve asking, "Chui gum? Chui gum?" We didn't have chewing gum, but we distributed the food we had for our safari and they were just as happy. They retreated into the village comparing the food they had received, waving goodbye, and wishing us "*Safari njema!*" (Good trip!) We paid the fundi more than he asked (five dollars), and he knelt on the ground to thank us, but it was we who should have knelt down to thank him.

Having given away our food, we arrived in Dar tired and hungry, but thanks to the fundi, we had no more flat tires.

In Dar, I visited Henrietta. We were next to each other in the dorm at middle school and in most classes because of the alphabetical order of our last names. She had been thin then, but now she was heavy and was raising her three children by different fathers. After her year of service to the country, she got a job at the Bank of Tanzania. She was building a house in a suburb of Dar, which she planned to rent to supplement her income.

Kjell flew to Oslo to pick up our daughter and return home to Minnesota while I went to Nairobi to spend time with Thecla, my high school friend, and her husband, John. They had four children and were doing well by Tanzanian standards. Her husband worked for a British pharmaceutical company. They had purchased a large house in an upscale neighborhood of Nairobi, which they rented out while they lived in a small apartment in another part of the city. We talked about our high school days at Marian College and what our classmates were doing.

Thecla had a nanny for their kids and two maids, so she was able to work as a secretary at the same company as her husband. Compared to salaries in the United States, theirs were quite modest, but like other educated families with two salaries, they enjoyed golfing, shopping in upscale stores on Kenyatta Avenue, and membership in opulent, colonial era private clubs, where semiformal attire was mandatory. They wined and dined me at two such clubs, and we danced the night away to a live African band at yet another club. It felt good, though strange, to see that most of the clientele were African. Before Independence, the few black faces at these exclusive clubs would have been those of waiters and other workers.

Consesa, Thecla's cousin, who worked in tourism at Momella Lodge (of *Hatari!* movie fame) in Arusha National Park, took the bus to Nairobi and joined us for lunch one day. Consesa said she had discovered something strange about the *wazungu*. "They use things from the dead." She seemed horrified at this. After questioning her, I realized she was referring to wigs!

Thecla agreed. "How can you walk around with something from the dead on your head?" She and Consesa were both from the Mbulu tribe. Maybe they had a tribal belief about not using articles from the dead.

"*Hizo si nwele za maiti?*" Consesa asked. (Isn't a wig made out of dead people's hair?)

"I don't know how they get the hair, but people grow their hair to sell," I interjected. "I have a synthetic Afro wig I wear to parties. And don't forget Maasai men wear wigs."

"But their wigs are made of strings rolled in grease and ochre that they wear on their shaved heads," Consesa said. "Maybe Bob Marley and the Rastafarians are imitating the Maasai. His music is so popular—I hear it played on big cassette players everywhere."

"Do you mean 'boom boxes'? That's what we call them in America. You don't say 'boomi boxi' here?"

They both laughed and commented on my American accent and my use of English words when I couldn't remember the Swahili word. Although they preferred speaking English, I insisted on Swahili. I didn't want to lose fluency, and I needed new vocabulary to talk about contemporary issues.

"I'm intrigued by how Americans have 'discovered' herbs and natural foods," Consesa said, changing the subject. "In Africa, our food has always been natural, and witch doctors have been using herbs to cure for thousands of years."

"Call them medicine men," I said. "We can learn much wisdom and knowledge from indigenous cultures. One day our medicine men will be working with Western doctors."

"Once you've been helped by a medicine man, you return to them even though *wazungu* doctors insist their medicines are better. Many educated Africans, even government officials, regularly confer with native doctors and elders," Thecla declared. "Have you ever had acupuncture? Many Kenyan doctors are in China now, studying it alongside American and European students. Tell me Maria, are Native American medicine traditions still practiced in America? From what I read, it looks like they suffer from racial and cultural discrimination even worse than the Blacks."

"Native American traditions are practiced. Discrimination is a complex issue! I could talk for hours about being Black in America and tell you many stories. The mix of peoples from every culture in the world in America is amazing, but there's also great injustice. Think about it—whites killed Indians, took their land, and then imported thousands of Africans to work for them as slaves. I love living in America, but the injustices I see every day and everywhere, stick in my throat."

Thecla and I also visited Imelda, my friend from the orphanage and Marian College. She was working for Pan Am Airlines and living in a spacious flat in downtown Nairobi with her American husband, Dallas, who was studying anthropology in Kenya. As always, whenever we Kifungilo girls got together, we talked to exhaustion. We had so many stories to recall, most of which were funny now. Yet beneath the laughter, we lamented our lost childhoods.

"The abuse that seemed so inevitable in Kifungilo," I pointed out, "is prohibited by child protection laws in America. The laws help, but abuse still occurs in America."

"Dallas seldom discusses his family or life in Chicago. We'll be moving to the States someday, and I'm uneasy about it."

The last time the three of us had been together was at Marian College in 1962. Now, in 1974, that seemed so long ago. Though I was the one who had traveled the farthest, we agreed that I was the one who had changed the least when it came to the African way of looking at and interpreting life. Physically, we had all changed; I was now thin, and they were both heavier.

By the time my trip to Africa ended, I had resolved to keep my Swahili alive in America. I brought back Swahili music cassettes and books and asked my friends to send me newspapers and magazines I couldn't get in America so I could update my vocabulary. Swahili had changed in the last ten years and added new words reflecting new technology and computer use.

Thecla and John reluctantly took me to the airport, not only because we were sad to part but also because the Nairobi airport is well known for its total confusion at check-in. We were advised to arrive at the airport three hours early, probably to allow time for bag inspection and interrogations. After East African countries gained independence, luggage was checked upon both entering and leaving the country.

"Name?"

"Maria." Thecla told me not to give any more information than necessary.

"How long have you been in Kenya?"

"Three days."

"What did you buy?"

"Kiondo baskets, brass and wooden necklaces, T-shirts, ebony carvings, books, tinned coffee and tea."

"Where did you buy the necklaces?"

"At *Nyumba ya Sanaa*, an art center in Tanzania where the Mary-knoll Sisters help African artists make and sell their work."

"Did you buy any precious stones?"

"No."

"No tanzanites?"

"No."

"No rubies?"

"No."

"Open that one." He had me open the duffle bag that Thecla and I had had to sit on to zip up. He fingered my possessions, then went over to talk to someone on the other side of the baggage area until an American tourist yelled angrily, "Let's get on with this, for Christ's sake!"

He came back to my bags. "Close it," he ordered. "Do you have Kenya shillings?"

"About one hundred fifty shillings."

"It is illegal to take money out of the country. You'll have to leave it with me."

I left the line, walked over to Thecla, and handed her the shillings.

He gave me an evil look, shoved my duffle bag and suitcase into the luggage chute, and snarled at me, "Bastard Americanized African!"

33

Ujamaa

After this first trip back to Africa, I came to terms with several issues about my life in Kifungilo and about Tanzania. When I left the country, it had still been called Tanganyika and was just beginning to emerge from British colonial rule. In America, I had followed developments and heard from my friends about the changes under African rule, so I was eager to see for myself.

Was the country better off now that the British had supposedly stopped plundering the country's wealth, exporting its diamonds, tea, and anthropological finds? Had the standard of living gone up as was promised during the campaign for independence that we had studied, discussed, and followed in school?

It was disturbing that every time I asked my friends about life in Tanzania, they pretended not to hear me or said that everything was great. Only in the privacy of their homes, after swearing me to secrecy, could we talk. They warned me that if I mentioned any negative aspect of the government in public, they would be jailed. But I could see with my own eyes what was happening.

The only true progress I perceived was abstract. It took place in people's minds and hearts. Now there were no *wazungu* to order them around. Being ordered around by Africans was more palatable than being ordered around by the British who didn't give a bloody damn about our culture and customs. Even cynical, educated people showed a sense of pride that a Black African was living in the State House in Dar-es-Salaam. Educated and less-educated Africans who once tolerated their foreign rulers had become chief ministers, members of Parliament, and officers of TANU (Tanganyika African National Union).

Independence was achieved in 1961, and Julius Nyerere began formulating and instituting *Ujamaa*, a social and economic development system loosely based on Chinese socialist ideas. *Ujamaa* can be translated as familyhood, extended family, or brotherhood and is a type of cooperative socialism intended to foster equality and growth.

As we drove around the country, we saw Chinese diplomats, technicians, and engineers everywhere in cities and rural areas. There were Chinese consultants in every branch of government; Chinese foremen and laborers worked side by side with Africans, building roads, railroads, schools, hospitals, and office buildings.

I had read President Julius Nyerere's three books, *Uhuru na Umoja* (Freedom and Unity), *Uhuru na Kazi* (Freedom and Work), *and Uhuru na Kujitegemea* (Freedom and Self Reliance), which contained Nyerere's doctrine of Ujamaa. I could picture Nyerere writing his theories of government in the belief that Ujamaa was suitable for Tanzania. His thinking was of great interest to me because I shared his Catholic beliefs and values and could see that his desire to create a just society was most likely motivated by those beliefs. He also adhered to the African tradition of caring for others, so I understood why he thought Ujamaa was the true path to a strong, vibrant, and independent Tanzania.

His teachings were inspiring: We are our brother's keeper, we have a duty to share our good fortune with our less fortunate countrymen, everyone should have the opportunity to work and provide for our families in accordance with our talents or skills, all should have equal opportunity for education regardless of financial or mental capacity, and our human and natural resources should be used to further our country's progress and the well-being of all citizens.

As usually happens in the leap from excellent theory to practical, day-to-day implementation, however, much can and did go wrong.

Overly zealous enforcers of the principles of Ujamaa, mostly TANU executives, eager to emulate the ruling style of their British predecessors, created laws and requirements going well beyond what President Nyerere intended. Villagization—the process of forcibly resettling people on land once owned by expatriates, tribal chiefs, or African entrepreneurs—was fiercely resisted and led to many revolts. Once removed from their farms, the formerly independent and self-sufficient farmers had to collectively grow and harvest crops that were equally distributed to everyone—both those who worked and those who didn't—and bosses could not fire workers regardless of performance, tardiness, or whether or not they showed up for work.

At first, people were glad to see that everyone had work, food, clothing, and could purchase building materials for housing. Though most people agreed with Ujamaa in principle, it was another matter in practice. Along with villagization, businesses and educational institutions were nationalized. Politicians and government officials quickly took advantage of the power of authority, no matter their level, and terrorized the populace by strictly and often unfairly enforcing the Ujamaa system. Fear and secrecy permeated people's lives. They never knew when they might be arrested for something they discussed after reading the TANU-censored newspapers or what they read in the foreign press.

I heard the fear and frustration in Sister Silvestris' voice when she talked about the newly empowered status of her Wasambaa workmen. I felt the disappointment of a friend in Morogoro when he told me that TANU had confiscated his tiny rental property. The secrecy and anxiety surrounding my visit with Henrietta in Dar-es-Salaam was palpable when we talked. From the fear I saw in her eyes, I knew she was telling the truth when she lamented the policies of Ujamaa.

I had always believed that Nyerere was one of Africa's finest statesmen and one of a handful of African leaders who truly put his country and his people before himself. He was a selfless idealist in a selfish world. But after seeing his Ujamaa theories of government at work, I was disappointed. I often wondered what Tanzania might be like if Ujamaa had worked.

Back in Minnesota, I suffered reverse culture shock. I just couldn't get back into the rhythm of my life in America. My shock was almost as bad as it had been when I first arrived in 1963. Then I had been afraid that everything, from the food I ate to American speech, would be unfamiliar. As difficult as it was to culturally acclimate those first years in America, I was thrilled, excited, and eager to learn everything about my new country. I often pinched myself when I realized I was living in my promised land, and tears of gratitude were never far away.

My culture shock this time was from contrast. I was overwhelmed by the number of material things I had accumulated and the wealth I saw in America. Things I'd come to take for granted—the smooth and wide roads, big cars, tall buildings, the amount and variety of food in the giant grocery stores, department stores selling everything, beautiful parks, well-dressed people, television—all hit me hard. When I compared my four weeks in Africa with my life in Minnesota, I could hardly function.

I looked around my house and felt crowded by its contents. After a few days of discomfort, I knew I had to do something about the paralyzing feeling in my gut. I began to sell and give away whatever was not absolutely necessary to friends and charities. I gave away most of my dishes, towels, pots and pans, jewelry, clothes, books, and even some of my African records. After a month of giving away stuff, I felt like I could breathe freely again.

I survived in this peaceful state for a full two weeks before I realized I couldn't live like an African in America. I had to replace much of what I had given away because I had guests coming who would need dishes for eating and towels for bathing, I had to dress a certain way for teaching, I needed books to read and pots and pans to cook for my family and guests. My husband dreaded subsequent trips to Africa as I repeated the purge-and-restock routine a few more times before I was cured.

34

Swahili at Central

I met someone at a party who not only became a lasting friend but who also shifted the course of my work. Margaret Wong, a beautiful young woman from China, said she was teaching Chinese at Central High School in Minneapolis—an urban "magnet" school. She urged me to meet with Dr. Joyce Jackson, the school's Black principal, to see about teaching Swahili there. Margaret assured me that Dr. Jackson would probably accept my suggestion as even Russian was taught at Central. Magnet schools were one means of remedying racial segregation in public schools and creating classes of interest to a broad range of students, especially minority students.

Dr. Joyce Jackson was a beautiful and intelligent no-nonsense woman who could be intimidating, but I believed I could offer something that Central needed. "Tell me what's on your mind, Mrs. Bergh," she said looking up from her desk as I walked into her office.

"I notice no African languages are taught at inner-city American schools," I began, "and because Central's student population is largely Black, I'd like to teach Swahili here."

"Well, an African language would certainly be supported by the Equal Education Opportunity Act for students of African heritage. I'd like to offer Swahili here. Margaret Wong's Chinese classes are very popular, and she's one of the reasons Central has such a successful magnet program. Many students come from other schools just to take our nontraditional courses. Now, if this is your first time teaching at an inner-city school, it might be challenging."

"Swahili would definitely be a nontraditional course, and I'd relish the challenge."

She told me to prepare a Swahili curriculum and said she would take it to the Board of Education.

"Mrs. Bergh, it will happen," she assured me as I left.

I knew that the intimidating Dr. Jackson liked me, and with her on my side, Swahili would be offered at Central High School. But what was I getting myself into? I had no idea how to write a curriculum, much less a curriculum for the first African language class in a public high school in Minnesota and maybe in any state.

My biggest obstacle to writing the curriculum was a lack of resources. The libraries I visited had little about Swahili. I did find one book put out by the Foreign Service Institute of Languages to prepare diplomats and Peace Corp volunteers for service to East Africa. Although it was traditional and dry and had little about the culture, it became my basic text. I dug out the curriculum for teaching French at Washburn High School that Harold Dunn, head of the French department, had given me when I taught there and came up with a three-page curriculum for teaching Swahili, including one page on culture comparing American and African music, dance, religion, and customs. Students would have no textbook, but by the end of the year we'd have made one based on my lesson plans. Compared to how I was educated in Kifungilo, where we wrote our textbooks by copying every word the teacher wrote on the blackboard, this was easy!

Three months later I found myself standing in front of forty loud, mostly Black seniors, who totally ignored me. One male student wore a big-brimmed, black-velvet hat, dark glasses, black jeans, a black button-down shirt and carried a walking cane. Another had on orange platform shoes, lilac satin pants, and a red woolen V-neck vest with no shirt. The multicolored caps at different angles on their heads represented every football, baseball, and basketball team in the country. They paid no attention to the bell and continued talking and laughing. Half of them faced the back of the room.

"Would you please turn around so we can begin class?" A few heads half turned, checked me out, and turned back. The few white students in class and a few Black ones faced forward.

"Let's just start class," said a white student.

"What you doin' here?" a Black student asked the white student sitting next to him. "Go take German or Spanish or that commie language."

"I'll take any class I want!"

The students facing me argued with each other, and the rest ignored me. I picked up my notes and walked to the back of the class.

"What's wit her?" asked someone.

"I'm the teacher, and I'd like to start class," I replied.

"Lez be good, man," commanded one. "Miz Ber' is from Ooga Booga country, an' she don' know nothin' bout teaching at Central."

Most of the students followed her example and turned to face the front at which point I ran to the front before they changed their minds. I started taking attendance, and they mimicked my accent with each name.

"You can correct my pronunciation of your name, but there's nothing I can do about my accent."

"She be serious!" someone said, and they broke out laughing. They then corrected every single name I called. I made a point to repeat the correct pronunciation after them, but sometimes with a name such as Duane, I had to repeat it several times. By the end of roll call, which had taken the entire forty minutes of class, all the students were facing front and happily teaching me how to speak English.

I was grateful that I had to teach only one African Studies class. I came home exhausted, bewildered, disillusioned, and discouraged. I wondered whether I had made my life more difficult than it needed to be by requesting to teach in a predominantly Black school.

Regina High School had been a great place to teach because students behaved as respectfully and courteously toward their teachers as African students did. Unfortunately, the pay was very low, and I had had enough of all-girl schools. Washburn High School had greater diversity than Regina, and the students seemed fairly well off, but there I learned that students were not as disciplined as we were in Africa. The pay was much better, and the few Black students I had were interested in learning about their heritage. I often stayed after school to teach them African dance and to be available if they needed to talk.

Central High School, though, was like nothing I'd ever experienced. Obviously my life in America so far had been very white, and the only affinity I had with Black Americans was that of pigment. I dreaded the next day, but I'd signed a contract and there was no turning back.

On the third day in my new school, I had to do a sight count. Teachers were supposed to report the racial makeup of the class and be discreet about it. According to the number of minority students enrolled, the school would receive an education stipend from the federal government.

I studied each name on my class list and then stared at the student to try to figure out what ethnic group he or she belonged to. The Caucasians and some Blacks were easy, but I had no idea how to classify the majority. I figured my students were either white or Black, and I seemed to have no Hispanic or Asian students. Anyone who was not obviously white or Black I put in the "other" category. Since this was my first time doing a sight count, I must have looked bewildered and not at all discreet. Before I knew it, students started blurting out their names and categories for me. I thanked the class and quickly changed the students I had put in "other."

The same girl who had helped me on the first day by telling her classmates I was from Ooga Booga country marched up to my desk and loudly asked, "Whatchu put me in, Miz Ber'? I ain't no honky."

"I'm sorry, but I don't understand what you're trying to tell me."

"I say I ain't no honky." She grabbed the sheet from my hand and searched for her name. "I knowd it! You call me honky."

"What is honky, and why are you talking to me like that? I'm your teacher."

"She says she's not white," said a white girl.

"Okay, I'll change it. What are you?"

"I'm Black."

"What? No way!" More laughter from the class.

The girl arguing with me was as white as the white students. She had curly blond hair and bluish-green eyes. She was also quite big, and when she grabbed the roll-call sheet from my desk and ripped it to shreds, I did nothing.

"What's your name?" I asked her softly.

"Sharon, Sharon Smith, and I ain't no honky."

"Okay, you ain't no honky. And you ain't Black neither." I tried to imitate her, and she and the class laughed uproariously.

"Miz Ber', you funny!" Sharon went back to her seat.

"My name is Mrs. Bergh. Even though I came from Africa, I speak better English than you. There's no use trying to teach you Swahili when you can't even speak English. Why did you sign up to take this class?"

"We hear you some stupid forner come from Ooga Booga lan', an' we thot we gonna have us some fun! We be havin' lotsa fun?" she asked her classmates, and they agreed, laughing and giving high fives.

"I love this class," someone said.

"I love it too, but it's the third day and we haven't had class yet," I said. It was as if I'd waved a magic wand over their heads. They were silent for the first time. "Is true you be from Africa?" Sharon wasn't finished with me.

"Yes, I'm from Tanzania." I showed them where it was on the map I'd hung on the wall. "You've heard of Mount Kilimanjaro and Lake Victoria, haven't you?"

A few students nodded.

"Well, they're both in my country."

"How come you come to America?" someone asked.

"Because I was lucky enough to get a scholarship. I am married, and now I live in Minneapolis."

"Your husban' white?"

"Yes. He's from Norway."

"Dem white Norwegeeeans ain't too bad."

"Why you marry a white man?" a guy asked.

"None of your business," Sharon defended me.

"Look who's talking? Dat be cuz ya momma be white?" asked the male student.

"Oh shudup!" They were raising their voices.

"Fuck you!"

"You mothafucker pimp!"

Before I could do anything, Sharon picked up her chair and hit the speaker on the head.

"Stop it!" I commanded, not expecting to be obeyed.

"I don' wan no trouble for Miz Ber' here. I deal wit you outside."

"Thank you," I said.

"You're most welcome, Mrs. Bergh," she replied with perfect pronunciation.

It wasn't until the second day of the second week I finally was able to start the Swahili lessons. By that time I had won their confidence by asking them to teach me a few Black expressions and words. They filed past my desk, greeting me with "Whuz hapnin'?" and actually sat down facing me more or less ready to learn something. They still laughed at my accent, but I noticed that anytime someone got out of line or was disrespectful to me, Sharon took care of them. With fierce Sharon on my side, I felt I could successfully teach Swahili at Central High School.

Things got much easier as the year progressed. We established that they couldn't care less about speaking Swahili. They were mostly interested in the cultural aspects of East Africa and Africa in general.

Just when I was growing weary of spending all my free time in libraries trying to find material for my class, the television series *Roots* came to the rescue. I had read Alex Haley's book and was debating about discussing it with my students, but as it turned out, I had no choice.

A few years earlier I had spent many days at the Macalester College library doing research for a summer course on African heritage I was teaching there. The course was a special project of the Equal Education Opportunities Act, which prohibited racial segregation of students and discrimination against faculty and staff; it also required school districts to take action to overcome barriers to students' equal participation.

At the library, I often noticed a man also working through a stack of books on Africa. Alex Haley spent considerable time at Macalester lecturing students and World Press Institute journalists. He told me that he had been researching his African ancestry for years and wanted to know about mine. Although I knew nothing about my ancestry, we had some lively discussions about Africans currently and during the period he was writing about.

Holding his book in my hand and discussing his masterpiece with my students was almost surreal. A few days after the initial installment of *Roots* aired, I had to break up verbal fights and deflect killer body language between my Black and white students. I put my Swahili lesson plan book away for the duration of the TV mini-series and focused instead on the students' questions and responses to *Roots*. It was like opening a Pandora's box of racial distrust, misunderstanding, stereotypes, and hatred. Everyone had something to say and insisted on being heard. The handful of white students in class stood up and fought as best they could, refusing to be blamed for historical sins of race. I placed myself among them (they sat in one section) to discourage arguments, but it didn't help. After one white student was called a cracker-bitch, all four walked out of class.

I followed and begged them to return. I told them it was a cowardly thing to do. Running away from a necessary discussion was not going to solve the problem.

"You don't have to convince us. Talk to the primitives."

"I resent that word," I said. "In Africa, white colonizers called us monkeys and primitives, and if you ever use that word to describe my Black students, I'll take it as a personal insult."

"I'm sorry, Mrs. Bergh. We really like this class, but it's hard to sit there when we're constantly being attacked for being white."

"When you signed up for a Swahili class, you must have known that the majority of the students would be Black, that they would be defensive and resentful toward you for taking their class."

"It's not their class."

"Of course it's not a class just for them. But you can understand that they would feel possessive of the class because finally they have an African language offered in their school."

"I don't care. They're not going to make me drop the class. I have every right to be here."

I opened the door, and one by one they entered. The silence inside was deafening.

"In order to learn, we must have clear and open minds—minds that are free of prejudice and ignorance. Every student here has the right to discuss whatever is on his or her mind without fear of being attacked verbally or physically. Do you agree?"

Silence. "All those who agree with me raise your hand." Slowly but surely every hand in the room went up. "If you promise to keep your cool whenever we discuss *Roots*, we'll continue to discuss it. Otherwise we won't. Is that clear?" Silence again. "All those who agree with me, raise your hand." All hands went up. "Thank you! Your assignment is to watch *Roots* tonight. Take notes and prepare two discussion questions. If you don't think you can discuss the racial issues in *Roots* calmly, you must still come to class, but I'll give you an excuse slip to go to the library for the hour. Understood?"

"Yes, Mrs. Bergh." The reply was quick and unanimous.

The next morning, and for the entire two weeks that *Roots* was on television and most of the remainder of the year, I had almost perfect attendance. Not only did we discuss the racial issues of *Roots*, we talked about many other aspects of life from Black and white points of view. We had some heated moments and sentences cut short when I interrupted with a reminder of what they had promised. Teaching *Roots* provided me with more knowledge of American history than any course I took in college.

With the help of *Roots* and my students, history came alive and awakened in me a desire, long shoved to the back burner, to learn about my own roots. Apart from being both white and Black, I knew almost nothing about my parents. Had they really died as I had been told? What tribe was I from? Maybe I too should actively search for my roots. No, I decided. Not now. I turned those thoughts and feelings over to Fat Mary to safeguard them for me.

"Fat Mary, should I try to find my roots at this point in my life? Is that even possible? Wouldn't I first have to know my parents? I know one was Black and one was white, but who were they? Where were they born? Where did they come from? Even if I knew my parents, would I one day be able to trace my roots over many generations as Alex Haley did?"

Human beings hunger for an identity and for roots. It is important to know your collective racial or tribal roots but not absolutely necessary. You will be a shining example to your students of how one can become whole even without that knowledge.

I thought about how lucky I was to have my Fat Mary. How many children do not have anyone to support their life journey to self-knowledge and loving themselves?

I learned to love and respect my students, and they let me know many times by words and deeds that they loved and respected me too. They invited me to their homes, and in one of them I choked on my first and last marijuana joint. They taught me how to roll the joint, how to inhale and exhale, the correct etiquette for passing the joint. They forgave my failure to master this art and told me I should never learn to do it right because I might like it. I went to weddings with them and ate food like greens and chitterlings in their homes. They introduced me to Black music, musicians, and the radio stations that played their music and took me to nightclubs to dance their dances. I realized again how little I knew about Black culture in America.

Once a week we had what I called "culture day," during which we compared and contrasted life in Africa and life in America. I took the opportunity to tell them that when I was a student in Tanzania we practically adored our teachers and did anything we could to please them. Opening our mouths to argue or even disagree with a teacher was unheard of. They shook their heads in disbelief and asked if my school was in a prison.

Sharon told me one day that in the beginning of the year I'd thrown out a brilliant musician from my Swahili class.

"No way!" I said. "I've never thrown out a student from class."

"Oh yes, you did, Miz Bergh. Remember the fourth week when you told Prince Nelson to get out?"

"Was he the guy who sat in the back of the room with his head on the desk the entire time and pouted when I asked him to look at me and sit up straight?"

"Yeah!"

"I didn't throw him out. I asked him to come and see me after class, and I was surprised when he did because he had acted like I was invisible and didn't participate in discussions or hand in any assignments. I wanted to talk to him privately because I thought maybe he was just shy. Since he was a senior and needed only one more credit to graduate, I told him he'd better transfer to another class because if he didn't start doing the work, he was going to fail and wouldn't graduate."

"Well, I hear that he got some sponsors. They think he got a lotta talent, and they gonna produce his records."

"Wonderful! Doesn't it feel good when someone you know gets a break?"

"We oughta go and listen to him sometimes. Me and my friends think he's real good. One day Prince might be famous."

As I look back at my teaching career, I see the years I taught Swahili and African Studies at Central High School in Minneapolis were the best of all.

35

Young Audiences

After Kata was born, I took a break to stay home with her until she was four. Then I went back to teaching part time and working for Young Audiences. I felt a need to teach children about Africa because by the time they got to secondary school it was much harder and, for the most part, students weren't as open-minded or interested.

Many of the questions I got from my high-school students and from adults convinced me that Americans knew little about Africa. They thought it was one country and not a continent with over fifty independent countries; they thought we all spoke one language rather than the more than 700 languages not counting dialects; they thought we lived primitively, probably in trees, and that some African tribes were like monkeys; they thought we ate our food raw and ran around naked.

One night, I saw on the news that a string quartet was going to perform for the children at a nearby elementary school as part of a program called Young Audiences. I decided to see what it was about. The program was sponsored by the Minnesota Orchestra and WAMSO (Women's Association of the Minnesota Symphony Orchestra). Children were sitting on the cafeteria floor, listening intently to the musicians. After explaining each number and demonstrating the instruments, the leader answered questions. This seemed a great way to introduce classical music to grade-school students, so I asked the presenters for information about Young Audiences.

A nationwide nonprofit organization, Young Audiences worked with educational systems, the arts community, and private and public sectors to provide arts education to children. The brochure, I noticed, offered no programs on any African art form. I'd already decided to correct misconceptions Americans had about Africans whenever and however I could, and that the best place to start was with children.

I met with the program director of Young Audiences in the Twin Cities and proposed teaching African dance to children. She reminded me that Young Audiences traditionally worked with the classical arts. I responded that children needed to be exposed to nontraditional forms of artistic expression to have a more rounded education. And children from minority cultures needed to see artists from their ethnic group as role models. The director told me to prepare a program and audition at the end of the month.

Where to begin? I knew the dances of my childhood and those I'd learned at Marian College, but they required live music, and I would probably be the only one-person presenter in the Young Audience roster of offerings, if accepted. I went through my old Miriam Makeba records and found songs with a beat I could use for my dances. Based on what I'd seen at the Young Audiences string quartet program, I choreographed the dances, breaking them down into simple repetitive steps that children could follow. I picked up basic rhythms from Makeba's songs and beat them on my drum so that children could clap the rhythms. I practiced simple Swahili children's songs and planned to teach them to count in Swahili. I created a fifty-minute presentation and rehearsed daily for my audition.

On the day of the audition, I walked into the room carrying the drum I brought from Tanzania on my 1974 visit. I also brought African artifacts—dolls, ebony figurines, and beaded necklaces—to show the children. I wore a bright red, black, and white khanga tied around my waist over a red leotard and wrapped a headpiece from the same khanga fabric. Around my ankles, I tied a leather cord with little cowbells that would jangle as I walked. The program committee liked my attire and my presentation. I was accepted, and "African Dance" appeared in the fall brochure.

"You'll be a great asset to Young Audiences," the program director told me. "How lucky we are, and I know the children will love you!"

Not quite! The schools I went to my first few months almost broke me. I dreaded the initial ten minutes of my program in any school. Standing in front of three hundred screaming children was almost as bad as my first weeks at Central High School. When I presented my program in the inner city, the students were overly excited and rowdy for most of my program, but eventually I was able to settle them down and get to dancing before my time was up.

The suburbs were a different story! Little children wore their prejudices on their sleeves, and their body language told me they didn't know what to make of me. It was obvious that they seldom, if ever, had seen anyone who dressed, talked, or moved like I did. They usually made foolish, clownlike movements when I asked them to imitate my movements. About six months into my work with Young Audiences, I was at a suburban elementary school near Minnetonka when, for the first time in my entire teaching career, I almost walked out.

As I entered the gym, there was a big hush and loud whispers. Going up the stairs to the stage, I stopped dead in my tracks because I heard a child yell, "Hey, Nigger!" taking me completely by surprise. The other children laughed while their teacher pulled the offending boy by the collar out of the room.

"My name is Mrs. Bergh." I tried to swallow the insult.

"Me Tarzan, you Jane!" yelled one of the kids.

I swallowed hard again and continued my introduction. I asked for volunteers to learn a dance, but since no one volunteered, I picked several students to come up on stage. Two of them made monkey faces at me. I made monkey faces back at them. At first they stared at me, then they laughed and started making other animal noises. I imitated them. We went back and forth making faces and animal sounds, until they forgot I was imitating them, and they instead imitated everything I did. When I looked up, two hundred children were making monkey faces and noises and laughing!

When I got tired of playing that game, I stopped and told the children on the stage to go back to their places. I changed my demeanor and asked them why they had acted like that toward me.

"That's how Africans act," they said.

"But I'm from Africa, and I don't know any Africans who act like that."

"They do in the movies," was the answer.

"Let me tell you something, girls and boys. Not everything you see about Africa in the movies is true. I want to teach you about my country. Do you have any questions about Africa?

"Do you eat people?"

"No, we do not!"

"Africans walk around naked and put bones through their noses."

"We have many tribes with different customs. I have seen pictures of Africans decorated like that but not in my country."

"Do you live in trees?"

"No!"

"A program about Africa on TV showed Africans killing people and throwing them to crocodiles."

"I saw the same program. Remember how they explained that offering a human being as sacrifice to the crocodile god was an ancient custom of one tribe?"

"Why were grownups learning the alphabet just like children?"

"Grownups were learning the alphabet because when they were children there were no schools in their villages. In my country, after we gained our independence from Britain, the new African government made it possible for everyone to learn to read and write. When I went back home after living in America for ten years, I saw old people having classes under the shade of a mango tree or out in a field now that education was available to them."

"Our pastor said our church gives money to help build schools in Africa."

"Your church probably works with Operation Bootstrap Africa to raise money for cement and roofing to build houses for the teachers and schools."

I looked at the children now listening eagerly to me. They seemed to brighten up as they replaced ignorance and misinformation with a real and genuine connection to people of another culture. In that moment, I saw how my work with Young Audiences directly connected to my efforts as a board member of Operation Bootstrap Africa, which was working with the Tanzanian government to help Africans build school themselves. Operation Bootstrap Africa was founded by Reverend David Simonson. He and his wife Eunice worked with the Maasai tribe and other Africans in Tanzania for many years as Lutheran missionaries. Because of my lifelong belief in education, Operation Bootstrap Africa provided an opportunity for me to fulfill my mission of fostering education in Africa.

By this time I had the children eating out of the palm of my hand. I spent the entire hour answering their questions, not all of them easy. To my surprise, when the bell rang they clapped and said, "Thank you, Mrs. Bergh! Can you come again?"

Like the many lessons I learned from my students at Central High School where I still taught each morning, I learned a lot from the children. Once I showed them they could ask me any question about Africa and that there was no right way or wrong way to dance, we got along beautifully. For eight years, I was booked so often that I sometimes had to turn down requests because of fatigue and back pain caused by dancing barefoot on linoleum-covered cement floors in gymnasiums and cafeterias.

To give my Young Audience an authentic visual sense of Africa, I always wore colorful African outfits and exotic jewelry when I performed. Depending on the grade level, I also brought fabric and had the students dress as Africans. They loved this, and I had all I could do to get my fabrics back to use at another school.

One afternoon while I tying my colorful head wrap before leaving for a Young Audience performance, Kjell called. "My friends just returned from hunting and gave us two ducks. You'll be in Edina this afternoon, so can you drop them off to be cleaned at Westgate Lockers on France Avenue?"

I put on my large, beaded African necklace, earrings and bracelet, put my drums, bells, whistles and African artifacts in my car, picked up the heavy brown bag at the door, and headed for Edina. As I approached 50th and France, I saw a big sign for Westgate Lockers on the left side of the road. I pulled in, parked, took the brown bag, and headed for the door. But then I saw another sign, for Westgate Cleaners, on the other side of the road. "Kjell must have meant

Westgate Cleaners," I said to myself. "The ducks are already dead; they don't need to be locked up."

I got back into the car and drove across the street, grabbed the ducks, and entered the building. A friendly, middle-aged lady behind the counter asked, "What can I do for you?'

"I brought these to be cleaned," I said setting the bag on the glass counter.

"What are they?" she asked.

"They're ducks. I think there are two of them."

"What?"

"These are two ducks that need to be cleaned."

"What did you say they were?"

"Ducks! Two of them!"

"I don't understand."

"I'm sorry. I have an accent, and sometimes it's hard to understand me."

"That's all right. Let's see." She opened the top and reached into the bag and asked, "Is it a hat?" Finally she'd see what I was telling her, I thought. She pulled a duck from the bag by the neck, dropped it on the counter and jumped backwards, screaming, "Oh my God! You really did say ducks! Are they alive? What in the world? Where did you come from?"

"They're dead. They were shot this morning, but they might still be warm."

Two young girls came running in from the back room and rushed to the woman.

"What's going on? Are you okay? Why are you shaking?"

The attendant simply said, "Talk to her."

They looked at me from head to toe checking out my outfit, huge bold and bright beaded jewelry, and finally rested their gaze on the fabric wrap on my head.

"I brought two ducks to be cleaned."

"Did you say ducks? Lady, we don't clean birds here."

"They are not birds. They are ducks," I said, overly annunciating every word. I didn't know how else to make myself clear.

"You should go to Westgate Lockers across the street. They clean and process wild game for hunters."

But why did dead ducks need to be locked up, I wondered, and tried to explain again when the three of them ran to the back room, leaving me alone with my ducks. I dragged them off the counter and decided Kjell would have to take them to be cleaned himself! Americans are strange. Imagine locking up dead ducks! It wasn't until much later that I finally understood the concept and purpose of food lockers.

My car was surrounded by people peering through the windows at the items on the back seat: two three-foot-tall goatskin drums, painted ostrich eggs, ebony figurines, a black-and-white fly swatter made from a wildebeest tail, painted masks, beaded calabashes, and a big sisal bag full of kitenge fabric. They backed off the car in tiny steps, staring at me as I opened the trunk and threw the ducks in. As I pulled onto the road, I looked into the rearview mirror at the clump of people in front of Westgate Cleaners glaring at my car, shaking their heads, making gestures and facial expressions as if they had just been visited by an alien.

Alien or not, my performance for Young Audiences that afternoon couldn't have been better! The children were excited and had prepared for my coming by learning the Swahili numbers from one to twenty. And they sang "Jambo Mama," a song I had taught them a year earlier.

A few things I will never forget about the Young Audiences experience: First is the innocence of children about matters of race. Once I corrected the institutionalized racial and cultural stereotypes they learned at home and elsewhere about Africans and other minorities, they accepted what I told them and treated me with respect.

Second is their unawareness of what did or did not constitute an insult. Once a fourth-grader raised her hand and admiringly asked whether I'd ever tried out for the *Gong Show*! Well, the Gong Show was one of the few TV programs I watched—because it was often funny. Aspiring amateur singers, actors, musicians, dancers, and performers presented their acts to a live studio audience. If the act got so bad the audience couldn't take it anymore, they groaned and made comments until the show's host hit a big gong and the competitor left the stage. My little admirer spoke her truth, giving me an often-remembered lesson in humility.

Third is the depth of truth in their direct questions and answers. Once, after telling the children that the giraffe was the national symbol of Tanzania, I asked them what the national symbol of America was. A little boy in the second grade raised his hand and answered, "The dollar!"

Instead of correcting him, I heard myself say, "Amen!"

36

The Letter

The question I found hardest to answer for my Young Audiences was whether I was white or Black. They were puzzled because they thought all Africans were black. Whenever they asked me that question, I asked them, "What do you think?"

"Black. White and Black. No, yellow. No, brown."

When they settled down, I told them I was all of the above. One little girl, who understood that race and color were often used interchangeably, said, "She's Black. We have a maid who cleans our house. She's whiter than Mrs. Bergh, and my mom said she's Black."

"The only important thing for you to know about me right now is that I am your teacher," I said. I wished I could answer the children's questions without skirting the fact that I really didn't know my racial makeup. I'd seen people who looked like me, but their parents were usually both mixed-race, white and Black, Indian and Black, or white and Hispanic. The many interracial combinations produce offspring of such variety of color. Is it necessary to classify everyone?

One morning Cathy, my American mother, called. I could tell from her voice that something was wrong. She was sniffling and coughing as she spoke, but after a couple of sentences all I could hear were sobs.

"Is someone dead?"

"Nnooo . . . It's a lett . . ." Sobs, more sobs, and plenty of her trademark loud nose blowing.

"A what?"

"A letter I got from . . ." More sobs, more nose blowing.

"Do you want me to come over?"

"No, I'll come. I want to . . . have . . . a . . . a family meeting. Is Kjell there?"

I couldn't figure out what was going on. Why a family meeting? As long as I've known Cathy, she'd never asked for a family meeting. After nine years of marriage, she was pregnant for the first time, and I was afraid she'd had a miscarriage.

"He's on his way home."

"And Katarina?"

"Yes. She's watching *Sesame Street.*"

"John and I will be over."

"What is it? Did you kill someone?"

Cathy laughed in spite of herself and said, "It's not that bad, although I'm not so sure. We'll be over in half an hour."

I feared that she'd had a miscarriage, and I felt heartbroken for her, remembering my miscarriage two years earlier, when I hadn't even known I was pregnant. It was an ectopic pregnancy that ruptured one morning as Kjell was leaving for work. I was waving goodbye to him from the top of the stairs in our little Japanese house when I fainted and tumbled down the steps. Lucky for me, Kjell heard the heavy thumping and rushed me to the hospital emergency room.

When I woke up, I had tubes and wires all over me. I recognized a pale Kjell, who, I was told later, fainted when my doctor couldn't find an adequate vein to insert the IV for the four pints of blood I had to receive after severe internal bleeding. I stayed in the hospital for a week and didn't get back to work for another six weeks. Every time I think of that scary day, I count my blessings. If Kjell had left even a minute earlier and I'd not been in America where excellent health care is readily available, I'd probably have bled to death in my own living room.

I wondered what news Cathy had for us now. When I heard Kjell arrive, I called to him. "Cathy and John are on their way here. They want to have a family meeting."

"A family meeting? With John and Cathy? What did I do to deserve this?"

"Cut it out, Kjell. Whenever we spend time with them, you act like you're under torture. If your parents lived closer, I bet we'd see them often."

"What will it take to convince you that they are not your parents?"

"Nothing, because to me they are. Especially Cathy. She came into my life when I needed her most. God always answers our prayers. In my case, he brought me Cathy to take the place of my mother, and nothing you say can change that!"

"I know she means a lot to you, but pretending she's your mother is pushing it too far. She's only four years older than you."

"Four and a half," I corrected him. "Because you were raised by your mother, you will never understand the emptiness inside without anyone in your life to call Mom. I choose to confer that honor on Cathy."

By this stage in our marriage, I had learned that he didn't like hearing details about my life. He always changed the subject.

"Oh no, here they are. I guess I'd better be on my best behavior."

"Something major is bothering her."

"Don't get me wrong. I've nothing against them. They've always been wonderful to us and to Kata, but I think your devotion to Cathy is way out of proportion to what she's done for you. She probably needed you more than you needed her."

I went to the door to greet John and Cathy. Their grave faces reflected worry and fear. I hugged Cathy for a long time. "What is it? What happened?"

Cathy resumed crying. Good old disparaging Kjell, who in spite of himself, could not stand to see anyone cry, assured her, "It'll be okay. Let's go in and talk about it."

We climbed the four steps that led to our living room and sat down. Kjell carried Kata over to the couch, and I sat facing Cathy.

"Well," Cathy began, then proceeded to cry and produce her usual whistle nose blow. This time, no one—not even Kata—laughed. "Well, I received this letter," she continued, still crying. Then John took over. Kjell and I looked at each other because we knew with John's love of detail, we'd get a dissertation about how the letter arrived.

"We got this letter that was first mailed to Onamia, where it sat in the post office for a long time. Then someone crossed out the Onamia address and forwarded it to the address in St. Paul where you used to live when you went to St. Catherine's. From there it got sent back to the Onamia post office until a friend of Cathy's happened to see it and mailed it to our new address. Here it is!"

"What is it about?" Kjell asked.

"Read it!" Kjell reached for it, but Cathy suggested I read it first. Sure enough, the envelope had seen a lot of Minnesota. I opened the beautiful Maurice Utrillo notecard and began reading. There was nothing alarming in the letter, but it was obvious Cathy knew the writer. She whimpered as I read it. "Who is Dorothy?" I asked.

Cathy huffed and puffed, sighed and coughed, and blew her nose a few more times then said, "Your mother."

"What?" Kjell and I asked incredulously.

Silence. No one spoke. Cathy had stopped crying and was looking at me like she expected me to say that since I had a mother now, I didn't need her any more. I looked into her deep, soulful eyes brimming with tears. Despite the impact of what I had just learned, I went to her and hugged her.

"Cathy, you're the only mother I've ever had. Nothing will ever change that." I wanted to give her more words of assurance, but I could hardly think. It was as if I had just read the first chapter of someone else's life story. I gave Kjell the letter, and he read it aloud.

April 26th, 1976

820 College Avenue
Wheaton, Ill 60187

Dear Miss Murray,

Both Mary and you have been much on my mind lately, and I would like very much to have some news of her, if you could find it in your heart to send me some. I realize that whether to do so or not, is entirely your decision.

I am writing at this particular time because I am planning to move to Michigan, and if we are ever to meet, Wheaton is closer to Minnesota than Michigan is. My circumstances are such now that no one else is included in any decision I make. If you alone, or you and Mary care to come to Wheaton for a visit, I should be happy to see you. If you decide against it, I will understand.

My husband died three years ago. I retired from teaching last year, and am moving this summer to be near my sister.

God bless you all,
Sincerely,
Dorothy Reiner

"What shall we do?" Kjell asked.

"I suppose you can tell her that I'm alive and well and happily married with a beautiful daughter."

"Yes, yes! I'm the beautiful daughter." Katarina jumped from Kjell's lap and, not understanding the gravity of the occasion, went to watch TV.

"You have to meet her," Kjell said matter-of-factly.

"She doesn't specifically ask to meet me in her letter."

"Do you want to meet her?" Cathy asked.

In my childhood prayers to Baby Jesus, I didn't specify birth mother. The mother I found in Cathy had satisfied my childhood longing even though I was still curious about my birth mother. "I'm not sure. I have to think about it."

"What is there to think about? She is your birth mother, and there's no question but we'll have to meet her," Kjell said. He was savoring the opportunity to inform me once and for all that Cathy was not my mother.

"At this stage of my life, meeting my mother is not a priority, yet it would be nice to see what she looks like. She is mostly asking for information and inviting us to visit her. Do you think she would like to meet me?" I asked Cathy.

Cathy nodded. "But it's up to you, Mary." Cathy never quite got used to calling me Maria, as I now called myself.

"I wonder why she's thinking of me now?"

"I think we should invite her to come for a visit. Then we can take it from there," Kjell suggested.

"That's a good idea," John finally spoke.

"But it might not turn out the way you want. What do you expect?" Cathy asked.

"Absolutely nothing."

"Okay," Cathy said, seeming relieved. "Should she stay with you or with us?"

"I think she should stay with you. She might feel more secure. It's a big step she's taken, though I wonder if it's not mostly curiosity at this point. I have some questions, Cathy. How did you know she was my birth mother and how did she know your address in Onamia?"

"I was afraid you'd ask." She started to cry again. "You see, she's the one who gave me permission to adopt you and bring you to the States."

Kjell and I opened our mouths to talk, probably to ask the same question, but he let me go first. "So, all this time you knew about my mother?" I felt as if I didn't know Cathy.

"I was sworn to secrecy."

"By whom?"

"By your mother and the Sisters in Kifungilo."

"Oh my God, you mean they also knew my mother?"

"It was your 'favorite' nun, Sister Clotilda, the Mother Superior at the time, who really helped me."

"No way! The devil herself came to your aid for my sake. It must have been her way of getting rid of me forever."

"Actually, she said many nice things about you. And really, she took a great risk giving me the information about your mother. I wanted to adopt you, though in Tanganyika at that time you had to be at least twenty-one years older than the person you're adopting. It was worth a try."

"You adopted me illegally?"

"No. That's where your mother comes into the picture." Cathy sighed. "Mother Clotilda told me that I couldn't adopt you because you had a mother and she was living in Nairobi."

I couldn't believe what I was hearing. "My mother was in Nairobi all the time I was at the orphanage in Kifungilo?"

"No. She lived in Lushoto. She was a teacher at the European school."

"Lushoto? Just thirteen kilometers away? Did you meet her?"

"Oh no! Sister told me this. She also said that several families had tried to adopt you when you were little, but your mother wouldn't give permission. She had several reasons for agreeing this time, but most of all I think she felt better that I was an American who wanted to take you to America."

"Is my mother American?"

"Yes."

"I was right," I told my attentive family. "When I was small and we performed for the *wazungu* who used to visit Kifungilo, I overhead Mother Rufina mentioning something about an American girl. Although there were many children performing and she could have been talking about any one of us, I assumed I was the American girl. Remember, Kjell, when we visited Sister Eileen, she said that whenever somebody asked me for my name, I always said, 'I'm an Amelican gal!'"

"Unbelievable!" is all Kjell said.

"Is my mother an African or a European?"

"Neither. She's American," Cathy said.

"You know what I mean. Is she white or Black?"

"I'd guess she's white," Kjell said, with the smirk he always had when he thinks the answer is self-evident. "Her name is Reiner."

It suddenly dawned on me that the big girl who copied down the last names of the children had said my last name began with an *R* and had an *n* and maybe an *e* or *i* in it. Evidently she was right. I fought back tears of remembrance. This was the first time since seventh grade that I'd mentioned anything to Cathy or anyone about my hard life at middle school in Mhonda.

"See? There's a reason I kept changing my name," I joked. "It was inevitable I'd stumble on the right one someday. I had no name, so I had nothing to lose."

"You've got me, babe!" Kjell said.

"Now that I finally have a name, how ironic to find out my real name."

"I don't want to rain on your parade," Kjell said, "but Reiner is your stepfather's name. You probably have an African last name."

We were all silent. I'm sure that each one of us was speculating about the circumstances of my birth. "Your mother will tell you whatever you want to know," Kjell said.

"I don't know. A mother who can put her child in an orphanage and live only a few miles away yet never come to see her or bring her toys is a mother who doesn't love her child—or is forced to hide her."

"We don't know what life in Africa was like back then. She must have had a very good reason for giving you up," John spoke again.

"I suppose," I said, "but try explaining that to a little girl."

"Mary, I believe circumstances were such that your mother couldn't raise you. After I received this letter from her, I went through our correspondence in 1963, and I've brought a couple of letters I'd like you to read when you're alone. I believe your mother really loved and cared for you even back then."

She handed me a registered airmail envelope with a lavender one-shilling stamp of a young Queen Elizabeth. I put it down to read later.

"So, Cathy, you're going to write her and ask her to come soon," Kjell said.

"I've waited thirty-three years. I think I can wait another year if necessary. Invite her when it's convenient for you," I said.

Cathy collected her mound of spent Kleenexes, and stood up to leave. She came over to my chair, gave me a kiss, and cried some more before she and John left. I got Katarina ready for bed and Kjell sang his original composition for her.

Sleep, sleep little girl.
You are daddy's special friend.
Sleep so tight tonight,
You are daddy's plight.
Sleep, sleep little girl,
You are daddy's special friend!

As I listened to them talking and laughing and Kata begging him to sing again and again, I wondered if I had turned out different from the children whose daddies tucked them in at night. For once I enjoyed listening to Kjell do what he and Kata thought was singing! He sang so out of tune, so hoarsely, so irregularly, taking long breaks between the lines, that it was difficult to listen to, yet Kata loved it. I dreaded the many times he had to travel for business because then I had to sing his song to Kata, and she pleaded with me to sing "just like Daddy!" Try as I might to imitate his toneless, off-key singing, I couldn't please Kata. I finally solved the problem by taping a singing session and playing it for Kata when he was away.

When all was quiet upstairs, I reached for the first envelope and turned it over and over, wondering what great revelations it held.

February 13, 1963

Strictly confidential.

Dear Miss Murray,

Thank you for your letter about Mary, which has just reached me, and for your interest in Mary.

I assure you that I will do anything you ask in order to make it possible for her to become an American citizen. You will realize that it has not been easy for me to carry out the path decided on by my husband and myself, but it was necessary for the sake of other members of the family. I feel that the Lord has brought you into Mary's life so that she will not have to pay the whole price of being sacrificed for others. May God bless you exceedingly!

I am enclosing particulars of my passport and parentage of Mary, who was born on Dec. 30th, 1943, at the Tanga Hospital. Her father was a Tanganyikan, presumably of the Lake Province, since that was where the incident occurred.

I am dismayed by the time which has passed since your letter was written, and hope the enclosed information is sufficient. If not, please do not hesitate to contact me again at the address below.

I realize that I have no right to make this request, but it has been a relief to me to hear about Mary, and I would be so happy if you could let me know through Mother Clotilda how she is getting along. It would be a source of unhappiness to me to have a complete silence surround her, but that is a decision you have the right to make, and I leave it to you.

We plan ourselves to be in the States this year.

Yours sincerely, and with deepest gratitude,
(Mrs.) Dorothy Reiner
P. O. Box 580, Nairobi Kenya

My God, how could Cathy keep such a secret for so many years? And Dorothy? She knew all along that she was sacrificing me for the good of others, but it was only Cathy's courageous and selfless act of adopting and taking me to America that had prompted her to do something about me not having to "pay the whole price" for her indiscretions. Wasn't it in her power all along? Why did she wait so long?

The second letter was in a small gray envelope and was also sent to Miss Murray at Marian College.

April 12th, 1963

Dear Miss Murray,

Acting on instructions from the Embassy in Dar, I have been to the Consulate here about three weeks ago and signed the statements he asked for, so I hope everything is in order now for Mary's American Passport.

We are leaving for Europe on the 'Europa' Lloyd Triestino Line, sailing from Mombasa on April 18th. I had planned to write sooner, but Mr. Reiner came down with a bad go of malaria, in the midst of our packing, so I have been very busy.

I am sending Mother Clotilda our address in the U.S.A. and you can reach me if necessary through her. After discussion with my family after we arrive in America, I shall probably send you the address there too.

I can't tell you how much I appreciate the photo you sent of her. I considered asking for one, but didn't want to presume in any way, so I indeed thank you sincerely. I shall treasure it and any news you may send me of Mary and her new life. May God reward you and bless you both.

Yours sincerely,
Dorothy Reiner

I took the letters and put them upstairs in my desk drawer, reflecting on how complicated Dorothy must be. She hadn't mentioned anything to her family about me until thirteen years after she returned to America! By the time Dorothy decided to write, Cathy had married, changed her last name, moved several times, and she seldom visited her childhood home in Onamia. It was only a miracle that the letter finally reached Cathy's hands.

Fat Mary had her hands crossed on her chest and was staring at me with her big brown eyes. I asked her, "Can you explain this?"

There is nothing I can explain. Dorothy might reveal herself in bits and pieces or not at all. Your longing for your mother would have been unbearable if, as a child, you knew that she was alive and lived only a few miles away from you. You were protected by what you knew in your soul—that you had to love yourself above all and take good care of yourself. You took charge of your heart, soul, and mind. You didn't blame others because you knew that, ultimately, you alone were responsible for your happiness. Dorothy will change little or nothing about the person you are because her absence is what formed your character.

"Well said. I have always known I would not have survived without you, my beloved one. You are the one who will guide me through this encounter with the woman I longed for my whole life. Do you think that seeing her now in flesh and blood will help me forget the void her absence left in my childhood soul?"

You couldn't forget that if you tried. It is not about forgetting but about not letting the past define you. It is about learning from it and embracing its role as your lifetime teacher.

When I knew Kata was asleep, I tiptoed upstairs to our bedroom. Kjell was awake. I cuddled in his arms and we held each other for a long time before I could speak.

"I don't know where my tears are when I need them. Whenever I talk about my childhood, tears are my constant companions, just like they were back then. They flow over my cheeks, and I bask in their warmth. I doubt whether meeting my mother will be very emotional for me. The well from which I drew my childhood tears of missing and needing her has been dry for a long time."

"Try to put everything in perspective. I agree with John that we don't know what she had to go through when you were born. The 1940s and '50s were the height of the color bar in colonial Africa."

"Probably she was permanently affected by whatever she went through, but I also have the feeling my mother was ashamed of me."

"She hasn't seen you for thirty-three years. You must understand her situation and try to forgive and forget."

"How can I forgive what I don't know? How can I forgive her for what she hasn't told me? I've spent so much of my adulthood trying to forget the pain of being an unwanted and unloved child, but I tell you, Kjell . . . it's impossible! Time helps me forget the physical hardships, but I'll take the mental, spiritual and emotional pain to my grave. Pain, in whatever form, becomes the thread that weaves the color and textures in my life's tapestry. There really is no good reason to forget what made me who I am. Each time I look closely at my life's tapestry, the pain is just below the surface. It is the pain and what I've managed to coat it with in order to survive that holds the tapestry together. It is a deeply hued, multitextured, beautiful tapestry that can't and shouldn't be forgotten or ignored."

"I hope this won't be a meeting you'll regret. I know you want to know your roots, but if your mother doesn't feel she can answer your questions, you have to let her be."

"Do you think I'm going to torture her if she refuses to talk?"

"You can be very persistent. You'll have to give her an out."

"Whose side are you on?"

"Yours."

"You could have fooled me."

"The only thing I'm not so happy about with you meeting your mother is that now there's more family to interfere in our life."

"Oh? One member of my family would interfere, but your whole family doesn't? Forgive me if I forget that my mother appearing on our marriage scene is all about you!"

"My family lives across the ocean where they belong. The odds that they would interfere are almost nil."

"You're not close to your family at all, and it's no big deal for you to leave them across the ocean and visit them once a year. But for me, I feel like someone brought me news of something I wanted to know long ago that's now no longer relevant. I could take it or leave it."

"Take it, at least for Kata's sake. I'm sure she'd like to know her grandma."

37

My Birth Mother

A week later the phone rang late in the evening. It was Cathy. Dorothy had answered her letter right away and wanted to know whether she could come the following week. I told Cathy it was fine with us. I reassured her that nothing about our relationship would ever change. "Giving birth can be as natural as breathing, but when an adult chooses to call you Mom, it's a privilege you've earned. The years with you have filled the empty spaces in my heart that longed for a mom. There is no vacancy now."

Cathy blew her nose and I jumped! Her nose blowing had interrupted many tender moments, but I still wasn't used to it. "Do you believe me?"

A long pause with more sniffling and nose blows. "I do. And thank you for telling me that," she answered.

It surprised me that Cathy felt insecure. Did she really think that I'd ignore her, or have little to do with her, or stop loving her just because my mother decided she was curious and wanted to know what had become of me? I was a little sad that she didn't give me more credit, but then I realized how much Cathy and I needed each other. In the past, I had needed her more, but now, for whatever reason, she seemed to need me more. Was I a living reminder of what she'd accomplished in Africa? As her memories of Tanzania faded, did she cling to me to prove that she'd been there? Or was what she told me one day really true? That no matter how long she lived she believed that what she did at age twenty-three—adopting me, bringing me to America, and loving me like her own daughter—would be one of her greatest achievements in life? Did she think that this woman who said she was my mother could diminish the sacrifices she made in bringing me to America?

I tried to prepare Katarina for Dorothy's impending visit, but it was harder than I thought.

"Kata," I began, "next week my mother is coming to visit us, and I think she'd love to hear you play your favorite Suzuki piano pieces. What do you think?"

She looked at me doubtfully and said, "Do you have two moms?" When I hesitated with my reply, she answered her own question, "Oh, I see, Grandma Cathy is my grandma, and your mom is coming!"

"Yes, Grandma Cathy is your grandma and my mother is coming." I was grateful that at age six she was satisfied with that.

"Can I play "Twinkle, Twinkle Little Star?"

"Of course, and then you can play some of the longer pieces you know."

I have always been happy that Katarina played the piano. At Marian College I taught myself to play simple songs on the one and only piano I'd seen in Africa. With much practice and lots of help from my teacher, the two of us played the overture to Gilbert and Sullivan's *The Mikado*. Recently a family friend gave us an old upright piano, and now Kata took Suzuki piano classes. When I had the piano to myself, I played the old songs I'd learned in Africa such as "Long, Long Ago" and "Starlight Waltz." I couldn't wait for Kata to be able to read notes because I'd hoped she'd teach me.

Instead of teaching me to play the piano, Kata taught me nursery rhymes and how to read like her teacher. Together we watched *Sesame Street* every day, and learned the alphabet with her correcting my pronunciation and accent every time I didn't say it right. I knew nothing about Mother Goose rhymes.

"Our teacher told us that everybody knows about Mother Goose!"

"I've heard of her and seen the book, but because I was born in Africa, I never read it."

"Could you read this for me?" She opened her book to "Little Miss Muffet."

I started to read, "Little Miss Muffet sat on—"

"No, Mom! Read like the teacher!"

Poor Kata, she just couldn't understand why I had an accent, and I couldn't explain it to her. I wondered if having parents who were both foreign-born would end up being a handicap in her life or an asset. For the moment, it was definitely a handicap. I learned a lot about the typical American childhood from Kata, *Sesame Street*, and *The Electric Company*. I got so good at imitating her teacher that once she sat through my reading of the entire *Three Billy Goats Gruff* nursery tale without corrections.

Cathy told me again over the phone how Dorothy described herself so we'd recognize her when she got off the plane. Cathy read: "I'm short and fat, with ear-length wavy gray hair, usually frumpy looking, but for the occasion I'll wear my slimming pink suit and carry a large black handbag. I shall also be lugging my traveling pharmacy—a small zippered bag on wheels that contains all my medications."

"A traveling pharmacy? Do you think she's very sick and we'll have to give her medications every hour?"

"If she's well enough to travel on her own, I'm sure she'll have everything including her medications under control," Cathy laughed.

"She must be quite a character. Short and fat and lugging a suitcase full of medicine! Not the way I pictured my mother."

"I'll pick you up on Thursday, and we'll go to the airport together. I hope I can control myself. Mary, I'm really happy for you. Finally, you will know your birth mother, and she must be dying to see you after all these years."

I couldn't sleep for several nights in anticipation of meeting my birth mother. I envisioned our reunion from different points of view. When I was a child, I had imagined myself seeing my mother at last and running to her. She would kiss and hug me, hold me tight, and tell me she had come to take me home, far away from the orphanage. I would ask her to have my friend Elizabeth come and play with me at our home, and could she please give her a doll like her mother had given me? I'd ask where she had been, and she'd tell me she had to travel far away, and she got lost, and that is why no one could find her. I would reply that I knew she was telling the truth because Baby Jesus had been looking for her for a long time.

I had imagined her coming to the African hospital when I was sick with typhoid in the ward full of patients of every age in various stages of dying. She would be so glad that she found me before I died. She would sit at my bedside and pray for me, feed me, and watch over me just like the other African mothers watched over their sick children. When I died, she would bury me behind her hut in her village. I had envisioned her coming to Mhonda when I was delirious with malaria. She would take me to a hospital and then far away to another school, where the headmistress would not ridicule me for being half-caste.

But I was a child then. Now, as I walked around Lake of the Isles in Minneapolis, I realized I had stopped dreaming of my reunion with my mother when I found Cathy. I was certain she was Baby Jesus' answer to my childhood prayers. Yet the truth of the matter was that in a couple of days I was going to meet my birth mother. How could this be? Even though I honestly didn't know how I felt about her impending visit, I knew a lot about such reunions from watching TV.

Would she run to me with wide-open arms and hug me as if she'd never let me go? Would tears of joy and happiness bathe her face while she fervently kissed me? Would I cry along with her? Would there be TV cameras and reporters to record the event and share our story with the world? When we were finally alone, would she beg forgiveness for not raising me and tell me why? Did I even want to know? Would she answer all my childhood questions? I was secretly hoping my reunion with my birth mother would be like the TV reunions, but because we can never truly forget emotional and psychological pain, I prayed that our reunion wouldn't revisit the dried-up well of my childhood tears and fill it up again.

I knew for sure that I was not bitter or mad at her. Objectively speaking, I was curious about her life in Africa. I wanted to learn firsthand what it was really like to live as a *mzungu* in Tanganyika. She lived there during colonial times and probably had quite a story to tell.

I was hoping that after we met neither of us would do or say things to hurt each other. From her letters, I felt she loved me enough to give Cathy permission to bring me to America. I will be eternally grateful to her for that.

Memories are your personal history, and you need them now. Fat Mary was expressing her important role in my life. *The joy of meeting your birth mother might influence how you interpret her absence in your childhood. You will be more understanding of her than she will be of you because that's who she is.*

38

Meeting Mother

I was watching for Cathy's car when she pulled up. She got out of the car and slowly closed the door behind her. She wore her favorite, blue-denim maternity dress that beautifully concealed the blessing she was carrying. She trundled over the weather-worn, wood bridge that connected the pagoda on the sidewalk to our Japanese house. She had two weeks to go before delivery, and I prayed that the stress of the occasion wouldn't cause her to give birth on our way to the airport!

She greeted me with "I think I need another box of Kleenex!" She then began a series of nose blowings. Her red face and her puffed up blue-gray eyes under her thick glasses told me she'd done a lot of crying since we'd last seen each other. The emotions I was supposed to have about meeting my mother for the first time didn't bring tears to my eyes, but the sight of Cathy crying made me cry.

"I know you hate driving," she said, "but you'll have to today."

"No problem. I'll drive on the condition you don't cry all the way to the airport. When you cry, I cry. And please don't blow your nose so loudly when I'm driving. Other drivers might think I'm blowing the horn."

"Come on, it's not that bad!" We laughed and Cathy was calm for a while.

"Do you think I want to cry? I'll feel so silly if I cry in front of her," she said.

"Then try to get all your tears out now."

We got into the car, and Cathy started sobbing just as I turned on the ignition. I pretended not to hear her. She rubbed her always-present nylon hankie so hard and fast I was sure she was going to start a fire. I kept my promise and let her cry.

"How can you be so calm?" she asked.

"Do I have a choice? Look at you! One of us has to drive."

I was too calm for my own good. I think I would have been less surprised when I saw Dorothy if I'd worked up some emotion. Any emotion. I was feeling nothing. I asked God as I drove to clog Cathy's tear ducts, and it seemed my prayers were answered. Cathy was smiling as we watched the passengers deplane. Since I was taller than Cathy, I saw her first.

I saw a vivid image from my childhood walking in slow motion toward me. I knew this woman. I'd seen her somewhere. I wasn't sure where, but there was no doubt I'd seen her before. My heart started beating fast. Cathy approached her, but for some reason I couldn't move. I felt my heartbeat in my head. My feet seemed as heavy as tree trunks. I watched Cathy greet her. They were both smiling, and I noticed that Cathy wasn't crying. A bolt of lightning lit my brain, and my heart almost stopped. I remembered where, why, and how I knew this woman.

With this affirmation, I walked toward them with my arms outstretched, ready to greet Dorothy with a hug, but she stretched out her hand, saying, "I'm glad to see you."

"Glad to meet you! Do you have luggage?" I asked.

"Of course I have luggage. You don't think I'd live in this suit for four days, now do you?"

"Knowing that you lived in Africa, I wouldn't be surprised," I answered.

For a moment Dorothy looked as if she wondered how I knew she had lived in Africa. Then she replied, "You're right. The Africans of my time seldom changed their clothes. They often smelled so bad it was hard to be in the same room with them."

"It's because they have no other clothes to change into," I said, annoyed by her typical *mzungu* comment.

"I suppose."

"Here's the escalator," Cathy said, squeezing my hand. I gathered she didn't think it was a good idea to start arguing when we had just met.

We picked up Dorothy's large bright red-and-gold-plaid suitcase and walked to the car. Cathy was quite cheerful by now, asking Dorothy about her trip. They hit it off and I was grateful. I think Cathy no longer felt threatened when she saw this nondescript woman who was even shorter than she was. As they happily laughed and chatted, I allowed myself to be transported back to Tanzania, where I'd seen this woman before.

She was the one who had come to Kifungilo several times, who I had thought would adopt me. She taught me how to drink tea from a cup and saucer and sit properly on a big *wazungu* chair. She let me drink all of her tea and eat all of her biscuits while silently staring at me. And the most vivid memory of all—she was the lady who had come to visit me every night in the Lushoto European hospital when I almost died from typhoid.

So this woman, Dorothy, who knew me when I was in Kifungilo, who arranged for me to be transferred from the African hospital to the European hospital so I wouldn't die, who stayed by my bedside every night for two weeks, who always knew where I was, now comes to tell me she's my mother. What kept her from telling me before? If she had cared so much for me, why had she given me up, and why hadn't she brought me toys, pretty dresses, or bright ribbons for my hair when she lived so close by? She's pretending she's seeing me for the first time. Probably the last time she saw me I was nine or ten years old because that's when Sister Silvestris stopped dressing me up to be shown for adoption.

So many feelings and memories were playing in my head that I didn't hear whether Dorothy or Cathy said anything to me on the way to her house. Kjell and Kata had already arrived. I didn't know what Kjell had explained to Kata, but she was subdued and solemn as she approached Dorothy. She curtsied (I've no idea where she got that from—probably from the fairy tales she loved to read) and reached up to hug Dorothy, but Dorothy caught her hand in midair and shook it instead. Kata hesitated for a moment, then gave her the tiny bouquet of flowers she'd picked from John's garden. She quickly walked away from her, came to me, and asked, "Is she your mom?"

"Yes."

"She doesn't look like you."

"I know."

"She isn't like a real grandma because real grandmas bring presents."

We went inside where John was preparing dinner, and I watched Kjell and Dorothy through the window. Dorothy was laughing and carrying on about how funny Kjell was and how wonderful that he was Norwegian. You'd think it was their reunion.

"Your mother and Kjell are really getting along well," John said.

"I'm glad. She seems like quite a conversationalist. She's well-read and well-informed about current affairs. You don't expect a person like her, having lived as a spoiled *mzungu* in Africa, to be interesting or interested, but she's definitely with it."

"Dinner is ready," John announced.

The conversation around the dinner table was light and pleasant. I joined in, and we talked about life in America, the news, the bicentennial celebrations coming up, and the coming birth of John and Cathy's baby. We said goodbye and made plans for the next day. I could see Dorothy was happy to be staying with John and Cathy this first visit.

Dorothy stayed for several days, but when she left, I didn't know anything more about her life in Africa or about my father than before she came. She did tell us she graduated magna cum laude from Wheaton College, with a double major in Latin and Classic Greek, and she was class valedictorian. She also talked a lot about her two sisters, but it was obvious she loved and admired Marion more than Marjorie. Marion and her husband Bill were Christian and Missionary Alliance missionaries in Indonesia and China, and Marjorie lived in Muskegon, Michigan, where Dorothy was going to live. She wanted me to meet Marion, even though she was thousands of miles away.

"I've always wished to be like my sister Marion. She's the best of us three. She's led an unselfish life of service to God and to her fellow human beings no matter how destitute."

"How about you? I thought you were a missionary too."

"Oh no! My husband was working for the British government in mosquito and tsetse fly control, and I just taught school."

"I assume your husband was not my father."

"No!" Dorothy stood up abruptly and headed for her room to get her nitroglycerine pills. She told me she'd had heart problems most of her life and her medication helped her live a normal life. It was like that for the whole visit. Every time I mentioned anything even remotely related to Africa, and especially when she thought I was interrogating her about my father, she got physically ill. Her color changed, she ran out of breath, and she rushed for a fix from her traveling pharmacy.

Apart from being her daughter, I also wanted to know what life in Africa was like for a *mzungu* in the 1930s and '40s from her perspective. Except for basic questions, conversation about Africa was taboo and inevitably brought out her nitroglycerine pills.

"Where did you live in Africa?"

"We lived several places because my husband Marshall had projects in many districts. We lived in Kahama by Lake Victoria, Kibondo, and in Kondoa."

"Did you ever live in Lushoto?" I didn't want to tell her outright that Cathy said Dorothy had worked at the European school there.

"Yes, I taught all subjects up to the sixth grade to children of European families. My husband lived for months on end in the bush and was gone a lot of the time." She really wanted me to understand that.

"He went to remote areas to do research and spray for tsetse flies. He was given a very old and inaccurate map of Tanzania and told where to spray. Once he showed me a rough map of Tanganyika with patches of green indicating forests, wide blue lines for rivers, and a few black dots showing cities like Dar-es-Salaam, Tanga, Lindi, Mwanza, Moshi, and Arusha. The map didn't show roads, railroads, or lakes."

"How did he find his way?"

"The Africans knew how to get around. Because of Marshall's work in the bush, a British cartographer worked with him to update maps. On one old map, the letters *MMBA* were written in all the areas with no rivers or cities. The cartographer told us that *MMBA* meant 'Miles and Miles of Bloody Africa'!"

"I love the British, don't you?" I quipped.

"Mind you, these were official maps used by all government agencies in Africa and abroad. I can't believe that Africans never questioned the meaning of MMBA. Strangely, they seldom questioned anything European."

"Not so strange when you've never needed a piece of paper to navigate, and you've never seen a map before, and government authorities and missionaries treated Africans as an inferior race. The Africans understood that the only way to get ahead was to become 'civilized' and emulate the European way."

"You seem more African than I thought you'd be."

"Oh? What else could I be other than African?" I asked her.

"You went to a European school when you were little and have lived in America for so many years, I thought you'd be more American in your views."

"I'm American on certain issues and African on most. Just because the orphanage was run by German nuns doesn't mean it was a European school. We were often reminded by word and deed that we were children of sin and nobody wanted us. If children in European schools in Tanganyika were treated the way we were, those schools would have been closed and the teachers jailed."

"How were you treated?"

"Sometimes good, sometimes bad. As children, we mostly felt that the nuns hated us, though that changed as we grew older and understood more. They often called us names like *Ziguener* (Gypsies), *schwarze Teufel* (black devils), and unwanted children. If you had a brother or a sister at the orphanage, or if you had a mother or father who sent you things or who gave the Sisters money, you were treated much better. Actually, most of the abuse at Kifungilo came at the hands of the big girls. They used to beat us and make us do hard physical labor and take our food as well as—"

"Stop!" Dorothy looked at me intently. "If you're trying to make me feel guilty, it's not going to work."

"Guilty? What do you mean?"

"I took very good care of you while you were in Kifungilo!"

"You did? In what way? How so when I didn't even know that you existed?"

"I sent money to the Sisters every month. They told me you had everything you needed and that you were a very happy child. They sent me pictures of you once a year, and I could see that you were being well taken care of."

"You sent money to Kifungilo for me?"

"Yes. Every month. Granted it wasn't a large amount, but it was enough to provide you with everything you needed. I even sent more money when they told me that you were going away to school and needed extra money for your school fees."

I really didn't know whom to believe—Dorothy or the Precious Blood Sisters of Kifungilo. If she knew I was in Kifungilo, why hadn't she come to visit me as my mother? And if she was teaching in Lushoto, only thirteen kilometers away, what kept her from taking me home for weekends and holidays like my friend Elizabeth's mother did? She seemed visibly shaken by our conversation, and I was afraid she'd need a handful of nitroglycerine pills, so I decided to save my questions for later.

"When I saw you at the airport. I knew I had seen you before. You used to come to Kifungilo when I was really small, and I would be dressed up for the occasion in hopes you would adopt me."

"Adopt you? How could I adopt my own child? Yes, I came to Kifungilo to see you whenever I could, and every time I saw you I was satisfied you were at the right place. You were always well-fed—you were quite plump, actually—and you were clean and seemed to be intelligent. I knew that the sisters would educate you, which is more than I could do for you at the time."

"Didn't you come to visit me in the hospital when I almost died of typhoid?"

"I made the arrangements for you to be transferred to the European hospital. I had seen you in the African hospital. I can never forget that. You were lying unconscious in a ward full of sick people. The ward stunk like a sewer, and patients were on the bare floor. I was sure you were going to die."

I wanted to ask her why she didn't tell me she was my mother, why she never touched me, and why she hadn't put her hand on my burning forehead in the hospital when she came to see me every night. I had thought she was one of the *mzungu* nurses on night duty.

"Thanks to you, I didn't die."

"I did what I could for you. Didn't the nuns buy you special toys and clothes with the money I sent? Didn't they give you sweets and take you on trips like they said they did?"

"No. But for Christmas we all got a dress from the boxes of donated items from Europe. On feast days we got a piece of candy, and sometimes when the *wazungu* came to visit Kifungilo, we got another piece of candy. I was fed, but I was always hungry. I ate anything I could get my hands on. That's why Sister Silvestris called me 'Fat Mary' and the children called me 'Piggy.'"

"Did you ever get things that the other children didn't? Several times I sent you parcels with clothes, dolls, and candy, and I sent you children's books too."

"No. I got nothing. I wonder why they didn't give me what you sent me. The other children who had parents or relatives received what their parents sent. Could it be because the children knew their parents? Most of the parents who came to visit were the African mothers, but I remember Ellen's father was a *mzungu*, and he came to see her and always brought her presents. She was very kind and shared with me."

"And when you went away to school, did they give you the money I sent?"

"Not only did they not give it to me, but they also made me sign a contract to repay all the money they spent for my school fees. No wonder they didn't ask me for it when I went back to say goodbye before coming to America. I was sure they were going to ask Cathy for it, since I hadn't paid them back."

"I don't know what to say. I tried my best to do what I thought was right. And now I find out that my efforts were in vain. It was hard for me to save money for you. I'd promised my husband that once we took you to Kifungilo, I'd have nothing more to do with you. No matter what it must have looked like to you, I never once forgot you. I'm getting ill . . . I need a pill."

That was a signal she couldn't handle more stressful subjects. I made us a cup of tea, and she started on a crossword puzzle. She did those British ones that require thinking backwards and knowing and finding words no one cares about. The rest of the visit was filled with pleasant conversation on non-nitroglycerine-inducing topics. She had a great sense of humor and could be a lot of fun with her many stories of the "olden days," which kept us in stitches. Dorothy was easy to be with so long as I didn't ask her about her life in Africa. She liked Kjell a lot, and she told me that being married to a Norwegian was the best thing about my life. Lord help us if Kjell ever heard that! Her opinion really surprised me. I thought it was obvious to everyone who knew me that Cathy was the best thing to happen to me.

"Help me, Fat Mary! This is all too much to take in."

I am hearing all this for the first time too. I think sometimes you forget that I do not initiate anything in our relationship. I am you, and you are me. We experience everything simultaneously, though I have the added task of deciphering the problem, putting it into perspective, and saving it for you.

All week long, I watched the interaction between Katarina and Dorothy. I could tell that Dorothy wasn't the nurturing type. She had trouble hugging Kata or even holding her hand for any length of time. She talked to her as if she were an adult and insisted there was a right way to do everything. We were having lunch with John and Cathy at their home when Dorothy suggested that Cathy come and visit her in Muskegon.

"How about us?" I asked.

"Well, you can come too. But it will be difficult."

"We won't all come at once."

"It's not that. What will I tell everyone?"

"About me?"

"Yes. You see, I told my sister and my neighbor that I was going to see an old friend from Africa in Minneapolis. My sister, especially, was very inquisitive: 'Who is she? What's her name? How come you've never spoken about her before?' You know, it would be easier to tell my sister Marion, because she'd have the sense to mind her own business."

"Do you think people care that much who comes and goes in your building?" Kjell asked.

"Maybe they don't, but I do."

"Don't you think it's too late to start worrying about what people think?" Kjell continued. "Unless you never want to see us again, it's just a matter of time before you'll have to tell your family and friends, and we'll have to tell ours."

Dorothy had managed to keep me a secret her whole life, and now she acted as if she had the power to control the kind of relationship we would have. She was the puppeteer, and we were all her puppets. She would determine when, if, and who would be privy to her big secret. As intelligent as she was, did she know that once you tell your secret to one person, it is no longer a secret? It was obvious she didn't want to tell anyone about us.

A couple days later, Kjell suddenly said, "I can't understand your mother. She waited thirty-three years to see you, and instead of shouting it from the mountaintops and telling everyone and anyone who would listen that she's found her daughter, she's worried about what people will say. Screw the people!"

That's typical Kjell. He couldn't wait to tell the whole world about Dorothy and couldn't understand why I didn't have his urge to make a public statement about her.

"Whomever I choose to tell about Dorothy, I'd like to do it in person. So Kjell, please give me the honor of telling people before you do."

"I'm afraid I've already told some people."

"I knew it! I knew you wouldn't understand. It's not easy to sit down for dinner at someone's home where you know only the host and hostess and have some guest blurt out, 'So Maria, I heard you found your mother.' What am I supposed to say? Where do I begin? Do they understand how personal and private my feelings about my mother are? Do they understand that I can't do superficial discussions about a lifelong source of pain? Do they even care about what I might say? Why is this part of my life another juicy tidbit to be exploited? And how can I tell people about my mother when she herself isn't ready to accept me unconditionally?"

I could see Kjell formulating an answer, but I cut him off. "Don't even try to answer me. Unless you've walked in my shoes, your logical answers will be empty and wrong for me. Unless you've walked in Dorothy's shoes, you cannot understand her either. Hopefully time will heal our wounds, and we'll both be able to talk about each other and our lives to anyone we choose. I'm not there yet."

"I didn't know you felt so strongly about this."

"How could you? I've always been grateful that I was married to an optimist, but there are times when your optimism underscores your naiveté and lack of empathy."

39

No Answers

When I took Dorothy back to the airport, I wanted to be alone with her to ask her one more question, no matter how forbidden.

"Dorothy, could you tell me anything about my father?"

She instinctively reached for a pill, took it, waited a few seconds, and then said, "No."

"Why not?"

"I just can't, so please don't ask again."

I ignored her and continued, "What happened? Did you have an affair?"

"Well, ahhh . . . maybe."

"Were you raped?"

"Maybe."

"Did you know him?"

"Maybe."

"Did you love him?"

"Maybe."

"Has your guardian angel whispered in your ear that 'maybe' was the only answer for today? How can you 'maybe' be raped?"

"I forgot."

"What did you forget?"

"Everything."

"So, you mean that you will never be able to tell me anything about my father because you've forgotten everything?"

"I've forgotten everything."

"How come you didn't forget about me?"

"You can never forget giving birth."

"But you can forget who planted the child in your womb?"

"I was really hoping that we could continue to see each other, but if you're going to put me through an inquisition every time I see you, I won't come again."

"Don't you think it's natural for me to want to know about my father? And what better person to ask than the person who says she's my mother? Am I to believe that you are really my mother but that you know or remember nothing about how you came to be my mother?"

"I really didn't want to have it end this way."

"Do you think you can come waltzing into my life and tell me something I've wanted to know since I was a child and then waltz out again, and nothing in your life will change? I thought I got my brains from you!"

"I just wanted to see you."

"And you hoped I would be a deaf-mute!"

"Don't be angry. I really have nothing to tell you about your father. Even if I could tell you, I have my reasons. The only thing I'll say is that I'm doing it for you."

"For me?" I realized it was useless to pursue the subject, so I asked, "If you really cannot talk about it, could you write it down for me?"

"No."

"So you mean you'll never, ever, tell me, even in writing?"

"That's right."

We drove quietly the rest of the way to the airport. Since Dorothy wanted to leave at least three hours ahead of time, we had two hours to kill before her plane left. She told me she didn't mind waiting alone and I should go home. I didn't want to say goodbye on that note, so I swallowed my disappointment and looked on the bright side of her visit.

"I don't want to open whatever wounds you've been nursing over the years, but I'm asking you to do this, and then I'll forever hold my peace on this subject. Would you write down the information about my father, who he was, how you knew him, and whether he's still alive so that my family and I can have closure about my background? Would you please, please, write it down and put it in a safe, maybe with your last will and testament, so in case you die before me, I'll have it? Please, Dorothy, you owe me this."

"We'll see."

In my disappointment, I told myself that whether or not I knew about my father didn't change the fact that at this moment I knew my mother.

"I'm grateful you looked me up. It must not have been easy. Given everything you've gone through on my account and everything I've gone through in my life, there's no way I'm not going to see you again. I hope we'll take whatever time God gives us to develop a mother-daughter relationship that will be the best for both of us."

"I hope so too. But please promise me that you'll never bring up your father again."

"I promise. Let's not exhaust your supply of nitroglycerine pills!"

With this assurance, Dorothy's manner changed back to the way she was during the visit—pleasant, talkative, but cautious about the things she didn't want me to know.

"When Kifungilo wrote to inform me that an American wanted to adopt you, it couldn't have happened at a better time. Marshall and I were leaving Africa to return to America for good, and it seemed that if I wanted to see you again, my chances lay with this American woman. The letter from the nuns said she wanted to take you with her to America and that you'd already received a scholarship for college, so I decided it was time to give my permission. As I told you, I had promised my husband that once we took you to Kifungilo I'd have nothing more to do with you. He never knew about the money I sent or my visits to you. I also did not tell him I'd written to the American embassy to confirm that I was your mother and an American citizen."

"Now I understand why I have an American passport. I thought that it was because Cathy was an American. She spent many months trying to get me a passport. It was only after the intervention of Senator Hubert H. Humphrey of Minnesota that I finally obtained one."

"You are an American citizen by birth, even though you were born and raised in Tanzania. Cathy needed Hubert Humphrey's intervention to speed up the process and make sure the State Department and the American embassy in Dar-es Salaam issued you a passport, based on my testimony of your birthright."

"You've done many things for me over the years without my knowledge, but the most important thing you did was give me my American citizenship. Soon I will have lived more years in America than in Tanzania. Strange as it might sound, though in my heart and soul I feel African, in my mind I know I'm also an American. I love both! When I'm in Africa, I'm an American ambassador, and when I'm in America, I'm an ambassador for Africa. I'm taking advantage of this unique position. I don't have to be one or the other. I can be both! Maybe, if I ever get to know my father, I'll have the opportunity to get a Tanzanian passport."

"I don't think so. America doesn't recognize dual citizenship."

"It's their loss."

"The good Sisters didn't teach you about modesty and humility, did they?"

"They did. But I knew better. Humility is when you know every aspect of yourself, the good, the bad, and the ugly, and you accept it. Nothing more and nothing less! Humility is not going around singing your own unsolicited praises, but it's also not going around pretending that you're not worthy of something or that you're not good at something when you know you are. Cathy has often pointed out my seemingly immodest self. I spent a lot of time, especially as a child, taking an objective look at myself and reinforcing what I thought was good about me. If I hadn't done that, if I had focused only on the many negatives directed at me—that I was a child of sin, nobody wanted me, I was ugly and stupid—my self-image would have been miserable, and I would have self-destructed by now. I know I'm a child of God, I am smart, and I'm pretty. I'm proud of my achievements, and I'm not going to play false modesty games. I hope I always see the truth about myself and don't exaggerate or invent an image of myself that I know is not true."

"I never knew that your life in Kifungilo was that hard. Whenever I thought of you, since I couldn't raise you myself, I felt that you were in the next best place."

"It was much harder on the personal level, though the everyday life was no piece of cake. Considering that I turned out normal and that I like who I am today, they must have done a lot that was right."

We said goodbye on that note. I gave her a huge hug and kiss and thanked her for coming back into my life. She just stood there with her arms at her sides, holding on to her purse and traveling pharmacy. It seemed she didn't know what to do. I understood she couldn't hug me because she wasn't into hugging and kissing. It was only when I looked into her eyes that I got a glimpse of a guarded softness and warmth that had difficulty surfacing. Yet she had loved me enough to fight for my American citizenship. She had opened an important door for me so my childhood declaration—"I am an Amelican gal"—became reality.

"*Safari njema!*" (Good trip!) I said as she disappeared into the plane. People turned to look at the Black foreigner speaking her language to a gray-haired, middle-aged, white woman.

When I got home I went through my box of treasured keepsakes and found the holy card that Cathy had given me when I got my American citizenship.

To Mary Rose Ryan—American Citizen—20th May 1963

GOD BLESS YOU

God bless you each new day and give you His Love,
God prosper your every year with His help from above,
Be His strength in your arm and His grace in your soul,
His smile to be your reward, His glory to be your goal.

40

Karl

Cathy gave birth to her daughter Eleanor the same year I met my mother. I wondered whether Cathy felt a difference between being a biological mother and an adoptive one. As far as I was concerned, she had always treated me as her biological daughter, and now we both had to accept and make room for other intimate relationships in our lives—a child for her and a mother for me. By giving birth, Cathy became Eleanor's mother overnight. It must have taken time for her to feel like my mother, but for me it felt like I became her child overnight.

Because of Dorothy's anxiety about telling the whole truth of how I came to be, I knew we would have to be cautiously patient with each other if we were going to have a good relationship. She did stay with us when she visited us in Minnesota for Thanksgiving, bringing her books, her crossword puzzles, and her knitting. I thought it strange that she never brought a present for Kata when she came.

Since I didn't mention my father, her visit was enjoyable and less stressful for both of us. I told her I'd always wanted another child, but my ectopic pregnancy had raised havoc with my reproductive system. One fallopian tube had ruptured and the other was infected, so my chances of getting pregnant were not good. Kjell was satisfied with one child, and it made no difference to him whether we had another.

"Why do you want another child?" she asked.

"Well, the biggest reason is that I was so alone in Kifungilo. I was jealous of the children who had brothers and sisters. If I can

217

help it, I won't do that to Kata. We've talked about adopting a little boy and have already attended two orientation meetings with the county adoption agency. We figure we shouldn't have to wait too long because biracial children are often the last ones to be adopted. They have several little boys waiting."

"I thought that in Kifungilo you wouldn't feel alone with the other orphans as your brothers and sisters."

"There's something I need to tell you. Kifungilo was not a true orphanage. You must have known that. There were the 'haves' and 'have nots.' The 'haves' were the ones with brothers and sisters and maybe a parent, sometimes both. While I was in Kifungilo, I really felt alone. Now when I see former Kifungilo girls, I guess what I feel is like a relationship between siblings, but I wish I had felt it then."

"I'm sure Kata would like a little playmate," she said matter-of-factly.

Dorothy often got fidgety and changed the subject when I talked about family. Was she afraid I was going to ask her about other children she might have had?

It seems that when you've given up trying to have your own child and decide to adopt, you become pregnant. Kjell was thrilled when I announced that I was pregnant. We decided I should cut back on my Young Audiences presentations so as not to jeopardize our baby by dancing on hard, concrete floors in school cafeterias and gymnasiums. I also knew that this was going to be my last child, so I settled into taking care of myself and indulging in some serious eating and relaxing—I gained sixty-five pounds with this pregnancy!

I wanted a boy since I already had a girl. I was sure the baby would be a boy because God always answered my prayers—eventually. Our son, named Karl after Kjell's grandfather, was born in October, seven years after Kata. For his birth, I wanted nothing to do with the Lamaze Natural Childbirth method I'd practiced for Kata. I asked the doctor to give me everything he could legally give me. My labor was five hours long, and this time I had no complications. All I remember about Karl's birth is straining to look between his legs. "Yes, yes, yes! He has a penis. Hallelujah!"

Kata was a baby from heaven, and Karl was a baby from purgatory. It was only faith in *Baby Care* by Dr. Benjamin Spock, my baby bible, that assured me his round-the-clock crying from colic would end. For the first three months, my baby and I took turns crying. A pediatrician friend of ours checked him and to comfort us said, "Yup, he has colic, and it will end in about three or four months. You know, some of the greatest men in the world were colicky babies."

"Name one."

"President Nixon had colic." That wasn't helpful.

In the spring of 1978, Cathy, Eleanor, Dorothy, Karl, and I went to Montserrat for two weeks. Kata stayed in Minnesota with friends because of school. Montserrat is a gem of an island, a dot on the map of the world, on the leeward side of the Caribbean islands. Twelve miles long and fifteen miles wide, it has a population of twelve thousand around Christmastime, when Montserratians living abroad return home for the holidays and carnival, and nine thousand the rest of the year. Kjell discovered it in 1974 when he and another Norwegian businessman traveled to several Caribbean islands in search of an outlet for their prefabricated wood cabins. After having a great time on the islands, they decided it wasn't wise to feed the beautiful Norwegian pinewood cabins to hungry Caribbean termites! But he fell in love with Montserrat and told me the people, climate, and topography reminded him of Tanzania.

That year Kjell, Kata, and I spent Christmas at the View Pointe Hotel in Montserrat, and I fell in love with it too. The people made me feel at home not only because of their hospitality but also because the population was a mixture of many ethnic groups. Arawak Indians, Africans, Irish, British, Spaniards—Montserratians came in every shade. Although black was the dominant color, my light-brown shade was just as common. Until they heard my accent, everyone thought I was Montserratian. I loved their easygoing style, how they danced, and how they used their bodies to express everything. I loved how they steupsed. That sucking sound instantly took me back to the orphanage and how we steupsed to express annoyance or anger. I loved how they made your business their own! One day I was enjoying a walk along the street in the warm rain when I heard voices coming from all directions. When I looked up, someone at every window and door was admonishing me to get out of the rain: "You go e ketch cole, chile." "Chile, go ow tof da ra'n!"

We returned to Montserrat twice more, staying at the View Pointe Hotel and the Emerald Isle Hotel in Plymouth, the only town on the island. I had already made up my mind that I was going to spend winter, or some of it anyway, in Montserrat. It also occurred to Kjell that it might be cheaper to send me away for the winter, as I'd crashed a car each of the past three winters driving on icy, snow-covered Minnesota roads. The next time we went to Montserrat, we bought a small condominium on Richmond Hill and rented a townhouse for Kjell's sister Berit and her son Eirik, who joined us from Norway.

When Dorothy and Cathy came, we all stayed at our condo. What a trip! First of all, Kjell raised hell because he didn't think Cathy should come with us. He felt the trip was a private time for Dorothy and me and that Cathy just didn't want to miss anything. I knew that Dorothy was coming to Montserrat because she had a priest friend who lived on the island of Guadeloupe (twenty-seven miles away) and she was hoping to see him. Private time or family bonding time was never a priority with her. Whatever she did, she did because the time was right for her. As it turned out, the priest had left Guadeloupe years earlier and no one knew how to find him. Eleanor, twenty-two months old, was a holy terror. Every day she put on the mother of all tantrums as a matter of course. Cathy was miserable and helpless most of the time, and Dorothy snored all night. Whenever I asked her to turn over, she said, "I couldn't have been snoring. I wasn't even sleeping."

After that trip, Dorothy was a little more comfortable around me, so long as I wasn't near someone she knew. She invited John and Cathy (not me) to visit her in Muskegon, where she'd moved a few months earlier to be near her "nosy" (her word) sister Marjorie.

On returning from her visit Cathy reported that she'd tried to convince Dorothy to tell her sister, as well as her new friends, about me. The report from John was, "Marjorie is still beautiful, even at sixty-eight, but she reminds me of an actress who knows she's admired and is intoxicated by that knowledge."

Again Kjell was upset that John and Cathy visited Dorothy before I did, and again I told him Dorothy was not ready to publicly claim me. Cathy was paving the way. I often wondered why Dorothy was so afraid to talk about me. Did she think people would think less of her? Did she think her friends would judge her morals? Or did she fear that her friends and relatives would blame her for having a child with a Black man and then leaving her at an orphanage?

I too was reluctant to talk about Dorothy to just anyone. I believed that few people really cared deeply about me and that whatever had happened to me as a child was for them just tantalizing secrets and gossip. I hadn't talked much about my childhood the first fifteen years I was in America, but now with my mother appearing, I had no choice. I told my close friends my story only when I was alone with them. Every time I talked about Dorothy, the physical pain and mental stress from long ago returned. The pain manifested as tears, and the stress turned my voice into short, whispered phrases. It hurt just as much to talk about my mother at those moments as it did to think about her when I was a child. Why as a child had I believed that when I found my mother all my suffering and loneliness would be erased? Though she was the one who had come looking for me, she wanted total control of our relationship as if I were still a child.

I went for a walk around Lake Calhoun and had a long talk with Fat Mary. She listened without interrupting and finally spoke.

At long last you've found your birth mother, and of course she resurrects the pain of her absence. Time does not heal all wounds. Time especially cannot heal those childhood wounds when they are reinforced by the same person who inflicted them. Dorothy is denying this aspect of her past. Because of your experiences, you are in a better position to help her face it.

41

Larry and Judy

Three years had passed since I met Dorothy. Her third visit was for Thanksgiving, and this time she was quieter than usual and sighed a lot. One evening as I was enjoying my sherry and she, her Earl Grey tea, she hesitantly said, "The reason I'm not going to spend Christmas with you is that you have a brother—well, a half-brother. His name is Larry, and he's a pediatrician in Boston. He's married and has three children—two boys and a girl who is Kata's age. If it's okay with you, I'm going to tell him about you this Christmas."

"I have a brother?" Somehow I wasn't surprised. "Does he look like me? How old is he?"

"He's eight years older than you and the only child I had with my husband. He was two years old when we left for Africa in 1936. He lived with us until he was seven, then we had to send him to boarding school in Nairobi. He finished secondary school there, and then we sent him to the States for college. He went into medicine and became a pediatrician."

"I see. Do you think he'd want to meet me?"

"He'd be delighted. I think Larry was happiest when he was in Africa. He has had problems in his marriage. He still loves Africa and is looking for a way to work in Tanzania."

"Is Larry the only sibling I have, or are there others in some corner of Tanzania?"

"Larry is the only one."

"Why did you finally decide to tell me?"

"Because you talked about how much you wished you had a brother or sister when you were in Kifungilo."

"How do you think he'll react when he finds out he has a sister who is half Black?"

"I don't know for sure, but my feelings tell me that he'll love you."

"Do it if you feel it's right. At this point it makes no difference to me whether I have a brother or not. And if he doesn't want to meet me, it's okay too."

Dorothy went back to Muskegon, and I didn't give Larry another thought. I didn't even mention him to Kjell or John and Cathy.

Shortly after Christmas 1979, Larry called, "Hey, Maria, this is your long-lost brother Larry. I don't care what plans you have—I'm taking a plane tomorrow morning to come to Minnesota. I'm counting the hours till we meet! It's about time. Mom showed me pictures of you. I can't believe I have such a beautiful sister. Unfortunately, your brother won't measure up. As much as I hate to, I'll have to describe myself, so you can spot me at the airport."

"Go ahead, but let me guess. You're bald and short and won't be wearing a suit."

"On the money. Did Mom describe me already? Did she say, 'Look for a short, balding forty-six-year-old man wearing a gray winter coat and carrying a beat-up overnight bag?'"

"That just about describes every other person who'd be crazy enough to come to Minnesota at this time of the year! Don't worry—we'll find each other."

"See you tomorrow, Sis."

Larry was the exact opposite of our mother. On the phone, he freely expressed his emotion and could hardly hide his excitement. I instinctively knew I was going to like him and that we'd easily develop ties that bind.

"Guess what, Kjell? At noon tomorrow I'm going to the airport to pick up my brother Larry."

"What? Do you mean there are more family members coming out of the woodwork? To think I married you because you had no family!"

"You're making fun of me and my newly found family! Dorothy says that Larry is the only sibling I have, and I suppose I should believe her."

"She should know."

"Yet she has a habit of forgetting important things about the circumstances of her children's births. She's not quite sure whether she had an affair or was raped when she conceived me."

"I wouldn't be surprised if there were more like you carefully placed and forgotten somewhere in Africa."

"I hope not. I'd hate it if she had other mixed children and put them in other orphanages or gave them up for adoption instead of keeping us together."

"She's a mysterious lady, but I do like her."

Larry and I gravitated toward each other as he walked out of the plane. We hugged as if we'd known each other our whole lives. He smiled, laughed, and talked intensely all the way home. He was as warm and cuddly as our mother was not.

We looked as different as salt and pepper. We just had to take Dorothy's word that we were related. He was as fair as I was dark. He had blue eyes and mine were dark brown. He had graying blond hair and I had black. He couldn't care less what he wore or how he wore it, while it mattered to me that I was neat and classy and well-groomed. He called me "Sis," and I called him "Larry." He called our mother "Mom" and I called her "Dorothy."

Larry brought calm just by his presence. Though he had a mischievous air, he made me feel there was nothing in the world more important than spending time with me. I loved hearing him talk about his life in Africa. He told me he had been sent away to boarding school and that he saw his parents only three or four times a year. They were stationed by Lake Victoria, and he spoke fluent Kisukuma, the language of the tribe living there. Larry clearly loved his father. Every time he talked about him, he choked, though it had been six years since Marshall Reiner passed away. He regretted not seeing his father before he died. "My father was a saint!" he said whenever mentioning him.

I told him that I had gone the previous year to visit a priest, Father Harnett, in Nairobi. Dorothy had given me his address and phone number and told me he was a dear friend when she was teaching there. I was eager to visit him because I hoped he would tell me something about my father or about Dorothy's life in Tanzania.

"I should have known Dorothy would have sworn him to secrecy like she did the Kifungilo nuns and Cathy. Father Harnett was thrilled with my visit but gave me little information about the Reiners. He told me there were only two people in the world he truly admired—his own father and Marshall Reiner."

"Wow! Father Harnett was mom's confidant. She still communicates with him."

"He also said your father was a saint."

Larry's eyes watered, but he swallowed his tears. "I have a question for you. Did you ever change your name?"

"Often. Since I didn't know my parents, it didn't matter to me or anyone else if I changed names. At different times in my life I was Mary Rgyne, Mary Ryne, Mary Rose Ryan, and when I married, I changed my first name to Maria."

"Was your name ever Judy?"

"Never. I tried not to depart too drastically from the name given me by the nuns when they baptized me. My name was simply Mary the entire time I was in Kifungilo."

"I'm really puzzled."

"Why?"

"Please don't ever ask Mom anything about this. But when we lived in Kondoa—the area in Tanzania where there are prehistoric cave drawings—I had a little sister whose name was Judy. We loved each other. She was mixed race like you, so when Mom told me I had a mixed-race sister in Minnesota, I thought you might be Judy. Are you Judy?"

"No—at least as far as I can be sure about my birth and parentage, since Dorothy is not giving details."

"Judy must have been about four years old when I left for boarding school. I remember how she cried when the lorry pulled away. When I came home for the holidays that year, Mom told me Judy had died from pneumonia, and she took me to see her grave close to our house in a German prisoner-of-war cemetery. You know that many Germans died in Africa during the Second World War. The British thought that even though they were the enemy in life, in death the Germans should be spared the indignity of lying alongside Africans in public graveyards, so they let them have their own cemetery."

"Did Judy really die?"

"Now I'm not so sure. I thought you would be her and that Mom made up a story about her disappearance. But things don't match up."

"I couldn't be her. I was in Kifungilo as a baby. I don't know exactly how old I was, but I was small enough to have Sister Theonesta rock me to sleep in her apron."

"I see some resemblance between you and Judy. The last time I saw her was in 1945. What year where you born?"

"According to our mother, I was born in 1943."

"You can't be Judy then, because when I left for school in 1942 she was already two years old."

"Are you sure Judy existed, or was she an imaginary playmate for a lonely little boy?"

"I'm sure, Maria. I have pictures."

"They should solve the problem. I have a picture of me when I was about three that I got from the album in Kifungilo. We'll compare the photos."

"But please don't breathe a word about Judy to Mom. She's never, ever, mentioned her since she died.

"I wish I had access to Dorothy's mind. She must have a lot of information buried deep. Do you think she'd ever write a book?"

"I wish she would. She was a compatriot of Karen Blixen, though not being a novelist, she probably wouldn't romanticize the continent like *Out of Africa* did. There was nothing romantic about her life. She worked very hard and was alone in the bush most of the time. Dad was always away, and she was left in charge of administering to the needs of Africans who congregated at her doorstep day and night. Once when there was a famine in Kahama, she single-handedly distributed food and clothing to thousands of starving Africans who came to a nearby mission camp. She took care of all their needs— physical and spiritual. She buried the dead and delivered newborns in the camp. She was the only *mzungu* at the camp."

"Those are the things I'd like to know about her life in Africa, but whenever I ask her anything, she clams up. I once asked her if she'd like to return to Africa someday, and she didn't say she wouldn't. She said she couldn't—it would be too painful."

"To tell you the truth, I know very little about my parents' lives in Africa. Being away at boarding school most of the year and traveling when we were on vacation hardly gave me a glimpse into their everyday lives."

"Did you get along well with both of them?"

"I got along better with Dad. That's all I can say. I've decided to get to know Mom better. I don't want what happened with Dad to happen with her. I will have to work on it, and I know it will be hard because we're so different!"

"You can say that again!"

42

Whose Grandchildren?

I noticed that Dorothy was much freer in her conversation after Larry knew about me. She even invited me to go to Muskegon for a visit, but she was still nervous when she introduced me. To some she'd say, "This is my daughter Maria." To others she'd say, "This is my friend from Minneapolis."

I didn't know what to make of Dorothy's youngest sister, Marjorie. She acted superior to Dorothy and patronizing toward me. She invited us over for dinner at her house and constantly compared her style of serving, cooking, cleaning, talking, dressing, and decorating with Dorothy's. At times, I'd catch her looking at me as if I were a mystery thing who'd come to disrupt their lives. She didn't know how to treat me, and she acted like someone who hadn't had much contact with Black people and was overcompensating and fearful she might blurt out something racist.

"So, Maria," she said to me, "even though you were born in Africa and all that and we didn't know you existed, Dorothy is happy to have found you." As an afterthought she added, "And so are we, of course. We knew Dorothy had something up her sleeve with those visits to Minnesota to see her friend Maria. Just goes to show how you can't make judgments about race anymore because you might be related to someone like you."

"Fat Mary, help me! What am I supposed to do about Aunt Marjorie?"

Nothing. Just be yourself, and let her be herself. She is a stranger to you and you to her. Although you're unfamiliar with family dynamics, you already know that your mother isn't the mother of your dreams. You cannot decide not to be a member of her family, but you can decide what members of her family you will let into your life.

"Let me tell you, Fat Mary, I'm not sure about my mother, but I know I really do not like Aunt Marjorie."

When Dorothy came for Thanksgiving, she asked me what I thought about her sister Marjorie. I tried not to be my usual blunt self and spell out in detail why I didn't like her. Attempting to be diplomatic, I said, "It doesn't matter to me whether I ever see her again." Dorothy said nothing.

Every so often Dorothy would do and say things that made me wonder if she had a definition for daughter that no one else knew. One evening as she was knitting away in the living room, I asked her what she was making.

"Sweaters for my grandchildren. I hope to finish them before Christmas."

Seeing she was knitting a dull gray sweater that wouldn't be a color choice for my children, I tried to ease her worry. "Kata and Karl have several sweaters that their grandmother and aunts in Norway have knit for them, so don't worry if they're not done for this Christmas."

"Oh, I mean I'm knitting them for my grandchildren."

"You mean Larry's children?"

"Of course. They expect me to make something for them every year."

She hadn't ever made anything for my children, so I asked her, "What relation are my children to you?"

"Well . . . they are my grandchildren too, I suppose."

"What's there to suppose? Either I'm your daughter and my children are your grandchildren or we're not related."

"It's been so long since I've had my first set of grandchildren that I sometimes forget about your children. Of course, they're my grandchildren too."

"Are you sure?"

"I am."

I swallowed my hurt and pretended I understood her. "In that case, they really have lots of handknit sweaters from their grandmother in Norway. You told me how much you love hooking rugs and knitting afghans. If you want to make something for us, we'd love to have a small rug for the Norwegian room or an afghan for the guest room."

"Great! I prefer that to sweaters. Let's pick out the wool and the other materials tomorrow, and I'll begin right away. I can knit intricate sweater designs only for so long, then my eyes give out."

During another Thanksgiving visit, she told me that she'd bought the *Encyclopedia Britannica* for all her grandchildren because she felt there couldn't be a better gift than the gift of knowledge. I agreed with her. A little further into the conversation, she asked, "What would your children want for Christmas?"

Since she always worried so much about what to give Kata and Karl for Christmas, I answered, "I thought you already bought encyclopedias for your grandchildren. I hope you bought the junior encyclopedia for Karl since he is still so young."

She almost fell off her chair. "You mean I should give them an entire set of encyclopedias just like I gave my grandchildren? They're very expensive, you know!"

"You can give them whatever you want. I was just trying to help. But tell me again, are my children your grandchildren or are only Larry's children your grandchildren?"

"I already told you, they are my grandchildren too."

I couldn't help but compare Cathy's treatment of my children to Dorothy's. Cathy became an instant grandmother to Kata and Karl; she gave them all the love and care, hugs, and gifts that grandmothers usually give. Karl once asked me if Grandma Dorothy knew she was their grandmother. I told him I thought so but he should ask her because she would know for sure. It crossed my mind to ask Cathy to teach Dorothy how to be a good grandmother, but I could only imagine how their conversation might go should Cathy agree to it.

That Christmas, Katarina got her set of *Encyclopedia Britannica*, and Karl got a gift certificate for the junior encyclopedia when he was ready for it.

43

Perils of Parenting

We were looking for a house, and Margaret, the Chinese teacher and dear friend with whom I'd shared a classroom at Central High School, knew of a house we had to see. It was large and contemporary and exactly what we wanted. Windows on one entire wall overlooked Lake Cornelia. Kata and Karl had their own rooms and another room for a playroom. It was more house than I'd ever imagined living in, and the layout provided privacy and room to wander without running into walls every few steps.

At this point in our marriage, we could afford to furnish the house the way we wanted. We also had a growing and eclectic collection of African art. Every room in the house, even the bathrooms, had African masks, tapestries, woven baskets, pottery, wood statues, and sculptures of all sizes, plus folk jewelry, as well as contemporary and traditional paintings.

Kjell commented on the dominance of Africa in our home and understandably wanted equal time for his Norwegian culture. We hired Harley, a contractor, to turn one of the semi-finished rooms in the basement into a Norwegian room complete with pine walls and rosemalled furniture. We transferred the many gifts of pewter, needlepoint wall hangings (many stitched for us by Kjell's mother), and handwoven table runners to the room. When our little project was done, the contrast between the African decor upstairs and Norwegian decor downstairs was so great that one guest joked that passports were needed to go from upstairs to downstairs. As much as I loved the Norwegian room, whenever I entered I felt cold. It

231

reminded me how culturally and temperamentally different my husband and I were.

Harley, a fine carpenter, was nearly seven feet tall. His work uniform consisted of jeans, cowboy boots, and a cowboy hat, and he whistled loudly while he worked. He didn't need a ladder or stool to reach the ceiling, which was amazing to me and fascinating to sixteen-month-old Karl. Whenever he fussed, I took him downstairs to watch Harley, who paid so much attention to Karl that I was afraid he would never finish the job. When he was finally done, he gave little Karl the huge hammer he used. Karl loved that hammer! He tried to drag it everywhere he went, and he wouldn't fall asleep without it. I bought him a light-weight red-and-yellow Playskool hammer to sleep with, but he would have none of it! He cried until I gave him Harley's hammer.

Karl's first words were *buuuut* and *att*, which took us a while to figure out. Of course, he was asking for cowboy boots and a hat just like Harley's. Every night Karl snuggled into bed wearing cowboy boots and a hat and hugging a cold, heavy, fifteen-inch hammer!

Karl was a typical boy in that he got into all sorts of mischief. Once he crawled into the suspended open fireplace in the living room, and we couldn't find him. Only the cloud of ash filling the living room finally gave away his hiding place. When I discovered him, he was covered with ash from head to toe. His curly brown hair was as gray as an old man's, and he'd eaten enough ash and charcoal bits to produce a pile of ash and a pool of vomit on the living-room carpet.

Another time when he'd just learned to stand, I put him in a grocery cart as I shopped at Byerly's food store. I nonchalantly filled my cart with fruit, Pampers, milk, cereal, and laundry detergent. When I looked at the almost full cart, Karl was gone! I moved some stuff from the cart and checked inside it. No Karl! I panicked. I left the cart where it was and ran up and down the aisles, calling his name and asking everyone if they'd seen a little boy crawling around. No one had seen him. I asked for the manager, and he called the police.

I can't tell you what was going on in my mind. I think I went crazy. I had no idea where I was, and I must have been speaking Swahili because I remember the policeman repeatedly asking me if I spoke English. Everyone was searched before they left the store, but there was no Karl.

I went back to my cart to get my purse, which in my turmoil I'd left on top of the groceries. As I dug into my purse for a quarter to call Kjell, I heard something and saw the cart move a little. I quickly tossed all the groceries out of the cart, and whom did I find stretched out on his back, eating the last plum from a container of eight? A dirty-faced, smiling little boy. I kissed and hugged him, paying no attention to the crowd of Edina women gathered around the crazy woman who couldn't speak English, who was covered with purple plum chunks, and who had buried her child under a mountain of groceries. I didn't shop in that store for a long time afterwards.

When Karl was two years old, we sent him to a Montessori School in Edina. One day I was called to the Montessori Nursery School. "Your son bit a little girl on the arm. Her parents have taken her to the hospital for tests, and we hope she's all right."

"You mean he bit her so hard she was bleeding and had to be taken to the hospital?"

"She wasn't bleeding, but you could clearly see tooth marks on her arm."

Instead of apologizing for Karl's apparently aggressive behavior, I got angry. "Are you telling me you think my son has rabies or something? Is that why the little girl has to be tested?"

"It was her parents' decision. I'm afraid you'll have to take your son home until further notice."

I carried heavy Karl on my hip and stormed out of the building. The fight with the little girl he bit must have exhausted him, because he fell fast asleep in the car. I was furious! When I got home, Kjell had arrived.

"Do the school authorities and the parents think that American children never bite and that the only reason Karl bit another child was because his mother is from Africa?"

"Don't be paranoid. Children often bite each other," Kjell calmly explained.

"What are they expecting to find out from the test—that Karl has rabies?"

"I've no idea. Let's ask Karl what happened."

"There you go again with your stupid Norwegian rational ways of discussing with newborns what happened. Sometimes you have to go with your gut feeling and do what comes naturally. I doubt Karl will be able to discuss this to your satisfaction."

By the time Karl woke up, I had calmed down. Kjell sat him on his lap and asked him, "Why did you bite the little girl in school?"

"I bit-ed her 'cuz she kick-ed me."

Kjell then gave Karl a little lecture on fighting, hitting, and biting. I must admit I thought biting was novel, and I wondered why Karl chose to defend himself that way. Luckily, the little girl's pediatrician confirmed that there was no damage done and that he had seen many bitten children in his practice.

Kata seldom got into any mischief. She loved school and was always reflective, considerate, and eager to please. We watched *Sesame Street* and *Mister Rogers' Neighborhood* together while she sang along and drew and colored. One day she said her ears ached and she was feeling dizzy, and she pointed to her nose. She was breathing with difficulty, and her face was turning blue. Praying frantically, I rushed her to the ER. It turned out she had stuffed the eraser end of a pencil way up her nose, where it had broken off and expanded with moisture, making it almost impossible for her to breathe. The doctor sedated her and used a tiny tweezers to pull out the eraser bit by bit.

We had a big scare when Kata was four years old. She had been ill with what we thought were cold or flu symptoms—fever, headache, swollen neck glands, lack of appetite, and extreme fatigue. Her pediatrician told us to take her to the hospital, where we were informed that she had leukemia and would have to begin painful bone-marrow treatments right away. Kjell and I were numbed by the diagnosis. Leukemia in those days was like a death sentence with a long wait before execution.

We couldn't believe it and decided to get additional opinions. A good friend who was a doctor suggested she be tested for the other illnesses with similar symptoms. I can still remember how we hugged each other with tears of gratitude and relief when we learned she didn't have leukemia but mono—infectious mononucleosis. It was an unlikely disease for a child because it typically occurred in teenagers. The virus is spread through saliva, hence another name for mono is the "kissing disease." The cure was rest, rest, rest, and more rest. Kata remained home in bed for three months before she was able to go back to her Montessori preschool.

When Kata was thirteen, she and I went to buy her first bra. We picked out at least ten different styles and colors, and she went into the dressing room and locked the door. I wanted to go in with her, but she wouldn't let me, so I sat on a chair in the lingerie section.

Out of nowhere, I was overcome by a flashback to the trauma of my first bra. I was in middle school, showing off and having a great time dancing inside a circle of other dancers. The headmistress suddenly appeared, yanked me out of the circle, and took me to the infirmary, where she told me to remove my uniform. The nun then wrapped a three-inch-wide bandage tightly around my chest and budding breasts. She told me my breasts were dancing when I was, and since that was sinful, I would have to flatten my chest under that bandage every day. Otherwise I would be expelled from school.

Tears ran down my face as I juxtaposed that scene with the racks of multicolored silk and lace bras all around me in the store with Kata. Should I tell her the story of my first bra? Could I get through it without breaking down? I decided against it, wiped away my tears, and swallowed hard.

When she emerged from the dressing room, I put my arm around her shoulders as she showed me the ones she wanted. I congratulated her on her choices. I felt a profound relief that she was able to take this step into womanhood without trauma.

44

Apartheid

 By 1981 I was teaching a course called Third World Africa at Central High School, and we'd embarked on studying South Africa and apartheid. I was just as amazed as the students were about apartheid, the system of racial segregation enforced by government laws that ensured the dominance of the white population in that complex nation. The country was ruled by the Afrikaners, predominantly Dutch settlers who had arrived in the 1700s and 1800s. To do a good job of teaching about South Africa, I felt I should experience apartheid firsthand. Kjell and I knew we were asking for trouble as an interracial couple traveling to South Africa. Marriage between races was against the law.

For this trip, one of our longer vacations as a family, we took Kata out of school. We traveled with both children in Africa for two months, but the last week they stayed in Nairobi with Thecla and John because we didn't want to take them to South Africa.

On the flight, we met Cindy, a South African of British heritage. She invited us to visit her in Durban when we were in South Africa. Our first stop was Botswana, where we stayed with an American friend and his Chinese wife. He told us that as a mixed couple we'd probably have some trouble, but so long as we were tourists they couldn't do too much. He explained in an ironic tone that once his wife had been designated an "honorary white," they had no more problems.

I had a headache the entire time we were in South Africa. First of all, when we lined up to go through security in Johannesburg

236

airport for our flight to Durban, Kjell went through one door while I was told to go through another.

"She's my wife," Kjell protested. "We're both going through this gate!"

"Not in South Africa, sir."

I watched as he walked through. Once I got through the door, I was taken into a cubicle where the officials went through all my belongings, looking at my lipstick and compact powder case and throwing them on the floor when they were done. They searched and frisked my body so thoroughly that I wished I'd had my period that day to mess them up. It took me a while to collect my belongings from the floor and find my dignity.

"What's holding the bloody kaffir up?" somebody angrily asked, using a racial slur.

When I came out of the cubicle, I saw that Kjell was holding up the line. He refused to go to the other side of the door until he saw me come through. Now Kjell is a gentleman if there ever was one, but you'd never have guessed it that day. He used swear words I didn't know were in his vocabulary.

"I'm not leaving this fucking line until my wife is with me. For all I know, you prehistoric Afrikaner bastards have other plans for her. Why don't you grow up and admit you're so scared and insecure you'll do anything to make yourselves feel superior, fucking idiots."

I walked over to Kjell, wondering what had gotten into him. He didn't say a word to me until we were on the plane. Then it was like nothing happened, and he was back to being the even-tempered Norwegian I knew.

Our friend Cindy was gracious and took us to her country club. Durban was more tolerant than Johannesburg, she told us, "But I love to throw apartheid in their faces." She went out of her way to let everyone know I was her guest—and there were some looks.

At our hotel, the staff knew me. Early one morning we were out for a walk, when my headache got so bad I decided to go back to the room. As I approached the front desk, the attendant threw the room keys over the counter and onto the floor before I asked for them.

Shopping downtown we ran into decent Afrikaner shopkeepers, who warned us to be careful because it was against the law for us to

live together or be seen together in public. They said they personally didn't mind us. "To each his own, but we are definitely in the
minority. We know that marriages like yours occur in England and
America. My sister moved to London two years ago, but she's coming
back. She has to clean her own house, cook meals, and take care of
her babies. White people even wash their own windows there. Can
you imagine that?" he asked, shaking his head in disbelief.

In Johannesburg we stayed at the Carlton Hotel. Below the
Carlton was a classy shopping center. Since it was our wedding anniversary, I went to look for a present for Kjell and, upon Kjell's
insistence, a present for myself from him. The white shopkeepers
were friendly, talkative, and helpful. Then I asked for a restroom.
The shopkeeper whistled and a well-dressed Black woman appeared
from nowhere. "Show her the WC, would you?"

"Yes, sir."

I followed the woman to the WC. A few doors down I noticed
the WC sign on the door. I started to walk in, but the woman pulled
me away.

"Follow me."

I followed her the entire length of the mall, which seemed to be
at least a half-mile, down a stairwell, along a rough cement path, and
down some rickety wood steps. Then I smelled it. In a dark corner I
saw the door: "WC—Coloreds." My urge to pee vanished.

I turned around and walked the depressingly long distance back
to the shopping mall. Since I had already paid for them, I stopped at
the store to pick up my packages, refusing to answer any questions
from the shopkeeper, and went upstairs to my room. Evidently the
shopkeepers didn't mind taking my money, but sharing their toilets
with me was a different matter.

In the evening, we went to dinner at the hotel's fancy restaurant.
Since there was live music, Kjell had asked for a table toward the
front and told them it was our anniversary

"Yes, of course, sir," he was told. "The best table for the lovebirds."

We walked into the restaurant and waited to be seated. The
maître d' called our name, but when he saw us, he said, "Just a
moment."

He returned and told us to follow him. We followed him to the rear of the dining room, where he sat us five inches from the back door.

"Excuse me," Kjell said, "I called yesterday and made reservations to sit toward the front, where we can see the show."

"Sorry, sir, but the front is always reserved for our regular customers."

"There's got to be a better table than this. It's ten o'clock, and the place is hardly full."

"Sorry."

I was afraid Kjell was going to be ungentlemanly again, so I said, "It's our anniversary, and we won't let apartheid spoil it for us. As long as we're sitting together, it doesn't matter where we are. And there's no point leaving, because I'm hungry and I doubt we'll find another place as nice as this to eat."

"I don't like it."

"It's okay. Let's order champagne."

We ordered champagne and fresh lobster tails and had a good meal.

It's an understatement to say that Kjell is not as fond of dancing as I am. But on our anniversary he usually obliges. The band played a song we recognized, and we stood up. We were sitting so far in the back that we didn't notice how big the room was or the beautiful decor. As we approached the dance floor in the center of the room, we heard knives, forks, and spoons drop onto plates, and glasses clink. Once on the dance floor, the band quieted and just about stopped playing. All eyes were on us.

I squeezed Kjell's hand, hoping he'd understand that I didn't want him to curse them out and have us carried off to jail, but it was too late. In the deafening silence, his voice cut the air like the dropped eating utensils. "Bastards!" he shouted. I pulled him off the floor, and we left. I tried not to show my hurt, but I started crying and couldn't stop. I appreciated that Kjell let me cry.

I know why you're crying. Fat Mary's distant voice interrupted my tears. *You are crying for yourself, you are crying for your brothers and sisters in South Africa, you are crying for all the people—Black,*

Indian, and Colored—whose lives are ruled by apartheid. But you are also crying for the whites in South Africa. You know they must be fearful and insecure to deny their fellow human beings their humanity. Nothing about apartheid law can change the person you have become. You must understand that how they treat you is a reflection of how they feel about themselves.

In the morning, for the first time since I'd arrived in South Africa, my headache was gone. All that crying must have flushed out the apartheid toxins from my head. During our last days there, I was able to appreciate what nature had to offer, though in my heart I felt the sadness, suffering, and anger that enfolded the entire country. The native people and topography of the country were breathtakingly beautiful, but for the beholder without inner peace, beauty is often invisible, and without love, beauty can be seen but not felt.

On the plane leaving South Africa, I thanked God for the opportunity to see firsthand the reality of the devalued lives of my sisters and brothers. I prayed for enlightenment, mercy, and forgiveness for both the whites and the Blacks. Alan Paton's book *Cry, the Beloved Country* had exposed the Black South African experience to the world in 1948, but in 1981 I personally experienced the institutionalization and practice of apartheid in living color.

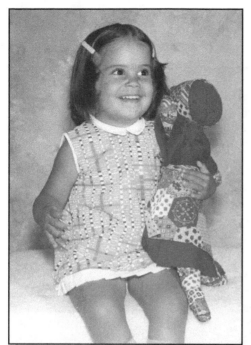

Katarina with African doll
made by her mother.

Karl and Kata.

Cathy, John, Eleanor.

Sister Silvestris with Kata, Maria and Karl
on convent steps at Kifungilo.

Natasha, Maria and Maureen on Trans-Siberian trip.

Teaching Aerobics With Soul® in Japan.

Young Dorothy,
Maria's birth
mother.

Kata and
Dorothy.

Larry, Dorothy and Maria.

Maria with her mother Dorothy

Maria, Karl, Kata and Kjell family portrait.

Family reunion with the Mamers, Berghs and Reiners.

Aerobics With Soul® instructors Diane, Anna, Valandra, Maria, Nedy, and Rachel (front).

Teaching Aerobics With Soul® in Moshi, Tanzania

45

Grandma Silvestris

We couldn't fly directly to Tanzania from South Africa because Tanzania's President Julius Nyerere was a fierce supporter of the African National Congress freedom fighters in South Africa and several other countries. There were military training camps for guerilla warfare in Tanzania. All other ties between Tanzania and the Republic of South Africa were severed because of the apartheid government, so we flew from Johannesburg to Addis Ababa in Ethiopia, then picked up our children in Nairobi and drove across the border to Tanzania.

Because of political disagreements, Kenya and Tanzania, once friendly partners in the East African Community, had closed their borders to each other. Tourists supposedly were able to get through without difficulty, but that was not always the case. Tanzania's foreign exchange reserves were depleted, partly as a result of sending and equipping an army of soldiers to fight in Uganda to overthrow Idi Amin. When Idi Amin became president of Uganda, he attempted to kick all Asians out of the country. They were the economic backbone of Uganda, so the depletion of skilled businessmen and the corruption that followed pitted tribe against tribe, depending on their loyalties. President Idi Amin and his army embarked on gruesome persecution and execution of Ugandans suspected of sympathizing with and benefiting from the mass deportation of Asians. The result was a civil war and the wholesale genocide of smaller tribes that couldn't defend themselves.

I dreaded the inevitable border confrontations with tourists at passport control. Upon entering the country, we had to declare every penny of foreign currency we had on us, and when we left, we had to produce receipts for everything we bought and all our expenses while in the country. If there was a discrepancy between the amount spent and the amount declared, which often happened because tourists couldn't be bothered to save every receipt, all hell broke loose. On departure, customs officials slowly and deliberately took all the time in the world to search bags and suitcases, regardless of how many people were in line. They confiscated whatever they needed or wanted. If they found money, they invariably gave a reason to keep it, the most common one being to accuse the traveler of having lied about the amount upon entering the country. These policies negatively affected tourism in Tanzania. Only businessmen, missionaries, and people who had ties to the country put up with the unbelievable inefficiency, bureaucracy, corruption, and mayhem at the border.

I'd promised Sister Silvestris that the next time we came we'd bring our children to see her. This visit we stayed with my childhood friend Betty and her husband, Frank who lived in Lushoto. They accompanied us to Kifungilo, and we made the usual visits to Gare, where we saw Father Kennedy, and to Sakarani, where we had lunch with Brother Fortunate before we returned to Lushoto for the night.

Sister Silvestris was so excited to see Katarina and Karl that I knew once and for all she had always loved her Kifungilo children. She had become old and frail since I saw her six years earlier, but her tired eyes lit up whenever our children spoke to her and she wouldn't let them leave her side. She held and kissed and hugged them as she had never held, kissed, and hugged us when we were under her care. Karl put on one of my long, bright-red, cotton skirts that buttoned down the front, over his shoulders, his Spiderman T-shirt and boots, and swooshed in front of the convent buildings to Sister's delight. Kata sang for her and read stories from the English textbook she'd taken along for her assignments during the three months she was out of school.

"I miss my children," Sister said from time to time. "Mr. Bergh, you have nice children. I'm happy my Fat Mary brought her children to see me. She was a very good girl and very clever." I felt this might be the last time I'd see Sister Silvestris, so I spent a lot of time just listening to her talk about Kifungilo, her children, and her Wasambaa.

Sister brought her diary to remind her of *zamani*—how things used to be and what she had done in the past. I had a tape recorder and asked her to read from her diary. I can still see her sitting on a Kifungilo-made, straight-backed chair, adjusting her glasses, eager to read her stories to us. On her lap, the red and gold box of Norwegian Kong Haakon chocolates (I called them "King Kong") we had brought for her contrasted with her white habit. Her veil was not the original heavy-duty, starched, penguinlike contraption she had to wear when I was little but a shorter, lighter cotton version. Her small, flat nose reluctantly supported her big black spectacles. She held her leather diary in her hands and laughed as she read. She hadn't written anything bad or sad or unpleasant—I was following along and could see she didn't skip days or paragraphs. She laughed until she cried as she read how we children had eaten the heated bacon strips she used to bring down the swelling from mumps.

Sister Silvestris was tired. She said she didn't want to go to Germany because she was afraid that, like Mother Rufina, she'd die there. "I want to die in Kifungilo. This is my home. These are my people."

She took us to the cemetery to visit the Sisters who had died since I'd left Kifungilo. We walked very slowly. What a contrast to the nun I remembered, who had chased me around the room when it was my turn to get a beating. How furious she'd been when I hid under the bed and she couldn't get to me!

The first grave she took me to was that of Sister Theonesta. "She was in Pemba for many years, but when her last days approached, she came to Kifungilo to die. She loved you very much, Fat Mary."

"I know."

"See, here's Sister Nerea, who ran the dentistry. Do you remember Father Gatang?"

"He died before I left for America."

"And here's Father Jaeckel, our first priest. How he loved you children!"

"I know. We used to go to his house and beg him for food."

"Yes, the children were always hungry. You stole food every day. Do you understand now why I had to beat you?"

"Yes, Sister."

"You always ran away when I beat you, and for that you got more sticks. I loved all my children. Some were really bad, but I loved them too. And here's Heini, our fundi who built so much here. He wanted to be buried in Kifungilo. He was playing the organ in church one day and died suddenly after receiving the Holy Eucharist. Maybe all our prayers for him were answered."

"I hope so. He was often mean to us. I'll never forget the day he made us crawl on our knees on the gravel all the way from the brick pit to the school, just because we tore down the wall he was building."

Sister always gave a *zawadi* (gift) to people before they left Kifungilo. Our *zawadi* this trip were a gold and silver crucifix for Kjell and me, a leather-bound prayer book for me, a small painting of Jesus with the little children in a gilded frame, several holy cards of the saints and the Virgin Mary for Katarina, and a colorful picture of Jesus in the Garden of Gethsemane for Karl.

We had one more week on our visas, so we decided to climb Mount Kilimanjaro, the highest peak in Africa (19,340 feet), the "roof of Africa." Kata and Karl stayed in the care of my good friends Fatima and Abdu Faraji on their thirty-two-acre coffee farm in Usa River, just outside of Arusha. Along with the arabica coffee that they harvested, roasted, and packaged, they had cows, goats, ducks, chickens, and every tropical fruit and flower imaginable. They sold their coffee, eggs, cheese, and yogurt to hotels and Tanzanian co-operatives, as well as to expatriates. They used bio-gas from cow manure for cooking and lighting when electricity wasn't available.

Despite our last-minute decision, we were able to rent used climbing equipment and clothing and leave with a group via the Marangu route. Expert guides and hardy, cheerful porters carried our tents, food, water, and bags, singing and laughing on the way. It takes a village—I doubt hikers could reach the peak if they had to carry their supplies and gear. The gradual hike lasts five days— three days up to reach Uhuru Peak and two days coming down. I had a hard time looking up at the beautiful, clear sky because my small backpack weighed me down. I finally asked a porter to help me. After the third day, hiking became a real effort because of the dwindling oxygen at higher altitudes.

With the ill-fitting rented clothing and boots, I was miserable and cold from the first day, and my fingers froze on the third day. Kjell developed a severe headache and was showing signs of high-altitude pulmonary edema, so when we got to the Kibo hut (at 15,520 feet), our guide suggested we hike back to Horombo hut (12, 205 feet) and descend with our group on the fifth day. We were disappointed not to reach the peak. Kjell vowed he would attempt the climb again the first opportunity he had, while I vowed just to admire this snow-capped mountain in Tanzania from a distance. He tried to assure me that Kilimanjaro was not a technical climb, and with enough mental preparation and our own hiking gear, we would definitely make it, but I had no desire ever to feel that cold again.

I will always remember my Kilimanjaro climb from the chill in my bones and the fear I would lose my fingers from frostbite. Then there was the Japanese tourist riding a bicycle along the "saddle"—a flat section of alpine dessert between Kibo and Mawenzi peaks—when I had all I could do to put one foot in front of the other. I won't forget that our group of six hikers were at first formal and shy about relieving ourselves, trying to hide behind a bush or small boulder. But somewhere along the road, we threw modesty down the mountain and squatted a couple of feet from the path in open air to do our business as other hikers passed by without notice. Finally, I treasure the overwhelming spiritual experience of the sunrise above the clouds, turning the moonlike landscape a majestic crimson and yellow of the deepest hues I'd ever seen and slowly piercing the clouds to greet and bless the population nestled on the slopes of Africa's majestic mountain.

Back in Arusha, I described my ordeal to Fatima, who declared that America had softened me up. "Students at Weru Weru Girls Secondary School at the foot of Mount Kilimanjaro have to climb to Uhuru Peak as a requirement for graduation—and they climb without porters or expensive hiking clothes and gear!" My admiration for girls studying in Tanzania increased even more, but I remained content with my memories.

Throughout that visit to Tanzania, I realized there was a hopelessness and feeling of despair in most of the people we saw, from Sister Silvestris to Sister Eileen to Betty and Frank. Nyerere's Ujamaa policies had bankrupted the country. Even in Lushoto, the fruit and vegetable basket of Tanzania, people walked about with blank faces and empty bodies. The country had become poorer and poorer with each year Ujamaa was in force. People were hungry, sick, and desperate. Shelves in the stores were bare. We drove everywhere, so we bought a loaf of bread wherever we could and used peanut butter and jelly I'd brought from the States. Even the hotels had little or no food. In one we were served a hardboiled egg and a cup of tea for breakfast. On the road from Namanga at the Kenya border, people stood on the road, trying to sell us a quarter bar of soap or dried up bread.

When we crossed the border to return to Nairobi, Kata and Karl were thrilled to enter a store and find merchandise on the shelves. With delight, they showed me a toothbrush, comb, pen, a box of biscuits, and they were ecstatic to find a packet of spearmint gum.

When we were visiting Betty and Frank in Lushoto, their housekeeper fell on his knees in front of Kjell and begged him to bring the *wazungu* back saying, "Nowadays in Tanzania, we are the poorest of the poor. Life was much better before independence. Nowadays we suffer too much. Everything is difficult. Finding food is difficult. We, the Wasambaa, are so poor, I am speechless."

How desperate must someone be to prefer the bad old days of white rule to independence and Black rule? Had he forgotten the human indignities we endured under the British, who believed they were genetically, intellectually, culturally, and morally superior to us? If a government cannot provide its citizens with their daily needs, the color of the official in charge is of no consequence. I personally believe, however, that poverty and corruption inflicted by one's own people is a tiny bit more palatable than poverty inflicted by foreigners who exploit you and insist that their race is superior to yours.

My trip to Africa provided lots of topics for classroom discussion. We studied each of the more than fifty African countries, and when we came to South Africa, we studied a play based on the life and death of Steve Biko. Like Nelson Mandela, who was imprisoned for treason on Robben Island, Biko, a radical student activist against apartheid, was arrested and imprisoned in Port Elizabeth in September 1977. They held him naked for eighteen days in a tiny cell, interrogated, tortured, and starved him. When he asked for medical attention, they threw him in the back of a Land Rover and transported him naked to Pretoria. He died in transit. Although there was a trial and his white guards admitted their part in his death, they went free. Biko's death was the catalyst that galvanized human rights activists around the world to become involved in the internal affairs of South Africa.

We discussed the economic sanctions imposed by the United States on South Africa, comparing and contrasting race relations in America and in South Africa. When it came to race and discrimination, most of my students felt the only difference between the two countries was that in America, it was against the law to discriminate against someone on the basis of color or race. In South Africa, Blacks said that at least they knew what they could and could not do. In America, the law says there's nothing you cannot do because of your race, yet in practice we know it is quite another matter.

Several students wanted to know what they could do to help the people of South Africa. I told them it was important to fight racism wherever and however it shows up in their lives.

"Will apartheid ever end?"

To answer them, I quoted Peter Gabriel's song "Biko":

You can blow out a candle, but you can't blow out a fire.

When the flame begins to catch, the wind will burn it higher.

46

Mommy Dearest

Larry invited me to Boston to meet his family and spend a few days at their vacation house in Nahant. Their beautiful brownstone in Boston had African carvings and paintings scattered among an eclectic collection of international art. His wife, Anita, was one of those reserved intellectual people who's not easy to have a conversation with, but I liked her because I could feel her soul. Her long-suffering expression made her seem older than her years, and her body language communicated pain. She talked to me about their early years and how Larry wanted children right away when she wasn't ready for them. She gave in and had three, but then Larry immersed himself in his work. Their children called me Aunt Maria right away and couldn't hear enough about life in Tanzania. Apparently their father, like their grandmother, didn't talk much about Africa to them.

While I was in Massachusetts, Dorothy came to visit, joining Larry and me at their vacation house in Nahant. I thought it would be a great time alone with my newfound family, but it was not to be. While with them, I felt a little strange calling my mother Dorothy when Larry called her Mom. I remembered how long I'd waited for the day when I too could call someone Mom.

The fireplace was glowing in the living room, and Dorothy and I were having a cup of tea as we enjoyed the ocean view. I was feeling warm and included, maybe even loved, so I decided to ask her, "Can I call you Mom from now on?"

"No," was the abrupt and firm reply.

I hadn't expected that. I tried to hide my surprise and hurt by jokingly asking, "Is Mother better?"

"No!" was her obviously premeditated answer. "Call me Dorothy."

Suddenly I was back at the orphanage. Wasn't this the woman who, for reasons I'll never know, did not want to raise me herself so sent me away to be brought up by nuns? What made me think that just because she looked for me thirty-three years later she was ready to claim me as her daughter? Was I a fool to have drawn conclusions, or would anyone assume that after looking for me and finding me she'd want to reestablish a bond between us that she had so abruptly ended when I was less than a week old? Her unwillingness to have me call her Mom explained her difficulty regarding my children as her grandchildren.

She didn't explain why she wanted me to call her Dorothy, and I didn't ask. To me she was the unknown and unattainable woman I'd longed to call Mom many years earlier. But to her, I was the unwanted and inconvenient daughter she had kept track of on the condition that she alone would define the relationship she'd have with me.

The rest of my time in Nahant I was miserable. The nightmares I'd had about life in Kifungilo came back full force. The feelings of being unwanted and unloved by my mother were so strong and real that I almost told Dorothy I didn't want to see her again. That would have been a big decision, and I needed to consult with someone—someone who fully understood me because she knew me better than I knew myself.

Fat Mary and I were in the presence of the woman who caused us much pain, sorrow, and confusion, and we were stunned by her rejection of me once again. Fat Mary took the time to count my present blessings and told me I was loved by too many people to let my mother jeopardize the growth in love, confidence, and peace I had attained without her.

Maybe she is consumed with guilt. Maybe she is keenly aware of her mistakes and regrets her choices in life. Above all, maybe she knows she's unworthy of that name. Don't try to understand her. Be grateful for everything she has affirmed about you. Calling her Mom wouldn't change your childhood. Her absence when you needed her most left a hole in your heart that not even she can mend. Maybe she knows that.

In 1983, we held a family reunion at our house in Edina. From the Norwegian contingent Kjell's parents, his brother and his wife and son, and one of his two sisters and her husband and son, were able to make it. On my side were John and Cathy, their daughter Eleanor, John's parents, my brother Larry with his wife and three children, my mother Dorothy, and my husband and children.

Dorothy and Liv, Kjell's mother, got along beautifully, though I don't think there's anyone in this world who wouldn't get along with Liv. For the first time, I heard Dorothy brag about her Norwegian roots. Her Norwegian father and German-Irish mother were married in Stavanger, Norway. She and her sisters had spoken Norwegian as children. She remembered several phrases like *takk for mat,* and she recited grace before meals in an old Norwegian dialect. As I looked at everyone at the reunion, I was reminded that we don't really choose our families, and we have no choice but to accept them. I was adjusting to my dream of having an extended family, but I must admit, it felt a little heavy.

47

Aerobics With Soul®

Right before the family reunion, I realized that most of the sixty-five pounds I'd gained carrying Karl still clung to me. I was chubby and chunky, flabby, and out of shape. If I wanted to keep my husband with his aversion to fat people, continue to dance, and get into the African outfits tailored for me in Nairobi, I had to do something. I registered at Lonna's Hot Workouts, an exercise studio in Edina, and began exercising in earnest. After a year of working out there five times a week, I realized that the minimal results I got from such dedication were out of proportion to the blood, sweat, tears, and money I'd invested.

I was still dancing for Young Audiences, but by choice my bookings were fewer, and the dance demonstrations I did for the children hardly burned any calories. At the workout studio, I felt like a fish out of water. The room was big, cold, and antiseptic looking. Students paraded in their latest dance leotards and checked each other out as they exercised. The class was mostly subdued, even when the movements warranted a groan or two or the music begged for singing the refrains.

One Saturday morning in the hip Electric Workout class, I was enjoying a music selection (ordinarily I did not like the music as it was too static, structured, and electronically synthesized), and I let it carry me into laughter and song, which automatically led me to do my own thing—African tribal dancing. Several others joined in, enjoying the break from the routine, but after class a man came up to me and asked, "Are you a maniac? Do you think you're back in Africa?"

I realized I did not enjoy working out there and must have been doing something wrong because every morning I woke up with a lower backache. I remembered how I loved my African dances and never felt as exhausted after dancing as I felt after a studio class. I decided to use African dance to get back into shape and stay fit.

I taped a series of songs on a cassette, mostly from Miriam Makeba and Olatunji, and danced by myself at home. I don't know if I lost weight or toned up those first months dancing alone, but I thoroughly enjoyed myself. And that's when I decided to create my own workout.

Off I went to the library to research guidelines for a dance-aerobics class. Lonna's Hot Workout classes served as an example of structure, content, goals, and safety tips for the class. I took slow movements from certain African dances I'd learned in high school and choreographed a fifteen-minute warm-up. I then did a thirty-five-minute aerobic section of faster tribal dances and a ten-minute cooldown. I knew that to get good results, a series of movements or exercises had to be repeated over a period of time. My biggest problems at Lonna's was that I didn't enjoy the spot-specific exercises for reducing fat, and I wasn't as focused on results as most classes demanded. I just wanted to dance freely, naturally, have fun, sweat, and lose weight.

I wrote down the choreography word by word, line by line, for the workout I'd put together. By the time I was done, I had twenty-one handwritten pages. I did the program twice a week at home and went to Lonna's three times a week. Eventually I went to the exercise studio only once a week, mostly to keep up with the new trends and guidelines from fitness organizations. I bought every record and cassette tape of African music I could find in the Twin Cities and combed libraries for music I could borrow and tape at home. I used this music for the five-minute free dance I incorporated into my otherwise choreographed workout. I didn't know it then, but I was embarking on a labor of love that would consume me for the rest of my life. I was giving birth to *Aerobics With Soul®*.

I am thankful for the classes I took at Lonna's because they showed me what I didn't want in my workout. I wanted *Aerobics With Soul®* to stress the process of getting fit rather than goals. It had to be joyful, natural, spontaneous, inclusive, social, and celebratory, and above all, it had to be soulful. Every participant would know what "soul" meant to them and be able to dance from that place.

I envisioned *Aerobics With Soul*® as a unique and innovative use of traditional African dance modified for exercise. I would use our khangas (multicolored fabrics worn by women and men in East Africa) to add visual ethnic flair and as weights to tone arms and upper body when we formed a circle to do the high-energy khanga dance. We would also tie them around our hips to give the illusion of big, desirable hips when we shook them. My program would be multidimensional and have several levels. I combined the guidelines of the American fitness industry with the magic and creativity of African dance that taps into the mind for inspiration and heart for feeling and expression. I especially emphasized the social aspect of African dance.

When we dance in Africa, we don't check each other out for age, size, or wealth. We all come as we are—from crawling babies to hunched-over great-grandmothers and grandfathers leaning on canes. We bring our personal uniqueness and gifts to the dance and take what others have to offer. We do not have to be the same. A two-year-old will dance as a two-year-old; a teen will show off; a great-grandma will dance slowly with dignity. We express our joy and sorrow, fear and courage, happiness and despair, and love openly and honestly to each other.

Another reason I created my workout was to expose Americans to African culture in a form that could be incorporated into their daily lives. For many, Africa is a spectator culture. People watch our dances and TV documentaries, observe and photograph us and our animals, but we remain distant and exotic. Using African dance as a form of fitness is a pleasant and natural way to expose Americans to African culture. I also realized that most Americans aren't aware of contemporary African music. As an educator, the educational aspect of *Aerobics With Soul*® was important to me. Was it possible to incorporate all these elements of African dance into a fitness program?

My family usually spent two weeks together around Christmastime in Montserrat, the sweet and beautiful tiny island in the West Indies where we had a small condominium. Because I barely functioned in the Minnesota winters and often crashed my car, Kjell felt it would be safer and cheaper for me to remain longer on the island. He took the kids back home with him, and I convinced myself it would give him quality bonding time with his children.

Three times a week during my time in Montserrat in 1981, I tried out *Aerobics With Soul®* on the Montserratians and expatriates who lived on the little island. It was the perfect place for me to polish my program because my clients loved to dance and loved African music. They encouraged me so much that I was sure I could develop a fitness program that would work in the States. While I knew that *Aerobics With Soul®* was not for everybody, I was sure it would fill its own niche, as other fitness programs did. Achieving the most popular fitness program status was not my goal.

The difference between *Aerobics With Soul®* and other exercise classes was captured by a young man who came to my classes in Montserrat that first year. Michael Milgraum was visiting his expat parents and as a farewell gift to me, he wrote a perfect definition of my new creation:

Aerobics With Soul®

Listen to the beat, listen to the beat.
Feel it in your heart, stomp it with your feet.
Hear the music playing for the melodies are sweet.
Listen to the beat, listen to the beat.

How can I describe it, how to even start?
Is that music drumming or the drumming of my heart?
Find my true potential, music is a key.
Mind and body dancing, set my spirit free.

Poetry of motion, beauty filled with poise.
Hear the inner music, quell distracting noise.
Living with one purpose, to find harmony,
To be whole and graceful, to be one with me.

Hips in constant motion, swaying to the sound.
Arms are undulating, chin swings up and down.
Skin damp and glowing, sparkling with the light.
Eyes alive and vibrant, joyful and so bright.

Music sings within me, music sings without,
Joins our souls together, conquers fear and doubt.
Dance my own variation, just unique to me,
Of eternal music in humanity.

Smiling with the song, listen to the beat.
Feel it in your heart, stomp it with your feet.
Hear the music playing, for the melodies are sweet.
Listen to the beat, listen to the beat.

On my return to the States, I immediately developed more workout levels, from beginner to advanced, and began holding regular classes in my home. To incorporate the important social aspect of my classes, I invited my clients to stay for tea after class. This turned out to be one of the best aspects of teaching *Aerobics With Soul*® at home. Many lifelong friendships developed because of the intimate setting, which opened the door to discussing not only the workout they had just done but also the happenings in their lives. This was one aspect of the "soul" in *Aerobics With Soul*®—the special feeling of being comfortable in our skins with nothing to fear and no need to prove ourselves to others.

Even though I didn't think being a certified instructor would change anything about my program, to give professional credibility to *Aerobics With Soul*®, I got certification to teach group classes from both the International Dance Exercise Association (IDEA) and the American Council on Exercise (ACE).

Before I knew it, I was being asked to perform and teach with my devoted and talented instructors in schools, private clubs, churches, organizations like the YWCA, and at fitness and cultural conventions. I did local, national, international radio, and TV interviews and demonstrations. I danced at the Governor's Residence in Minnesota and danced and taught in Japan, Kenya, Tanzania, South Africa, the Virgin Islands, Turkey, Norway, Mexico, Chile, Russia, Alaska, and even on an oil rig in the North Sea.

Three performances stand out. I did a solo opening dance with the Minnesota Orchestra at Orchestra Hall for Black History Month. When I went home that night, it seemed unreal that I danced with a world-renowned orchestra.

The second performance was one for the Minneapolis Society for the Blind. I was happy to do this even though a few of my friends questioned the appearance. I told them it wasn't necessary to see the performance to feel the dance in your heart. Unfortunately for me, several of the blind audience members had seeing-eye dogs with them. Halfway through the routine, I used a police whistle to mark the beat for a certain dance. Three German shepherds bolted towards the stage, barking at me and showing their teeth. Given my fear of dogs—and any animal for that matter—I instinctively jumped off the stage and flew out of the room faster than the dogs could run. It took the dogs' owners and the sighted organizers some time to subdue the dogs and even longer for me to compose myself enough to finish the performance. I was told that seeing-eye dogs are often trained with this type of whistle. At future performances, whenever I saw a dog in the audience, I asked to have it removed as a safety precaution.

An oil rig in the middle of the North Sea of Norway was probably the strangest and scariest setting where *Aerobics With Soul®* was taught. Einar, my brother-in-law, who worked for the Norwegian oil company, arranged a tour of the rig for Kjell and me and asked me to dance for the employees who lived and worked on the gigantic oil platform. We were outfitted in bright orange and black insulation overalls that made ghostbusters' outfits look fitted! Taken by helicopter from the mainland, we were deposited on the top-floor landing pad where a freezing wind whipped around us.

I have an abnormal fear of heights, and we had to walk down six long, narrow, meshed metal flights of stairs as the merciless wind assaulted us. If you dared to look down through the mesh steps, you saw nothing but the deep, dark ocean. My oversized suit with attached shoes made it impossible to see the steps, and I was sure I was going to miss one and fall into the sea several stories below. I turned around to slowly back down the steps, but the people behind me were piling up. Although they only spoke Norwegian, I understood they were getting impatient. I wrapped my huge mitt around the tiny rail, hung on for dear life, and let them pass. I watched in disbelief as five cheerful Norwegians ran down the steps, conversing and laughing as if they were dashing along a path to go fishing in a fjord. Kjell must have seen the petrified look on my face because he walked back up the steps, pried my hands off the rail, scooped me up, and carried me down to the hotel on the rig.

Before I gave my class that evening, there was another horrifying requirement—a fire drill. When I looked at the step-by-step instructions and illustrations of how to evacuate the rig in case of a fire, I knew that if an emergency occurred, it would claim my life because I would not enter the ejection capsule, no matter what. We had to put on a full-body life vest and enter a passenger capsule, which would be shot from the platform by a device that looked very much like a cannon and supposedly land near waiting lifeboats on the surface of the ocean far from the rig. When a crew member knocked on the door, announcing in Norwegian that everyone had to be up on the platform for the drill, I hid under the narrow bed and held my breath. He called and knocked several more times as if he knew someone was inside, but lucky for me, he didn't open the door. I think fear kept me from thinking straight because it was, after all, only a drill, and they were not going to eject people from the rig that day.

Uncharacteristically, the Norwegians on Gullfaks B oil platform really let loose for my class. Maybe it was because they worked on the rig for weeks at a time before returning to land and needed a release and some fun, but they did *Aerobics With Soul*® like pros!

48

A Leg Up on the Trans-Siberian

Maureen was one of my closest teacher friends at Central High School and a renowned magnet school English instructor. She was also an intrepid traveler, with an enormous sense of adventure and appreciation of other cultures—all this despite having a prosthetic leg. She had lost her leg due to cancer in her twenties. During our lunch breaks at Central, Maureen and I worked on a travel plan that started with a visit to Japan, where Natasha, an exceptionally bright student while at Central, was now a Rotary scholar in Nagasaki. The three of us planned to ride the Trans-Siberian train from Beijing to Leningrad in the summer of 1984.

Natasha's well-to-do and gracious Japanese host family invited us for dinner at an elegant restaurant, with the meal cooked hibachi style in front of us. I managed to eat the raw and almost-live things that were served and enjoy the wine and sake.

In Nagasaki, we visited the site where the atomic bomb was dropped by the American government during the Second World War. The videos at the museum made the horror of the bomb real—from the devastation of the population and the destruction of the land to the disfiguring, cancerous growths that survivors of the bomb suffered. The Peace Garden, with gut-wrenching sculptures of human torment placed among dancing water fountains, intricate landscapes, and manicured trees and bushes, was built as a memorial to those killed by the bomb. It was at once beautiful in its lament and remembrance and troubling in its depiction of the violent act it commemorated. On a sidewalk near the epicenter was the shadow of a man eerily and eternally imprinted into the concrete by the incinerating heat of the atom bomb at the moment of explosion.

Maureen, Natasha, and I boarded the Shinkansen (bullet train) and traveled to Osaka and Tokyo, visiting religious shrines, museums, and attending Kabuki Theatre performances. We even saw the uniformed and gloved "people shovers" packing commuters into trains at rush hour.

Throughout our trip, we witnessed the popularity of Michael Jackson and his music. Natasha's host family had a huge poster of *Thriller* and owned almost all of his albums. The family planned a dance party to say goodbye to Natasha and asked me to give an *Aerobics With Soul*® demonstration. Japanese and African ways of moving are spectacularly different. We all laughed as family and guests tried to imitate my moves. Maybe my class got things going, because the guests loosened up and danced the rest of the evening to Japanese and American popular music.

We flew to Beijing, and after a few days of sightseeing at the usual tourist attractions, we boarded a Chinese train to begin our Trans-Siberian trip. We traveled second class, which meant uncomfortable and narrow berths. Black soot covered everything from the dim bulb in the center of the ceiling to the screenless windows to our rock-hard pillows and rough cotton sheets. We tried to keep the window open during the trip, but clouds of pollution from factories along the railway rolled in. Having been spoiled by the material comforts of life in the United States, I was at first alarmed at the austerity of the train. But I quickly reverted to my childhood bare-necessity survival mode, and then little bothered me.

We were each given one sixteen-ounce thermos bottle of hot water to take care of all our needs for the day—drinking, bathing, and doing our wash. Water trickled in intermittent drops from the rusty faucet in the bathroom. The large windows in the corridor of the car provided a view of China and Mongolia that helped ease some of the unpleasantness inside the train. There was so little food in the dining car that if we weren't the first ones for meals, hardly anything worth eating was left. Unfortunately, everyone on the train caught on to this, so we spent most of our time lining up for the dining car and then lining up for the toilet.

Whenever in my travels I encountered unsanitary, smelly toilets like the one on the train, I longed for the African bush, where I could be free to relieve myself deep into the clean, dry ground, with only birds, lizards, ants, insects, and an occasional snake to watch me. In Swahili slang, we call relieving yourself in the bush *kuchimba dawa*, which literally means "to dig for medicine" or "to bury your medicine."

When we crossed the border into the Soviet Union, everything changed, including the gauge of the train tracks. The attendants were Russian and spoke only Russian. In China, the classes I had taken before the trip didn't do me any good because the only thing I could remember in Chinese was "Hello" and "Would you please show me your passport?" I used these Chinese phrases when body and sign language failed to break the ice, and people went out of their way to help us. In Russia, we depended on Natasha, who had studied Russian at Central High School and spoke enough to get us out of most jams.

We took on the role of informal ambassadors for the spirit of America. Here we were, three Americans: Maureen, a middle-aged, smiling, dignified white lady with a cane; a young freckle faced girl with short, straight, dark-brown hair and a Russian name; and me—a thirty-something brown lady with curly hair and an accent.

Our berth on the Russian train was even more austere than the one we had on the Chinese train. There were four beds—two on either side of an aisle that was so narrow we could hardly turn around. Maureen took the bottom bed away from the door. Natasha slept on the bed above her, and I slept on the bottom across the aisle.

The very first night we heard a knock on our door at 3 a.m. "Customs inspection," announced a Russian dressed in a tan uniform. We left the room and sleepily watched them search our room and go through our luggage. The only thing they took from us was our reading material. They confiscated Maureen's *Time* magazines, my *Ebony* and *Prevention* magazines, and all the books we had brought to read on the long Trans-Siberian trip. Natasha asked why they were taking our stuff. They told us that bringing subversive reading material into the country was forbidden. They ignored our argument that it was only for our personal use and insisted it was the law and there was nothing to discuss.

The second night, another customs official knocked on our door at 2:30 in the morning and demanded we get out while he conducted another inspection. We argued in vain that we had already been inspected and had nothing to hide. This time, he took some of my audiocassette tapes and tape player. He said music was subversive and that importing electronic equipment like my tape recorder was forbidden. There was nothing we could do. I was upset that they took my music. I could part with my magazines, but I couldn't live without my music. They hadn't taken my African music cassettes, but what use were they to me without a tape player?

The next night I took action. When my roommates were sound asleep, I quietly got up and put a stocking on Maureen's prosthetic leg, then hung it from the light bulb in the middle of the cabin. Sure enough there was a knock on the door at 2 a.m. No one stirred. Three louder knocks. I pretended to be fast asleep. The inspector then pushed the door open, causing Maureen's prosthetic leg to swing back toward the window and then forward to hit him in the face. In his confusion, he shut the door behind him. I heard his muffled shouts and grunts.

By then we had realized these weren't customs inspections; this guy was coming to see what else he could take from us. He struggled in the darkness, trying to grab whoever had kicked him. The more he reached for the leg, the more it swung away, only to return and smack him in the face, shoulders, and stomach. Confused and disoriented, he fell over our belongings piled on the floor. No matter which direction he turned in his panic, the swinging leg got him. Eventually he found the door handle and escaped down the hallway.

During the entire commotion, I prayed to God that Maureen and Natasha wouldn't wake up. He answered my prayers, and I congratulated myself on my brilliant idea. Then it occurred to me—what if the leg had gotten damaged? With all that swinging around, it could have been poked enough to make the filling spill out. Or its foot might have been broken or the ankle bent. What if Maureen couldn't use it? We still had several more weeks on the Trans-Siberian train. How would she have managed? Despite my momentary remorse I was pleased, because for the remainder of the trip we had no more midnight inspections.

Traveling in the Soviet Union under communism meant that we had to plan, book, and pay for our trip a year in advance. We stayed at Intourist Hotels, followed a strict itinerary, and could go nowhere without our guides, who all spoke excellent English. Helena, our guide in Irkutsk, took us to several quaint Orthodox churches and to the beautiful, clear, and deep Lake Baikal. Because Helena was so eager to accommodate us, I asked her to show us more of her city than what was prescribed by the Intourist organization.

Our second night in Irkutsk, she took us to a nightclub for dinner and dancing. The Russians danced their traditional dances to contemporary Russian, Beatles, and American Country Western music. Since everyone was doing the Russian thing, I danced my African thing to the fascination and cheers of the crowd. In America, after I married, whenever I did my own dancing on the dance floor, people watched and smiled with approval but few danced with me. Here, though, the Russians lined up to dance with me and had no inhibitions about trying to do what I was doing. They drank glass after glass of vodka straight up, and if standing was a problem, dancing didn't seem to be.

We met two young men who knew quite a bit of English because they worked as naval spies listening in on U.S. nuclear submarines. One of the men was a top gymnast who would have been at the 1984 Olympics in Los Angeles had it not been boycotted by the Russians in response to the U.S. boycott of the 1980 Summer Olympics in Moscow. They persuaded Natasha and me to join them on a night ride into the Siberian *taiga*.

I marveled at the eerie stillness and chilling beauty of the scenery of the immense coniferous forest. A car breakdown on the way back to the hotel, however, led to an encounter with two fearsome Communist Party officials, one with a missing eye and no patch over the eye socket, who bragged loudly about his party credentials and insisted on seeing the party cards of the two men we were with. The anticipated adventure in the Siberian taiga with locals turned into a nightmare and nearly caused us to miss our train!

In Novosibirsk, our guide was Alevtina, an elementary school English teacher, who took us to the traditional tourist sites but also to the ballet and the circus. Good seats cost next to nothing, and entire families of every social class attended the performances. Alevtina took us shopping at foreign-exchange shops open only to tourists and then to the market, where we were offered amber necklaces and religious icons in exchange for our jeans. I had no problem stripping down to my panties right there at the market place to exchange my worn jeans for a palekh troika box that would have cost hundreds of dollars in the States. I bought a brightly flowered fuchsia and green babushka for five rubbles and wrapped it around me like a khanga for the rest of the day.

At the market, there were Azerbaijani merchants with their wives and children, Georgian merchants and customers, and White Russian peasants. Everyone was friendly. We accepted with gratitude fresh fruit from the vendors as our meals at the Intourist Hotel almost never included fruits or vegetables.

Alevtina invited us to her apartment, and we were thrilled because we hadn't been to a home during our Trans-Siberian trip. As a teacher, she was able to get an apartment for herself, and she was happy with it despite the graffiti on the walls of her building and the dirty, forlorn, neglected look of the place. Her apartment consisted of a living room and a bedroom; she shared a toilet, cold-water bath, and stove with four other families. She was proud of her decorated living room—austere by our standards—and served us tea in a dull green tea set that she treated with reverence because it belonged to her grandmother. We were sad to say goodbye to Alevtina because she was so open with us and told us so much about daily Russian life.

The next morning, we boarded our rickety, dirty, overcrowded train and continued on to Moscow. The second week on the train, we met an African man who invited us to his compartment for vodka and Cadbury chocolates. We discussed politics, listened to African music on his brand-new cassette player, and tried to dance in the tiny space. It seems our inspectors mostly wanted American items, so the African traveler was not inspected and nothing of his was confiscated. To pass the time, I borrowed his player and often did *Aerobics With Soul®* in the narrow corridors of the train. It wasn't long before other passengers—men, women, and children—joined me, and we danced our way across Siberia to African music and Russian folksongs. One of the participants and her husband invited me to their cabin in first class. Wow! They had crisp white linens, towels, soap, toilet paper, and wine. The walls were of gleaming mahogany. They even had framed pictures on the walls. They asked me to join them for wine in the evenings, and I did, mostly because I wanted to use their wonderful toilet.

Along the way, we acquired a male roommate for the empty bunk above me. He was a quiet soldier in uniform who was also a doctor. Within minutes of our introductions, he started singing "Billie Jean" in barely recognizable English. Since he loved "Mee-kar-elle Chak-soon," I gave him my Michael Jackson cassette tapes, which the inspectors hadn't confiscated, and he kissed me with gratitude!

Moscow was full of history, art, museums, churches, tombs, department stores, and parks chock-full of statues. We visited them all and went to a performance of *Swan Lake* by the Kirov Ballet at the theater in the Kremlin. At our hotel, I met Anatole, a diplomat from the Democratic Republic of the Congo, who invited me for dinner at a restaurant exclusively for the diplomatic corps and then to a private violin concert at his ambassador's residence. I was so excited at the possibility of seeing real food and drink again that I accepted, then realized all I had to wear was the one skirt and washable silk blouse I'd worn for all the cultural events of our trip.

At the diplomat restaurant, I was surprised to see so many limousines, Rolls Royces, Jaguars, Bentleys, Cadillacs, and Mercedes Benzes—more than I had seen in my entire life in America! The restaurant was elegant; the men were dressed in suits, while the mostly foreign women wore designer couture. Anatole treated me to an opulent, extravagant dinner that I would never have believed existed in the Soviet Union—champagne, caviar, pâtés, asparagus, filet mignon, basmati rice, pastries, exquisite cheeses, crème brulée, espresso coffee, and liqueurs whose names I couldn't pronounce, all served by scantily clad waitresses. I was astounded and disconcerted. I couldn't believe I was in Moscow—the seat of communism and the enemy of capitalism. The concert at the residence was more of the same, except that the women were now wearing long evening gowns. More scantily clad waitresses and champagne flowing like water before the concert—then after the concert a live band played and the party began in earnest. Of course, I danced! Poor Anatole—we hardly had a dance together. Being the cultured diplomat, he stepped back when he was tapped on the shoulder and let others dance with me.

On the way back to the hotel, Anatole told me I reminded him of his wife and so would not invite me to his apartment. I was afraid he would expect me to pay him back somehow for giving me such a good time, but he was truly a gentleman. He also told me his three-year-old son had sickle cell anemia and was too sick to be transported to Paris for treatment. He thanked me for helping him end a hard day on a high note and hoped we could keep in touch. I thanked him for a memorable time, exchanged addresses, and he squeezed my hand goodbye.

In Leningrad, right outside our hotel window, we saw a parade of ships celebrating a Russian naval anniversary. The ships, historical and otherwise, majestically flowed by the hotel with bands, orchestras, and choirs on board. I watched as each one disappeared around the bend in the river.

Our next visit was to the State Hermitage Museum. I can't even begin to describe the effect it had on me. I couldn't get enough of it and all the magnificent art it contained. I'm well aware of the issues surrounding art masterpieces exported from their countries of origin to museums far away, but I was grateful to see such an impressive collection of the world's art in one place.

Maureen, Natasha, and I had a final fancy dinner our last night together before they left by boat for Helsinki and I flew to Oslo to meet Kjell. He had just arrived a few days earlier with a trade delegation from Minnesota but insisted on flying home with me. He said he had something to show me and wanted to be there when I first saw it.

49

Taj Ma Gym

While I was away, my beloved husband had managed to build a small but professional workout studio in our house so that I could exercise and have classes with friends. I was too thrilled and touched for words. My own gym—how absolutely fabulous! I no longer had to go to Lonna's, where people thought I was a maniac. I could exercise in my own space, at my own pace, and at my own time. Magnificent!

I walked around the studio looking at everything—the light hardwood floors, the floor-to-ceiling mirrors in the front, the two huge windows on either side, one overlooking Lake Cornelia and the other overlooking a fig tree with a decorative cast-iron turtle sitting on a rock beneath it. In the back, he built a shower, a toilet, and Jacuzzi—all tiled, wallpapered, and painted in my favorite earth colors of brown, gold, and rust. Now I could come downstairs and dance my buns off when I missed Africa and needed an African music fix!

I was too excited to fall asleep. I thought of all that Kjell had done to complete it in the nine weeks I was gone. Workmen must have started the minute we left for the airport. He'd also built another bathroom with a shower, bathtub, and sink at the other end of the basement so our many guests would have their own space.

Although it was exactly what I wanted and I couldn't have been more pleased and surprised, something bothered me. I finally figured it out before I fell asleep. To think that Kjell could tear up the house and do whatever he wanted with it without even discussing it with me made me feel insignificant and taken for granted. I knew very well that no matter how much money I had, no matter how much I wanted to surprise him, and no matter how certain I was that he would fall in love with whatever I was doing for him, it would never occur to me to rip up the house without discussing it with him.

A few months later, Kjell and I joined a tour to Nepal led by Jim Klobuchar, a Minnesota journalist, author, and travel guide. We flew from Katmandu to base camp in Lukla and then started hiking the Himalayas. For as long as I live, I will never understand why anyone knowingly and willingly gives up the comfort of sleeping on a bed for sleeping in a tent. I agree that sometimes discomfort is the price you pay for visiting exotic places and experiencing indescribable beauty, but I can't romanticize such adventures as others do. To me, they are educational adventures that the curious and daring want to experience to satisfy something within them. That urge is alien to me. Although I love walking, rigorous mountain hiking is not for me. But I endured the physical hardship because what we saw each day as we climbed higher up the mountain turned out to be worth it. Imagine how much more I'd appreciate the grandeur and spectacle had someone just dropped me from a plane!

We visited a factory just outside Katmandu where young women weave those beautiful Tibetan rugs that cost so much in the States. As they wove, they softly sang their traditional weaving songs, but when they heard we were Americans, they switched to singing Michael Jackson's "Beat It." These hardy Nepalese women with sun-kissed plump cheeks, dressed in their traditional long skirts, embroidered over blouses, wide sashes, and scarves wrapped tightly on their heads, clashed with what came out of their mouths. Listening to their rendition of Michael Jackson's song—they sang "Beeet eet! Jas beeet eet!"—reminded me of my Kifungilo days when we glued our ears to the gramophone and sang along with Doris Day, "Kay sad eye, sad eye" rather than "Que sera, sera." One woman left her loom and did Michael Jackson's moonwalk around the huge, woven-straw baskets filled with spools of colorful wool and cotton thread.

At the end of our official tour of Nepal, Kjell and I took the train back to New Delhi, India, and on to Agra to see the Taj Mahal, the mausoleum built by the Mughal emperor Shah Jahan in memory of his beloved wife, Mumtaz Mahal. We toured the magnificent and overwhelming Taj Mahal and surrounding forts.

When we were inside the fort that overlooks the Taj Mahal, where the king who built the Taj Mahal was later imprisoned by his own son, I said to Kjell, "Imagine loving your wife so much that you build her the Taj Mahal!"

"What do you mean, build her the Taj Mahal?" Kjell replied without missing a beat. "It can't compare to the Taj Ma Gym I built for you!" For a few years I referred to my dance studio as the Taj Ma Gym. The scale and materials were a little different, but the sentiment was the same!

50

Where There's a Will

Thanksgiving of that same year, 1984, Dorothy came to visit as usual. From the first day, I could tell something was on her mind. She started to say something several times but didn't finish.

She was tortured about what to tell people concerning me and still couldn't introduce me as her daughter. To most I was "a friend." She also must have been tortured about what her husband, Marshall, would have thought of all this. She waited three years after his death before looking for me and three more years to tell me about my brother, Larry. I wondered if she felt guilty for breaking her word to Marshall because she had promised him she'd never have anything to do with me after leaving me at Kifungilo. Yet she had apparently defied him and had plenty to do with me under the table. Not only did she send money to the nuns for my care but she visited me at the orphanage while I was growing up, and now, many years later, she had sought me out.

Whenever Dorothy visited my family, we took her to as many cultural events as possible. We went to the Guthrie Theater to see *Mary, Queen of Scots*. She loved the play and couldn't stop talking about the magnificent production, but on our way to the car, she suddenly blurted out, "You know, Maria, I'm rewriting my will."

"Good. I'm told we should update them, though God knows the last time Kjell and I did something about ours." She said nothing more, so I thought that was the end of that topic until she brought it up the next morning.

"I'm rewriting my will, and I want you to know there's nothing I can do about you. I have to leave it the way Marshall wrote it."

"You mean Marshall, Larry's father?"

"And my husband."

"How did he write it?"

"Well, whatever is left when I die will go to Larry and our grandchildren."

"That's fine." I hadn't expected a penny from her.

"You understand that Katarina and Karl are not our grandchildren together."

I didn't believe what I was hearing. "Do you think that Marshall would leave his step- grandchildren out of the will if he knew about them?"

"That's not the issue."

"What do you mean, that's not the issue! I'm sick and tired of the distinctions you're always making between Larry's children and my children. If you have not accepted my children as your grandchildren, then you obviously haven't accepted me as your daughter. It's as simple as that."

"I know for a fact that you're my daughter, but I don't want to penalize our grandchildren by sharing the little inheritance they're going to get from their grandfather with two more people."

"Didn't Marshall leave you everything in his will?"

"He didn't put it in the will, but he told me that when I die, everything should go to Larry and his three children."

"Let me get this straight. You're the sole beneficiary of his will?"

"Well, yes."

"Obviously you're making changes, because you just told me you're rewriting it. Why are you telling me this? Do you mean to tell me that you're going to leave nothing to my children—your grandchildren?

"More or less."

"All I have to say to you, Dorothy, is this. I can understand why you wouldn't want to leave me anything since you didn't even want to raise me, but I honestly don't understand why you would want to punish your grandchildren when it was you who came waltzing into their lives. They are separate entities from me, and whether you like it or not, they are your blood grandchildren. If you've ever wished you had done right by me, this is the one opportunity you have. It's too late for me, but at least do right by my children."

"You feel very strongly about that, don't you?"

"Of course I do! Why should my children also be punished for your mistakes? You must understand that there's nothing, absolutely nothing, I wouldn't do for my children—even if it is begging you to accept them as your grandchildren like your other three grandchildren. Having said that, I want you to know that you should follow your conscience on this matter, and do what you believe is right. I know you do only what you want. You must have wanted my opinion, since you brought up the subject. I just gave it to you."

That conversation with Dorothy brought up all the feelings of being unwanted, un-acknowledged, and unloved. With tears in her eyes, Fat Mary gave me back the old feelings from childhood she had kept for me. "Maybe finding my mother was a curse rather than a blessing," I told her.

You were wise to create me when you were a child. Yes, your mother has reopened all your wounds, but she has also given you your past. And you understand that she cared for you in her own way. Think about it. Your experience taught you what a child needs from a mother, and this has benefited your children. You're also giving your children their grandmother. This encounter, even though painful, will open your eyes to the blessing of having her in your life.

One of the reasons Dorothy was rewriting her will was that she'd decided to move into the retirement community in Kissimmee, Florida, that spring. Before she left Muskegon, her favorite sister, Marion, and her brother-in-law Bill came to visit her, and she wanted to bring them to Minneapolis to meet my family.

I could easily see why she liked them so much and why she felt so inadequate around them. Both Marion and Bill had peace, love, and acceptance written into the ridges of their gracefully aging faces. The years of missionary work hadn't hardened them into cynics and pessimists as it had some missionaries I knew. They had been missionaries in Tibet and China, and they also administered and founded schools and hospitals for lepers in Thailand. They expressed to me in words and deeds the love that Dorothy couldn't express. They wanted me to meet their three sons and their daughter as soon as possible.

Marion brought pictures of her mother, my grandmother, to show me. Ragna Knutson Isle arrived in the United States from Norway in 1905, when she was five years old. She was a full-blooded Norwegian married to a full-blooded German. It was evident in the crisp black-and-white photographs how meticulously she took care of herself. She looked like the photos of early settlers I'd seen in antique shops in the States and on the walls of Kjell's aunt's farm in Kristiansund, Norway. My grandmother's tense, determined, and God-fearing face stared straight from the portrait.

"Your grandma was very intelligent. I think you got your brains from her," Aunt Marion told me. I wondered why she thought I was intelligent when we had hardly met.

"No, she got them from me," was Dorothy's proud reply.

Aunt Marion showed me pictures of my cousins and hoped we'd all meet soon. She made an effort to make me feel part of the family, and I felt the same as when I first met Larry—loved and unconditionally accepted as a bona fide member of their clan. We had a chance to take them out to Lake Minnetonka on our boat, and they couldn't seem to get enough of our children. I wondered how Aunt Marion and Dorothy could be cut from the same cloth yet be so different in personality, body language, and outlook on life. I wished she lived near us instead of in Illinois.

When it was time for Dorothy to move to Kissimmee, I volunteered to fly to Muskegon to help her pack and then fly with her to Florida and get her settled. Even though she hadn't been well for a while, she wouldn't hear of it. "What am I going to tell people about you?" Her old refrain resurfaced. It was seven years since we'd met, and she still didn't know how to introduce me. I told her she should do what Kjell did when he introduced Larry and me as brother and sister. When people looked at us oddly, wondering how we could be related, let alone brother and sister, Kjell would clear up matters by saying, "Same family, different tribe!" I'd then say, "Same tribe, different family!"

Larry had to take time from his busy pediatric schedule to help her move. I wondered whether she'd ever be able to refer to me as her daughter. She'd sent me birthday and Christmas cards and presents, but they were always addressed "Dear Maria" and signed "Affectionately, Dorothy." I went to Kissimmee to visit her a few months after she settled in, and it was the same old story—I was her friend from Minneapolis.

In the spring of 1986, both Larry and I spent a few days with Dorothy in Kissimmee. A few months later Larry made arrangements for us to attend a classical music concert at Tanglewood Music Center in Massachusetts. The concert, along with the food, the sunshine, the green meadow with tiny white flowers bending in the breeze, and the chatter among family and relatives gathered to see their offspring perform, made this visit one of the best I'd had with Dorothy. She was relaxed, joking a lot, even playful. She acted as if a load was off her shoulders and she was getting ready to throw her hang-ups out the window and settle down to enjoying life. She even introduced me to one of Larry's friends as "my African daughter."

At the end of that unforgettable day, Dorothy announced that she was going to have open-heart surgery. She was tired of living with her chronic heart condition, and "By golly, I'm going to do something about it!" She said that a friend of hers had gone through quadruple bypass surgery that so enhanced her quality of life that she wondered why she hadn't done it sooner.

"Are you sure, Mom?" Larry asked.

"I've made up my mind, so now it's up to you, Larry, to get me the best doctors and the best hospital for the surgery. I'm ready whenever they can take me."

It seemed so final.

"If I get this done now, I might be able to get ten or more good years of life."

She was seventy-seven years old, and if the bypass could buy her ten or more years, I thought she should go for it. I wondered how bad her heart was, but I said nothing. A little later this thought crossed my mind: What if she didn't make it? Heart surgery was always major. Despite our many disagreements, I realized that I loved her and the thought that I might lose her scared me.

51

Karibu Video

I used my Taj Ma Gym a lot. I had been teaching my African dance workout for nearly five years and held regular classes for clients from Monday to Saturday and also trained an instructor, Yvette, to teach whenever I was away. Since my Taj Ma Gym was too small to accommodate all my clients, I started offering evening classes as well.

I was thrilled to train the first instructor because I had created *Aerobics With Soul*® from dances and a culture that were second nature to me and hoped I could transfer the knowledge and special feel of my program to another person. I created sixteen different levels, beginning with "Over Easy" and ending with "The Ultimate." I eventually trained nine instructors and offered classes at the Uptown YWCA, Pilgrim Baptist Church in Saint Paul, Calhoun Beach Club, Central High School, The Marsh in Minnetonka, and the College of Saint Catherine.

One day out of the clear blue I decided to make an exercise video to sell. I had no idea how to go about it or what it would entail. Someone told me that a production company would take care of everything—the location for filming, the videographers, costumes, setting, the talent, rehearsals, and so forth. Being a naive and trusting woman who knew next to nothing about filming or taping, I wanted to give the job to a Black-owned production company. I also wanted the company to provide me with a Black director. I went with the first and only Black company, which a friend of my husband had highly recommended.

Making my first video, *Karibu*, proved a nightmare! Everything that could go wrong did go wrong. I fought tooth and nail with the director over the script, the costumes, the talent, and even content. In retrospect, I realized the company had never made an exercise video and hadn't understood the critical differences between music and exercise videos. The director told me with frustration during the filming, "Maria, I'm responsible for what people see, not what people do." She wanted the whole picture, not isolated movements, while I needed to clearly demonstrate and give precise instructions on how to execute every move in each exercise sequence.

I hired a music composer who also came highly recommended and whose work I really liked. When the music finally arrived, it had been composed on a computer with no live African drums. I give the director credit for bringing in both the musician and the superb drummer who rescued it by singing and drumming over the composed synthesized music.

I don't know what I would have done without Yvette, the first *Aerobics With Soul*® instructor who helped with costumes. She and I combed through warehouses and fabric samples to find plain-colored Lycra® for leotards, which we took to another artist for tie-dyeing.

Halfway into the taping, I realized I'd bitten off more—a lot more—than I could chew! Just because I could dance and teach a quality, fun exercise program didn't mean I was ready to make a one-hour exercise video for mass education and consumption. Yvette held my hand throughout and stuck by me no matter what four-letter words the director, production company members, and video editors called me. My husband, Kjell, was busy with other affairs at this time, and I could not depend on him to be there for the heartache and confusion I was going through. He figured that paying the bills and showing up every so often at the taping was sufficient participation in my video. To him it seemed a fair exchange because he felt emotionally and culturally disconnected from my creative venture.

For some reason, the editing of the film was postponed for two months, and when we started, I wanted to strangle the director. She smoked like a chimney and made fun of the participants in the video. "Who'll buy a video where half the dancers are out of shape, fat, and ugly? I'm responsible for what people see. People will think I have no clue on casting."

"Oh, it's about you! I thought it was about me and the video I'm paying you megabucks to direct. I want an exercise video that is true to what I do in my classes and reflects those who attend. We have to start where we are and accept who we are in order to improve our health. My clients are not models, and they won't all have hard bodies and six-pack abs."

"You'll be hard put to sell a handful of videos. People exercise because they want to look like the people in the video."

"My video is not about looks. It's about health. Even if it takes me a lifetime to educate the public about my program and my approach to health, I'll do it!"

No matter what she said to unravel and upset me, I insisted on doing things my way. I was paying her to direct my video, and ignorant or not, I was the one who created *Aerobics With Soul®*, and she was not going to change it to suit her. She repeatedly told me, "I don't give a damn about your stupid choreography or African movements." She was talented but also very insecure and jealous as Fat Mary told me later.

After we finished the editing, I had to buy extra time at the editing studio because I got tired of fighting with the director about content. I did voice-over for the many places where my instructions were inaudible, and I cut out the footage in which my feet were not visible. I added sections that she said were "too repetitive" but that showed essential close-ups of me doing the movements. No wonder, when we had our champagne video premier at The Marsh, the director said she hardly recognized the video.

"I returned it to its original objective of being an exercise rather than a music video," I told her with satisfaction. She laughed and nodded. I thanked her for her work. Though I hated every minute with her, she was talented and creative. But she forgot who hired her, and my inexperience and respect for her knowledge almost let her get away with it.

Without a doubt, the filming, editing, jacket design, duplication, and packaging leading up to the champagne premier of my first video was one of the hardest endeavors I've ever undertaken.

52

Truth to Tell

For several months before the filming of my video, I'd suspected that Kjell was having an affair, and then an incident occurred when I was in Miami with The Black Expo.

I often went to conventions showcasing African American products, businesses, and services to perform and publicize *Aerobics With Soul®*. Two women in the convention booth next to me were going to a hotel in Delray Beach for lunch. My ears perked up because Kjell was building a car dealership in Delray, and I wanted to see it. I arranged to go with them.

The next day I dressed in my usual African attire and worked at the convention for a few hours, then left with them for Delray. The receptionist at the Holiday Inn looked at us intently. I wasn't surprised because we were three well-dressed Black women and my African outfit always turned heads. The other women went to the dining room while I stopped at the desk to ask the receptionist how to get to Federal Highway. As she was giving me directions, she read my nametag: "Maria Bergh, *Aerobics With Soul®*, Minneapolis, Minnesota."

"What a coincidence," she said. "There's a Mr. Bergh who stays here often. And a few times he's brought his wife."

"There are many Berghs in Minnesota," I said, struggling to dismiss the thoughts entering my head.

"You're only the second Bergh I've seen who spells it that way. You must be related."

"Are you sure they were from Minneapolis?"

"Positive. I remember him well, because I'm from the Midwest too, and he had a weird first name, something like Kay-jell or K-jill, and we talked about the Midwest. Let me show you."

As she fetched the reservations book, I thought "No, this can't be," but when I saw the signature—sure enough, it was Kjell's.

"Are you sure he was with his wife?" I tried to stifle the emotion in my voice.

"They were in the same room. She asked for the room key when she came back from the beach."

In short, choppy sentences I said, "You're right. I am related to that man. He is my husband."

"Oh, my God! I'm so sorry. I had no idea. Who would ever guess that someone as beautiful as you in that absolutely stunning outfit could be related to that Nordic type. Please forgive me. I shouldn't have said a word. I could be fired for this. I'm so sor—"

"It's okay. I'm sure you see a lot working in a hotel." I tried to be brave. "Thank you. I know you didn't mean to hurt me, but now I can't hide my tears."

She took me to a room in the back of the hotel, where I stretched out on the bed with the heaviest heart I'd had for a long time. Back at the expo in Miami, I managed to carry on as if nothing had happened.

On the return flight to Minneapolis, I racked my brain to figure out who the woman might be and how to deal with this, but for some reason, I decided to swallow it and not confront my husband. I think I was afraid of learning the truth.

My first video was just out, and I was busy with every aspect of *Aerobics With Soul®* from teaching, writing out the choreography, and preparing training material for instructors, to designing leotards and T-shirts. I also tried not to neglect my duties as a mother and wife.

I have been blessed or cursed with the ability to suppress my hurts and exaggerate my blessings my whole life. I'd put family heartaches on the back burner so often it was almost second nature to me. This time I made a conscious effort to overlook the situation and focus on all the good that could come from *Aerobics With Soul®*. If I'd confronted Kjell, I would have been a mess. I'd have lost the momentum of getting my first video out and probably for *Aerobics With Soul®* altogether.

Kjell always had to have a boat. His first one was a little wider than a canoe with a motor, which we dragged behind the car to Lake Minnetonka so as to "enjoy" the day on the lake. I hated every minute I spent on that and all of his other boats—until the one he got about fifteen years into our marriage. It was a thirty-six-foot Hatteras that made me forget I was on water. Kjell was so proud of that boat and decided to take paid charters for dinner or cocktails on the lake. I noticed that all of a sudden, he started taking showers every time he left the house to give his charter boat tours. He drove a red sports car, wore cologne and gold chains, and his "charters" often lasted way into the night.

One Sunday, Carly, who was working for Kjell at our travel agency, came to pick him up at the house for an early afternoon charter. Kjell was still getting ready inside, so I went out to the car to thank her for taking over the catering and hosting for the charters. I was expecting her to come out of the car to greet me, but she stayed inside, fidgeting. Her long, manicured nails trembled on the steering wheel. She was shaking so badly, she couldn't even push down the button to open the window for me. Her body language answered my questions and confirmed my suspicion that Kjell was having an affair and that she was the woman. She finally managed to get the window down and with trembling lips squeaked a "Hi." For all I knew, she might be the woman he'd been with at the Holiday Inn in Delray Beach.

"Thank you for always helping Kjell with the charters," I said. "I don't like dealing with food, and I especially hate to cater to and chitchat with people I don't know and will never see again."

"Ah, well, it's just a job, and I get paid very well."

I couldn't resist. "I'm sure you are paid well, very well indeed, and not only monetarily, should I say?" I saw Kjell rushing towards us, obviously nervous. "We're late. We've got to run!" He got in, and they drove away without saying goodbye.

One evening Kjell came home very late—around 3 a.m. I heard the garage door open and I got up to go to the bathroom. I heard him quietly walking down the long hallway that led to our bedroom. I turned on the hallway light to let him know I was awake and to keep him from bumping into furniture. As he approached, I saw a man I hardly recognized. His hair was in disarray, and his shirt was buttoned wrong and smudged with stains I recognized as make-up—foundation, lipstick, mascara, and God knows what! My heart started to beat faster, and I felt my temperature rising. I'm known for being emotional and expressive, but I'm also known for being calm under pressure. I controlled my urge to kick him in the crotch. Instead I asked, "Where have you been? What kind of charter lasts until three o'clock in the morning?"

"This group was all party people. If I hadn't insisted on coming home when I did, we'd still be out."

"And what are those stains on your shirt? Why do you look so disheveled and unkempt?"

"Oh, about an hour ago, a friend called me and asked me to help him move. Some of the items I moved for him were original paintings. I guess I didn't realize that the paintings were still wet, and I got paint all over me."

"Who moves at 3 a.m. on a Sunday, and who would move wet paintings?"

"I thought it was strange too, but that's what we were doing."

My instinct was to run away from him as fast as I could. I ran toward the front door screaming but heard Kata calling, "Mom, Mom, where are you going?" I stopped dead in my tracks. My daughter was calling me. Instinctively, I turned around and went back to our bedroom, walking past her and past Kjell without saying a word. On second thought, I decided to sleep downstairs.

Kata followed me downstairs and sat for a while with me in the dark silence. She asked if she could do anything. I shook my head no. "Mom, I don't know what's wrong," she said, "but I know that I love you and we all love you." She got up slowly and went back to bed.

Kata was sixteen and adored her father. How could I begin to tell her what was the matter? I decided right then and there I would say nothing to her. I would make her father tell her. It crossed my mind I was taking a big chance to leave it up to him to explain. I was hoping against hope that when confronted with his daughter's questions, her innocence and vulnerability, he would tell the truth.

Kjell came downstairs and I threw myself into his arms, sobbing till I choked. He said nothing.

"Is it Carly?" I asked him.

"Yes. I'm sorry. I have been trying to end it for a long time, and this was our final fling."

"Please leave me alone and go explain yourself to Kata. She's very upset."

The next morning, I didn't come upstairs to see Kata off to school as I usually did. My eyes were almost swollen shut from crying, and I hadn't slept a wink. I asked Kjell if he'd spoken to her and he said yes.

"Why did you do it, Kjell? Don't you love me anymore? Why couldn't you just tell me, if that's the case?"

"I love you. I love you very much."

"Then what happened?"

"Oh, I don't know. I guess that turning forty and losing so much of my hair made me insecure. And you were so busy with your *Aerobics With Soul*® classes and filming your video, I felt you had no time for me."

"And you thought a twenty-four-year-old employee would give you back the self-confidence you'd lost?"

"I guess I did it because I could get away with it, and I was also intrigued by the danger of it all."

"Intrigued by the danger of it all! Were you also intrigued by what it might do to your wife and children?"

"I'm so sorry. It's over. I promise it's over. I'll do everything in my power to make it up to you. You are the only woman I love and always have."

For the next few days I tried to keep it together, but I was devastated. I insisted that if I were to stay with him, Carly would have to go. She knew full well he was married, and she knew us personally. Eventually she was fired—with a new car and six months' salary. But in my heart I knew this was a pattern, and that it probably would not end despite his promises.

I asked myself if I could continue to live in constant suspicion and fear that the next affair would be the one to break up my treasured family? Should I leave him now? What about Kata and Karl? He did say he was sorry and that I was the woman he loved. Like every fool in love, I believed him.

Kata had been acting very distant towards me since that night—as though blaming me for the affair. She brushed me off when I tried to talk to her and locked herself in her room when she came home from school.

A few days later, as I was driving her to Suzuki piano lessons, I was hurting so much that I had to pull over to the side of the road to compose and orient myself. Kata wanted to know what was the matter. She wanted to know what was going on with her father and me. I told her I was having a hard time with the affair her father had told her about a few nights earlier.

I have always regretted sharing so much of my pain with her. She was a vulnerable teenager, discovering her blossoming femininity and longing for love, admiration, and attention from boys. Instead, she was looking at love's betrayal up close and personal!

"Kata, you seem to be mad at me," I said. "Do you think the affair was my fault?"

"What affair?"

"Didn't your dad explain everything to you?"

"He did."

"So why are you acting like this toward me and not him?"

"Like what?"

"Like the affair was my fault."

"Mom, there was no affair!"

"What? What did your dad tell you?"

"He told me the truth!"

"And what is the truth?"

"I was very upset when he came into my room. I wondered what was the matter with you and why you screamed like that in the middle of the night. Dad took my hand in his, just like he did when he used to sing for me. 'Your mother has somehow gotten the crazy idea that I'm having an affair.' He said he would never, ever do such a thing and I believe him."

"Is that what he told you?"

"Mom, Dad is the nicest man in the whole wide world, and I know he loves all of us. He would never do that to us."

When Kjell came home from work that evening, I told him to tell Kata the truth—and nothing but the truth. Otherwise, I said, I would go to his office to confront Carly and create the-mother-of-all-scorned-woman scenes. His employees would know the exact reason for the angry Black woman's rare appearance at the work-place. As it turned out, almost everyone already knew because Carly had bragged about her escapades with the boss to several employees, who obliged her by spreading the word.

I was so afraid Kata would forever believe I was prone to unpre-dictable bouts of mental illness, would disrespect me and dismiss whatever I said about her father. I wanted Kjell to tell her the truth in front of me. Deep down I feared his ego would prevent him from tell-ing the truth, but knowing how Kata adored her dad, I didn't want to be present when she found out, so I listened outside the door.

After that, the three of us went to see a marriage counselor, and it all came out. The affair had been going on for two years, including the time I was filming the *Aerobics With Soul®* video. I had sensed for a long time that Kjell was having an affair, but I couldn't face that added stress while dealing with the director from hell.

After a grueling eight-hour day of filming, I would come home and Kjell would be out on one of his charters, returning in the wee hours of the morning. Thank God I was so exhausted from shooting that I fell asleep soon after I wiped away the first stream of tears. I really needed to talk to him about the filming, but I knew he would dismiss my problems with something to end the conversation like "You're taking everything too seriously." Several times during the filming, he stopped on the set for a short while to watch and chat with me, the crew, and my dancers before taking off for the boat and his Carly.

Kjell had been supportive of *Aerobics With Soul®*, from building me a dance studio and paying the huge bills for the videos and other merchandise to promoting it afterwards. I think he was proud of me, but I was not sure. He sang my praises everywhere and to anyone who would listen. It was hard to understand how he had publicly said and done everything to show love for me and then secretly committed adultery. Everyone who knew us, including my director, believed that our marriage was made in heaven. She expressed her exasperation with me to the seamstress and artist who tie-dyed our leotards: "Maria has everything—talent, beauty, personality, and friends, and to top it all, she has a husband who has money and acts like the sun and moon revolve around her. I hate her."

After our therapy sessions, I still wasn't sure I wanted to stay in the marriage. It was difficult. I struggled for a long time, prayed a lot, and had long conversations with Fat Mary. Kjell had lost my trust and respect. If I stayed, he'd have to earn them back. I must say he tried very hard. Eventually I forgave him, but forgetting was another matter. I finally decided that everyone makes mistakes and that because I loved him he was entitled to another chance. The affair was particularly humiliating because all of his employees knew about it.

For several years, every time we made love, I saw Carly's face, her young body and long, thick brown hair, as if she were warning me it was just a matter of time before he'd find another. Little by little she disappeared from our bedroom as I made a conscious effort to kick her out. Kjell's cheating life continued after a short reprieve, but the few times I confronted him, he denied it, saying I had too much time on my hands and was imagining things.

Kjell had no idea how hard it was for me to stay in the marriage. He believed that because he said he was sorry, bought me weekly roses and several luxury items, and let Carly go, it was over and we were back to normal. Nothing was normal for me. I asked him not to send me roses anymore, but he begged to continue this tradition, and I gave in. Previously I had relished putting the flowers in a vase one by one, knowing I was loved and appreciated, but now I stuck them in the vase with water and rushed to the bathroom in case I threw up. He, however, quickly resumed business as usual—all business! What helped me the most was keeping my eyes on the prize. The prize was our children. They were worth my trying again and putting forth the enormous effort it took to rebuild our relationship. I was also afraid I might not be able to raise them on my own. He was a good father. The children loved him, and they would miss him. I knew I couldn't fill his shoes and felt a divorce was not in their best interest. My children, at that juncture in our marriage, came first.

As I look back, I see clearly that during Kata's teenage years, a lot was going on with our family. I was often emotionally unavailable to her. I did not know or realize how much guidance she needed from her mother to navigate those difficult years. In my culture the concept of teenager does not exist, and neither does the word. We generally go from childhood to adulthood to being elders; adulthood can begin at age fourteen or fifteen.

One incident comes to mind. Kata, who never cared much about school dances, was excited about her senior prom. When she told me how expensive prom preparations and the activities leading to the formal dance were, I couldn't make sense of it. I was involved only in helping her shop for her dress, shoes, and other accessories, and then I left her alone. Kjell and I were gone that weekend and missed her prom.

When she was sixteen, Kata fell madly in love. Instead of encouraging her to tell us more, we told her this was a passing sentiment and she would go through it several times before settling with the right person. Then we went back into our personal and family routines.

It's true I had a lot on my mind during her teenage years—insecurities about my husband's affairs, the challenges and stress of developing my *Aerobics With Soul®* fitness program. But I recognize now that I failed my daughter at a time when she was confused and vulnerable and needed my guidance and understanding. I regret that I put myself instead of her first at that particular time in my daughter's life. I lived with the pain and shame of my selfishness for several years. Eventually I was able to forgive myself for all my sins of commission and omission towards both my children.

Most of my past struggles had blended into my adult American life like a string of red yarn among the subdued colors of a tapestry. At certain intervals, the bold string jumped out in the form of a nightmare and took me back to my childhood. In America, I had nightmares that proved you can take me out of Africa, but you cannot take Africa out of me. True to my childhood coping mechanisms, I didn't let the stumbling blocks in my marriage blind me to the blessings around me.

About this time, I had a recurring nightmare. In the dream, Father Michael's little red devil—the name he gave his car—rolled into a ravine in the Usambara mountains with the two of us in it. He was killed and I wasn't. I wandered around in the ravine dragging his corpse and looking for a place to bury him. After two long weeks, I dragged him back to the spot where he had died and started crawling out of the ravine. As I approached the top of the hill, a sad voice from long ago spoke the last words Father Michael uttered to me when we said goodbye at Dar-es-Salaam airport, "Take care of yourself, young lady, and write, write, write!"

Two days after I had that nightmare, Father Michael, whom I hadn't heard from for twenty years, wrote and said he was traveling to America and would like to stop by and see me and meet my family.

We invited him to stay with us at our home in Edina, and when I saw him, I was sure he was the corpse I had dragged around the ravine in Tanzania. He was very thin, his once youthfully flushed rosy face was bluish-gray and bumpy, and his voice gurgled as if he had something stuck in his throat.

I asked him if he was well, and he said that one of the reasons for his trip to America was to celebrate his successful treatment for cancer. He told me he had left the priesthood, was married, and had children. He asked if I was happy in my marriage, and I told him I was—for the most part. We talked like old lovers who were now only good friends—happy to see each other but eager to return to our own lives.

After he left, I realized that my nightmare was a confirmation that what we had shared was indeed dead and gone and left in the ravine in Tanzania. A few years later I heard that he had passed away from a recurrence of cancer.

His parting words at the airport in Dar-es Salaam when I was nineteen turned out to be his advice to me: I am taking good care of myself, and I am writing, writing, writing—my memoirs!

53

No Admittance

Dorothy had her surgery the last week of editing the video. I had decided to ignore the director and make whatever changes I felt were necessary so the final product would be acceptable to me. Because of the video, Dorothy insisted I wait to go to Boston until her surgery. I arrived at Larry's house the day before, and we talked about options in case the surgery didn't go as planned. Dorothy did not want to be put on life support, not even a respirator if she lapsed into a coma, and she didn't want a long hospital stay if surgery left her handicapped. She wanted to recuperate in a nursing home, and she gave us instructions where to take her. Larry and I didn't pay too much attention to her requests because we were sure they weren't necessary.

That evening after dinner, Larry suggested we should ask her for information about my father, but I told him I'd given her my word never to bring up the topic again. I found out later that Larry asked her anyway, and the only answer he got was that she couldn't speak because she had to protect certain people.

"You did write it down for us, didn't you, Mom?" Larry asked her.

"Maybe," was the answer.

We were both encouraged by the "maybe," though in the back of my mind I remembered that she had answered my question about whether she was raped or had an affair with that word.

The surgery went well, and we left her to come out from the anesthesia in the Intensive Care Unit. We waited in the lounge at Beth Israel Deaconess Hospital. Larry choked up as he talked about his mother. "I realized a few years back that I hardly knew Mom. In Africa, I was mostly away in boarding schools, and then I came to the States for college and medical school, married, and got on with my life. I was much closer to Dad.

"When Dad was ill a few months before he died and I went to see him several times, I discovered how much I was like him. The last time I saw him, he was doing so well that we both decided I didn't have to visit again unless he took a turn for the worse. Mom would call me. Well, Maria, he died before I could say goodbye to him. I've always regretted not being with him when he died. I've never stopped missing him and thinking about him. He was a great man. He was my father, and I didn't say goodbye to him."

His mother just had open-heart surgery, and anything could go wrong. Yet Larry was sitting outside her door, missing his dad. That told me everything about his relationship with his mom. Larry let the tears flow. As I watched him cry, I knew that if I had to search the world over to pick someone to be my brother, I'd pick Larry. He was so unlike Dorothy when it came to emotions, and if he was like his father, I grieved for the circumstances that made it impossible for me to know him.

"You'll have lots of time to develop the relationship you want with your mom, starting the minute she comes home from the hospital to recuperate in your house," I said.

"After what happened with Dad, I've made a constant effort to get closer to Mom, and I know we've come a long way."

We sat in silence until the nurse summoned Larry. I wanted to go too, but she said only next of kin were allowed. I didn't argue with her. He was in such a hurry to go with the nurse that he forgot about me. I waited anxiously for forty-five minutes before Larry came back.

"Mom had a stroke while she was still under the anesthesia. She's in a coma, and they have her on a respirator! It doesn't look good, but it's too early to tell."

"What do you mean, it doesn't look good? Is she going to die?"

"I hope not. It's impossible to know what damage the stroke will do. She could be paralyzed on one side or from the neck down, and the longer it takes for her to gain consciousness, the more serious the damage. All those years in medical school, all the research I've done on heart disease, and I can't do anything for Mom."

Larry was not crying. He was upset, helpless, and afraid. "There's no way she could be all right when she comes out of the coma. There'll be some damage from the stroke, and seeing that she's just undergone major heart surgery, the prognosis is not good."

My mind went blank. I felt nothing—the same as when I had seen Dorothy for the first time. The idea that she might die or never regain consciousness didn't affect me. I was as calm as I always am in times of crisis. I knew I had to take care of Larry, who had lost all color and was staring right through me.

"We just have to wait. She'll be all right," I comforted him.

"If, when, she comes through—and it looks like she's going to end up living like a vegetable—Mom will never forgive us for it."

"Do you think she'll forgive us for having her put on a respirator?"

"That's pretty routine. If she has to be on it for more than a week, we'll have to do something."

Larry and I held hands and went to the ICU to see her. Different-colored tubes sprouted from all parts of her. There were machines and tubes and things I had never seen, but Larry knew exactly what each one did, and he patiently explained to me what was going on. All we could see of Dorothy was a section of her cheeks. The respirator was loudly breathing for her. This was exactly what she didn't want, but we decided to wait and see what the next few days would bring.

We'd been in the hospital since 8 a.m., and it was now 11:30 p.m. Since Larry had to make his rounds in another hospital early in the morning, he went home to try to sleep, and I stayed in the hospital. One, two, three, four days passed with no change in Dorothy's condition. We thought we saw movement where there was none. We brought a Walkman, put headphones on her ears, and played her favorite classical music. Nothing! The respirator kept on breathing like a beast.

On the fifth day, when Dorothy was no longer in the ICU, I returned to Minnesota to wrap up the video editing. I got an update form Larry every evening for a week. "It's almost two weeks now, Maria, and I think we have to decide whether to remove the respirator."

"Even though I know it was her wish, I don't think we should. Miracles happen, Larry."

"I don't believe in miracles, but I also think we should wait a few more days."

"It's not going to be any easier in a few more days. If she hadn't insisted and made us each promise to never keep her on any life support, I'd wait forever!"

"Me, too!"

The next morning Larry called and said her condition had worsened, and she was back in Intensive Care. I knew it made no difference to Dorothy whether I was present or not when she died, but it made a difference to Larry and me. I took the next plane out of Minneapolis and met Larry at the hospital. Dorothy looked bloated, especially her size-five feet she had bragged about, saying they were the only part of her without wrinkles.

"What now?" I asked Larry.

"We'll take turns staying with her. Since you just arrived, go home and come back at midnight."

When I came back at midnight, Larry had just left. I waved at him in the parking lot and walked into the hospital. I made my way toward Dorothy's room in the ICU but was stopped by a tall, blond orderly who ran down the hall after me.

"Where're you going?" he demanded.

"To the ICU to see Mrs. Reiner."

"Sorry, only immediate family is allowed."

"I am immediate family."

"I beg your pardon?"

"She's my mother."

"Well, of course," the orderly said, "and I'm Chinese."

I, who seldom get American jokes, replied, "Really? You don't look it. But truly she's my mother."

"Who's your mother?"

"Dorothy Reiner, in this ICU, is my mother, and she is dying alone in there. I need to be with her."

"I can't let you in. Hospital rules. I'll have to escort you out."

"You don't have to escort me. I know the way." I felt defeated and walked out the door. I called Larry on the phone and explained my dilemma. Since he knew almost everyone in the hospital, he had to make only one call and the same orderly came to escort me back to the ICU.

"Hi," I said to him. "Where in China are you from?"

"Dr. Reiner is very respected here, and I guess if he says you're his sister and that dying lady is your mother, we have to take his word."

He told me to follow him, and as we walked past the nurses at the station, I happened to look up and see that they were staring at me. I stared back. They averted their eyes and looked down at their desks, pretending they were minding their own business. I couldn't understand their problem as I had signed in with them the first day Larry and I went to the ICU.

Inside the ICU, the respirator was going strong, but its rhythm warned of a forever slumber. I touched Dorothy's forehead. It was warm. I touched her feet and hands. They were cold. I rubbed her feet and admired how perfect and tiny they were—they truly had no wrinkles.

I said goodbye to her with each touch. I knew we wouldn't have to remove the respirator. I knew that Dorothy Reiner would have her way, and her life would end on her terms. I thanked her for everything, kissed her on both cheeks, and said, "Sleep tight, Dorothy."

Two days later she died. Larry was with her. Being with his mother when she died made up for not being with his dad. He had the certain peace that comes from doing everything right.

I called home and told Katarina that her grandma had died.

"I'm so sorry, Mom," is all she said. When I told nine-year-old Karl about his grandma's passing, he burst into tears and sobbed loudly and uncontrollably.

I, on the other hand, felt as if I had witnessed a hurricane of emotions that were not mine. I searched for Fat Mary.

Remember the old nuns in Kifungilo and the African villagers and children whose funerals you attended so often as a child? How did you feel at the time?

"On the outside I was calm, I must say. In my heart, I imagined the place their souls were going and was often envious. I imagined most of them going to heaven."

What do you feel about the death of your mother?

"Nothing in particular. Is it because she had been dead to me for so much of my life, or because I understand somehow that death is the partner of life?"

Death is simply an ending. Life comes and goes. What makes death hard is that it seems so final. Yet for many people, the loved one continues to live in their minds and hearts, and they can talk with them at any time and place. The dead are never completely out of the lives of the living. You do not feel much emotion about your mother's death because you have no memories of being with her, touching and loving her. Your feelings at her passing correspond to the role she played in your life.

54

Daughter at Last

Dorothy was cremated, and her ashes came with Larry from Boston to Wheaton, where she was buried next to her husband, Marshall. At her funeral, I met the rest of my cousins and relatives on her side. I met Bonnie, Aunt Marion's daughter, and loved her right away. I knew I'd see her again. Except for Aunt Marion, I haven't seen the rest of the family.

There were about a hundred people at the service, and Kjell and I sat in front in the seats reserved for family. I wondered if in heaven Dorothy would be upset that I was listed in the program: " . . . survived by Maria Bergh—daughter."

Two weeks after the funeral, I went to Kissimmee to help Larry go through Dorothy's belongings and do whatever else was needed. The first order of business was for us privately to go through the papers she had left with her will in the safety deposit box. Larry waited for me to arrive from Minnesota before he opened anything. The two of us sat quietly on the couch in Dorothy's living room, and Larry read her will. My mind was set to hear only what I thought I would finally hear. I didn't hear it.

"There's nothing in there about my father," I said, disappointed.

"She wouldn't write that in her will."

"Sorry! Of course not! Well, I heard something about Katarina and Karl. What did she say about them?"

"Calm down and listen, Sis," Larry laughed. "My son Larry Reiner and my daughter Maria Bergh get equal amounts."

"I don't believe it! She actually called me her daughter in writing? In a legal document? And left me something?" Dorothy left equal amounts to her five grandchildren including Kata and Karl.

293

By now I was choking. It was as if Dorothy wanted me to know that she couldn't face the truth about me when she was on earth. But in death she unequivocally admitted that I was her daughter and Katarina and Karl were her grandchildren. Better late than never.

"Thank you, Mom. Can I call you Mom now that you cannot hear me?"

We continued going through everything in her safety deposit box—mostly the disbursements of her material possessions. She tried to divide everything evenly among all of us, with Katarina and Karl inheriting a few family heirlooms.

We found nothing about my father. Not even one line that might lead us to the information we had requested. We couldn't believe it.

"She must have hidden the information somewhere in the house," Larry suggested.

We started a frantic search. We went through every book in her many bookcases, thinking she might have tucked it between pages of a book. We searched through all the drawers in her dressers, every kitchen cupboard, every shoe box, old hat boxes, the pockets of her many clothes in the closet, some of which still had the price tags, through the pots and pans and silverware trays in the kitchen and every drawer in the whole house. We looked under the rugs, the mattress, inside pillowcases; we checked the lampshades; we even removed pictures from the walls to search behind them.

We found nothing. After searching for two days, we gave up.

I hadn't cried when I met her ten years ago. I hadn't cried when she forbade me to call her Mom. I hadn't cried when she told me she was disappointed that I emphasized my African rather than American heritage. I hadn't cried when we spoke Swahili and she used terms that a *mzungu* used only when addressing servants or inferiors. I hadn't cried when she died nor did I cry or at her funeral. But now I sat on the floor of her house and cried with tears that tasted the same as the ones that had rolled down my cheeks at the orphanage.

Fat Mary consoled me: *I really believe your mother couldn't be what you needed her to be. She placed you in the orphanage right after you were born because she believed it would be the best place for you. She believed she was doing the right thing.*

"But tell me, Fat Mary, doing the right thing for whom? Did she believe she was the only one who carried the burden of my birth? Was it the right thing to do for herself, her husband, her family, her church? How about me? By refusing to tell me anything about my father, she's still having her way, even in the grave."

No matter how it looks, she loved and cared for you from the moment she gave birth. We will never know what sacrifices she made or what private agonies she lived with her whole life. That she knew where you were and with whom your whole life means she always had you somewhere in her mind.

"Maybe in her mind but not in her heart. Her heart was cold and couldn't express love, joy, or gratitude. She was always in control—of herself and any situation that involved me. I think she wouldn't let herself feel a mother's natural urge to physically bond with her child. If she had, she would have held me, hugged me, and loved me when she came to the orphanage to see me."

No matter what she wished for, she knew she had to do what was right for herself and her family. You paid a very big price for her being "proper," but don't believe that she didn't love you. Like you, she did what she had to do to survive.

55

Destinies

I tried to put myself in Dorothy's shoes and imagined scenarios that might have kept her from giving even the slightest hint about my father to Larry or me. I wondered if he could still be alive. If my mother was seventy-seven years old when she died in 1986, then my father would be more or less the same age if he were alive, which didn't seem likely.

I even wondered whether Dorothy really was my mother. How could she not tell me about my father? Did she know anything about him? Was she raped in the middle of the night as she'd insinuated the first and only time I asked her about him? Were the heart palpitations she'd experienced a reason for me to believe she was lying? I didn't know what to think. It was as if she had appeared to me in a welcome dream that turned into a frustrating, never-ending nightmare. Should I be grateful she came looking for me? What was she looking for? Did she miss Africa and see me as proof she'd been there? Should I thank God for her or would I have been better off continuing to believe that I was an orphan? I spent the next two years in disbelief that Dorothy could take my father to the grave with her.

Then Larry called me one day late in 1988, two years after Dorothy's death, and said he too could not stop thinking about who my father might be. He suggested we travel together to Tanzania. I could show him where I lived, and he would show me where he grew up. That might help him remember some events in his childhood that he might have blocked out. Though we had the same mother, we knew our African experiences had been very different.

"For now, Sis, you're all the family I have. Let's get reacquainted with the continent we both love, spend time under the sky that knows us, and see what might be revealed. I have a feeling that when I'm there and see people from my childhood, things will come back to me."

"Are you suggesting we go to Tanzania to look for my father? What a brilliant idea!"

"But we shouldn't make finding your father the object of the trip. I'd hate to have you disappointed and hurt any further, since chances of finding him are slim."

I agreed. Our mother's reluctance to even talk about Africa with me certainly hadn't let me dream I would find my father one day. Yet the idea of traveling with my half-brother Larry to the places he had lived made me eager to go.

We didn't want to advertise the reason for our trip, so we agreed to tell family and friends that the trip to Tanzania was because of our curiosity about each other's childhood. But in our hearts, we both knew the real mission of our journey was to gather information that might lead to my father's identity.

A lot of the confusion about who I was and where I belonged had gradually lifted after I met my mother. Upon my departure from Africa the first time, Mama Africa had assured me that I was her child. Little did I know that my American mother was waiting for the right time to claim me as her daughter. Now I was returning to the country of my birth not only as Africa's child, but as America's daughter.

A few weeks later I flew from Minneapolis to Boston. The next day Larry and I boarded a plane for Tanzania where the mysteries of our intertwined destinies, conceived and nurtured in the same womb and etched into the African landscape, awaited us.

Acknowledgments

Without Catherine Murray Mamer, there would have been no hope, no love, no America, no college, no mother, no children, and a short, sad story for me to tell. How can I say thank you to someone like you? Your unconditional love has hovered above and around me and shone brightly for everyone to see since we met when I was nineteen and you were twenty-three. You have showered my children and grandchildren with the same love you gave to me. We are all indebted to you for your unwavering love, never-ending support and commitment to each one of us in your extended family. You are the spirit that flows through the generations, connecting us all with a bond that will never be broken. *Asante sana, Mama.*

Thank you, my children, Katarina and Karl. You made me a mother about the same time I discovered who my birth mother was. I knew little about motherhood, since I had no role model as a child. Despite my inadequacies, you made me feel I was a good mother. I thank you for being the catalysts that encouraged me to face the truth about my humble beginnings in Africa and for assuring me that my roots would enrich your lives. I thank you for cheering me on when I shared bits and pieces of the struggles I faced in America as a foreigner, as a mother, and as a wife. I thank you for always protecting me. I thank you for adding an unimaginable level of richness and blessing by making me a grandmother. *Nawapendeni sana!*

Jacqueline Mosio, my editor, my Best Friend Forever: When you looked at me, you saw my soul. Though we seemed oceans apart—culturally, linguistically, and ethnically—we were attracted like magnets to each other from the day we met in class at the College of Saint Catherine. You validated my uniqueness and encouraged me not to try too hard to become too American too soon. You stood by me through many years of doubt and insecurity about myself and my writing. Your brilliance in deciphering my poorly articulated thoughts and emotions along with your sensitive and sensible questions have enabled me to tell my story with courage, beauty, and even pride. I have no words to thank you for your steadfast belief in me and your insistence that my story be told. Thank you for letting me expose my vulnerability and showing me its reflection in your soul. You are my Soul Sister. *Muchas gracias!*

Asante sana kaka, Larry. Many thanks to my brother Larry. You appeared late in my life, but you were worth waiting for. If I were given the choice to travel the whole wide world to find the one person I would like to have as a brother, I would pick you. Thank you for loving and accepting me unconditionally and for making my inclusion into your and my family smooth and worthwhile. Thank you for making time to travel to Tanzania with me in search of my father.

Thank you, Sister Eileen for your many recollections of my childhood that made it possible for me to write *Africa's Child* and for your continued storytelling that carried on to *America's Daughter*. Thank you for welcoming me and my family to the dentistry in Lushoto and for going with us to visit our childhood friends scattered around the Usambara Mountains.

Betty, thank you for sharing your little sister, Imelda, with me. She and her family have become my family in America. I value the joy and laughter you brought into my life when you visited me in my American home. No matter how many years have passed, we always picked up our stories where we left off, proving that the bond we formed in Kifungilo is alive and well. Thank you for always opening your heart and home whenever I show up at your doorstep in Tanzania.

Imelda, we were together at the orphanage, so you know my story inside out because much of it is your story too. Though you are two years younger, we latched onto each other long ago, and now all these years later we are not only the best of friends but we are family. Many thanks to you and your husband, Dallas, for your faith in me and your steadfast encouragement during the writing of my memoirs.

A special thank you to Dr. Joyce T. Jackson, former principal at Central High school, for inaugurating a Swahili and African heritage class at your school. Your concern that the curriculum be inclusive and pertinent to the lives of your students set a far-reaching model of what public education can and should be. Some of my best teaching years were those at Central High School. I have you to thank.

Thank you, Kjell Bergh, for your patience, encouragement, promotion, and support throughout the many years of my developing the *Aerobics With Soul®* Fitness Program and making the *Serengeti, Karibu*, and *Kilimanjaro* videos.

I am indebted to my *Aerobics With Soul®* instructors Yvette Trotman, Nedy Windham, Diane Gayes, Rachel Soffer, and Salma Faraji for proving that my creation could be learned and taught by instructors other than me. When I count my blessings, you five are near the top of the list. Your understanding of the meaning and essence of *Aerobics With Soul®* affirms that race and culture cannot stifle what we feel in our hearts. Tears of love and gratitude fill my eyes when I watch you teach. I am overwhelmed by your courage, commitment, joy, and exuberance for the class. My deep and sincere gratitude for all you have meant to me personally, and to *Aerobics With Soul®*. *Asanteni sana!*

Rachel Soffer: I met you when you were in your teens. As a magnet-school student, you chose to open enroll at Central High School to take my African studies class. Little did I know our paths would cross again, and that you would become an *Aerobics With Soul®* instructor and my fearless attorney. Thank you for standing by me and supporting all my endeavors. You went beyond the call of duty to provide excellent counsel to me. Your love and enthusiasm for teaching and promoting *Aerobics With Soul®* is infectious. I am overwhelmed with love and joy as I say *Merci beaucoup, mon amie, bien aimée.*

Salma Faraji: We met at your parents' farm in Usa River in Tanzania when you were thirteen years old. We danced in your parents' living room, and you have been hooked on *Aerobics With Soul®* ever since. I have no words to describe how your loyalty and admiration of my creation have touched me. You have called me Auntie from day one and made me feel as if we have always known each other. Your unwavering dedication to *Aerobics With Soul®* and love for me is multiplied several times in my love and admiration for you. *Asante sana.*

Merci beaucoup to Sister Marie Phillip, CSJ, my college advisor, who took a personal interest in me and did everything in her power to help me graduate with a French major.

Merci beaucoup to my French conversation professor Marie Therese Reed, who took me under her wing and made sure my French major studies were cultural as well as academic.

My deepest gratitude to Sister Rosalie, CSJ, and all the Sisters of Saint Joseph of Carondelet for enabling me to fulfill my dream of a higher education by awarding me a scholarship to the College of Saint Catherine (now Saint Catherine University). Your tutelage, dedication, and commitment to women's education laid the foundation for the person I am today and inspired me to "be my neighbor's keeper."

A big thank you to my readers whose comments, corrections, and suggestions have been invaluable: Katarina Nhambu Bergh, Karl Nhambu Bergh, Ruth Brombach, Imelda and Dallas Browne, Janet Brownell, Janice Dickinson, Anna Fitzsimmons, Diane and Jim Gayes, Catherine Murray Mamer, Samali Mutazindwa, Grace Rogers, Denise Scott, Carletta Smith, Rachel Soffer, Rita Speltz, Natasha Vaubel, Margaret Wong and Walter Graff, and Ellen Blackman Green.

Thank you to Barbara Cronie, Editor, Editing Par Excellence, for your professionalism, enthusiasm, and support for *Africa's Child* and *America's Daughter.*

As always, to my friends, thank you for your friendship, encouragement, love, and belief in me. Thank you for your patience as you nudged me along over the years saying, "We'll be dead before your books come out!" All I can say to you now is "Better late than never!"

About the Author

Maria Nhambu—educator, dancer, writer, mother, entrepreneur, and philanthropist—was raised by German missionary nuns in an orphanage for mixed-race children high in the Usambara Mountains of Tanzania. A twenty-three-year-old American woman adopted her at age nineteen and brought her to America for college. Nhambu is the creator of *Aerobics With Soul®*—the African Workout based on the dances she learned growing up in Tanzania. She prefers to be known simply as "Nhambu," which means "one who connects" or "bridge person." She is the mother of two, grandmother of three, and lives in Delray Beach, Florida, and Minneapolis, Minnesota.

About Dancing Soul Trilogy

In *America's Daughter*, the second book of the trilogy, the author arrives in the United States in the company of Catherine Murray, an American high-school teacher. Her adjustment to a new culture includes shocking doses of American-style racial discrimination and Nhambu's discovery that she must learn to be a Black American. She graduates from college, thus fulfilling her dream of becoming a teacher, and teaches high school in the inner city. She marries, has two children, and establishes herself in the American way of life. Then a visit to Africa, and especially to Tanzania, reawakens the drumbeats and dancing that she carries in her soul. On her return home, she teaches Swahili and African Studies, performs African dance at schools, and creates *Aerobics With Soul®*, a fitness workout based on African dance. She both finds and creates the family she longed for as a child and connects with her unknown background. The first book of the trilogy, *Africa's Child*, was released in 2016. The final book of her memoir series—*Drum Beats, Heart Beats*—reveals more of Nhambu's life as she searches for her father.

Glossary

Pronunciation
    In Swahili the stress of a word almost always falls on the next-to-last syllable: **Tan-zan-I-a**. There are only five vowels and they are always pronounced the same. All vowels are pronounced. Two vowels together are each pronounced: **Haule = Ha-u-le.**

Amelican gal – American girl. Little Mary couldn't pronounce "r" and some African languages do not distinguish between "r" and "l"
apartheid – South African system of racial segregation enforced by government laws to ensure the dominance of the white population
Arusha – town in northern Tanzania, headquarters for northern safari circuits
asante – thank you
asante sana – thank you very much

Baba – father
Betty – a friend from the orphanage living in Lushoto
Bibi – Grandmother
Blessed Martin – a mulatto Dominican Brother who was the patron saint of people of mixed race
bwana – Mister, sir, husband

Color bar – discrimination based on color in South Africa ("Kalaba")
Consesa – a friend from high School

dawa – medicine
Don Bosco Home – name of orphanage and boarding school for mixed race children, Usambara Mountains, Kifungilo.
dudu/wadudu – any insect or creepy crawly bug (singular/plural)
duka – store

Eleanor – Cathy and John Mamer's daughter
Elizabeth – best friend at the orphanage

Far – Father (Norwegian)
Father Antonio – Italian priest who wanted to take Mary to Italy
Father Gattang – resident priest at the orphanage
Father Michael – Irish priest who helped Mary with her education and exploited her
Fatima and Abdu Faraji – Friends in Arusha, Tanzania
fundi – skilled person, expert, foreman
Gare – Mission station near Kifungilo

hafukasti – half-caste
Heini – building foreman and general contractor for the orphanage
hapana – no (Swahili)
Henrietta – best friend at Marian College, later worked at The Bank of Tanzania

Imelda – Childhood friend from the orphanage
Iringa – major city in the highlands of Southern Tanzania

Jambo – hello
Janteloven – the Law of Jante, set of social rules regarding behavior in Scandinavian countries
John Mamer – Catherine Murray's husband

Kaffir – a derogatory term used in South Africa to refer to a Black person, equivalent to "nigger"
Kalaba – Color bar, discrimination on the basis of color
kaniki – shinny, black, very cheap cotton worn by poor people
kanzu – white loose-fitting robe Muslims wear
karibu – welcome, near
Karibu – title of first *Aerobics With Soul*® video
kenedi – term used for flour donated by the United States (referencing President John F. Kennedy)
khanga – colorful cotton cloth worn by East African women and some men
kitenge – heavier, more expensive cotton fabric (often Java print) used for women's and men's shirts
Kifungilo – name of the little village where the orphanage is located. Pronounced 'key-foong-ghee-low'
Kihehe – language of the Hehe tribe
Kisambaa – language of the Sambaa tribe
Kisukuma – language of the tribe living by Lake Victoria
Kiuzai – name of a village near the orphanage
Kjell – name of Nhambu's husband. Typically pronounced 'Shell'

Kongei – African Middle School run by Precious Blood Sisters
Korogwe – town on the Tanga region's main railway and bus routes
kuchimba dawa – slang, to relieve oneself in the bush
kusindikiza – to accompany a parting person a short way along their journey
kusonya – a sucking sound used in East Africa and the Caribbean ("steups") to show annoyance or anger
kwaheri – goodbye

Lady Twining – wife of the British Governor to Tanganyika during colonial times, Sir Edward Twining
Lindi – the southernmost coastal town in Tanzania
Lizzy – one of the "big girl" orphans who became a nun and a dentist
Luguru – name of tribe living in the Uluguru Mountain range in central Tanzania
Lushoto – name of the small town closest to Kifungilo

Maasai – a Nilotic ethnic group of semi-nomadic people, located in Kenya and northern Tanzania.
Mabladifu – Bloody fools (plural form)
Magamba – little village in the Usambara Mountains where the British Governor's lodge was located
mdogo – little one
Mkuzi – village five miles away from Kifungilo
Mama yangu! – My goodness! (lit. Oh my mother!)
mapenzi – love
Marian College – high school in Morogoro run by American Maryknoll Sisters
Maryknoll Sisters – order of Catholic missionary nuns founded in New York in the 1920s
Mary Rose Ryan – the name Maria used until her marriage
maskini – poor people
matajiri – rich people
matata – trouble, problems
Maureen – traveling companion on Trans-Siberian trip
merikani – cheap, shinny, cotton fabric from America
Merikani – America
Mhonda – Middle school near Morogoro run by Precious Blood Sisters
Milele na milele – forever and ever
Miriam Makeba – South African singer usually referred to as "Mama Africa"

Miss Murray – name of volunteer English teacher at Marian College
Mombo – town near Lushoto
Mon petit chou – French term of endearment (lit. my little cabbage)
Mor – Mother (Norwegian)
Morogoro – large town at the foot of the Uluguru Mountains
Mother Ancilla – founder and builder of the orphanage
Mother Rufina – the Mother Superior of the Convent in Kifungilo
Mr. Murray – Catherine Murray's father
mshahara – salary, wages
mshamba – from the country
Mungu Ibariki Tanganyika – God Bless Tanganyika (title of national anthem)
Mungu wangu wee – Oh my God!
Mwalimu – teacher
Mwalimu Haule – name of supportive teacher in Mhonda Middle School
mzungu – white person (plural form: *wazungu*)

Natasha - traveling companion on Trans-Siberian trip
ndiyo – yes
nyumba ile – lit. "that house" or "that room" where orphans gathered for various activities and where clothes were kept in cubicles
nyumba mpya – new house

Olatunji – Nigerian musician and drummer
Onamia – Catherine Murray's hometown, 95 miles north of St. Paul
Operation Bootstrap Africa – organization dedicated to increased educational and healthcare opportunities in Africa, headquartered in Minneapolis Minnesota

Paulina – friend at Mahonda Middle School
Pemba – small island off the coast of Tanzania
pole sana – so sorry

Rangwe – Benedictine Order Mission Station in the Usambara Mountains
Reed, Mrs. – college professor from France
Rosa – big girl who first cared for Little Mary. She died after a brief marriage.
Rosminian – Catholic Order founded by Italian Antonio Rosmini. Most Rosminian priests in Tanganyika were from Ireland

Sambaa / Wasambaa – tribe living in the Usambara Mountains schwarze Kinder – black children

schwarze Teufel – black devils

schwarzer Ziguener – black gypsy

shenzi – pagan (often use as a derogatory term)

Simonson, Reverend David and Eunice – Lutheran Missionaries to the Maasai in Tanzania

Sister Clotilda – teacher at Kifungilo who became Mother Superior and supplied Cathy with information about Mary's mother.

Sister Eileen – big girl (Lizzy) at the orphanage who became a nun and dentist

Sister Jacinta – nun at Kifungilo in charge of cooking

Sister Marie Phillip – head of French department at the College of St. Catherine

Sister Martin Corde – African-American Maryknoll Sister at Marian College

Sister Nerea – dentist in Kifungilo and Lushoto

Sister Rosalie – instrumental in obtaining scholarship for Mary to the College of St. Catherine

Sister Silvestris – nun in charge of all the orphans

Sister Theonesta – taught elementary school at the orphanage and took care of Mary as an infant

Sophie – Murray family friend in Onamia

steups – a sucking sound used in East Africa and the Caribbean to show annoyance or anger

Swanglish – slang (mixture of English and Swahili)

Tabora – name of major town in central Tanzania

Tanga – large city on the East Coast of Tanzania, also a region

Taiga – Siberian coniferous forest

Tanganyika – name of the former British Colony which gained its independence in 1961 and became Tanzania.

Tanzania – a country located on the East Coast of Africa. The name Tanzania is derived from two countries—the mainland of Tanganyika and the Island of Zanzibar—that united in 1964 to form the United Republic of Tanzania

Thecla – a friend from high school

Tumsifu Yesu Kristu – Praise be to Jesus Christ, used as a greeting for nuns and priests

Turiani – little town near Mhonda Middle School

Tussebo – home of the female trolls, name of cabin in Norway

ugali – a stiff porridge used for lunch or dinner made of corn flour, water, and salt

Ujamaa – familyhood; concept that formed the basis of President Julius Nyerere's social and economic development policies after Tanzania gained independence from Britain in 1961

uhuru – freedom

uji – soft porridge used for breakfast, made of water, corn flour and salt

Uluguru – land of the Luguru tribe

ululation – a long, high-pitched vocal sound made by rapidly moving the tongue against the roof of the mouth used to signify joy or sadness

Usambara Mountains – range of mountains surrounding Kifungilo

Usa River – Small town on the outskirts of Arusha. Pronounced 'oou-sah'

wadudu – insects or bugs (plural)

WAMSO – Women's Association of the Minnesota Orchestra

Wasambaa / Sambaa – tribe living in the Usambara Mountains

washenzi – heathens, pagans (plural form)

wazungu – white people (plural)

wenyeji – locals

yeba! – hurrah!

Young Audiences – nationwide organization that brings performing art programs to elementary schools

Zami – big girl in charge of Little Mary after Rosa at the orphanage

zamani – long ago, old times

zawadi – gift, present

CPSIA information can be obtained
at www.ICGtesting.com
Printed in the USA
LVHW02s1800020918
588936LV00004B/363/P